REVIEW COPY

QUANTITY 1

DATE 4/18/85

7737-00811

TITLE NEWSWORTHY C

AUTHOR CREAN S

PRICE 24.95

CONTACT ELLEN WOODGER

TWO COPIES OF YOUR REVIEW,
WHEN PUBLISHED, WOULD BE
APPRECIATED.

STODDART PUBLICATIONS

30 LESMILL ROAD, DON MILLS, ONT.

M3B 2T6   TELE. (416) 445-3333

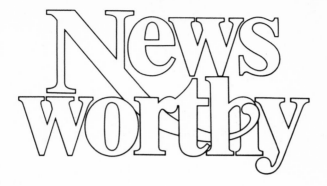

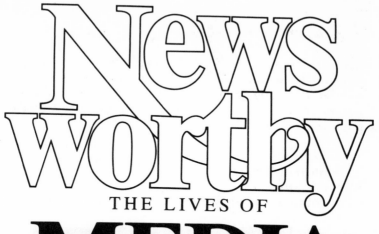

News worthy

THE LIVES OF

MEDIA WOMEN

SUSAN CREAN

Stoddart

First published in 1985 by
Stoddart Publishing
A Division of General Publishing Co. Ltd.
30 Lesmill Road
Toronto, Canada
M3B 2T6

Canadian Cataloguing in Publication Data

Crean, S. M., 1945-
   Newsworthy : the lives of media women

Includes index.
ISBN 0-7737-0081-1

1. Women broadcasters — Canada — Biography.
2. Women journalists — Canada — Biography.
3. Women in the mass media industry. I. Title.

PN1990.7.C73 1985 070.1'092'2 C85-098151-4

Printed in Canada

Table of Contents

This book is dedicated to two
extraordinary women

E. CORA HIND
foremother and feminist

MARGARET E. CREAN
my mother

Acknowledgements

The very first revelation I had when I began work on this book was that it would be impossible for me to interview all the women working in journalism, either in print or in the electronic media. I knew that there had been a time, not so terribly long ago, when that would have been possible. As one of the generation that came of age in the sixties, I had seen that transformation happening myself and played a bit part in it. The second relevation came when I was searching for a point of departure. After ten years of freelancing in television and magazine journalism and writing extensively about broadcasting, I discovered that I had no sense of where women came into the history. I had no sense of there being a past to remember. Worse still, for all my commitment to nationalism and feminism and the job of reclaiming the past for the present and future, it didn't occur to me until late 1983 to ask the question: Where have we come from?

I embarked on a journey in January, 1984 without a map, only a list of names. Over the next six months I talked with about a hundred women from all walks of media life — researchers, writers, reporters, producers, script assistants, secretaries, editors, directors, and vice-presidents. Only one person declined my request for an interview (and she has since left the profession); all the rest, without exception, gave unstintingly of their time, sharing with me their life stories, their ideas, opinions, and dreams.

Through them I have had a glimpse of the history I know now to be a colourful and amusing saga, chock-full of heroics, grand imaginings and larger-than-life characters. Through them I have developed a sense of the century-old history of women journalists in Canada (a history that still waits to be written) and a feeling for the shape and dynamics of the profession today. This book is a product of their collaboration and trust. My hope is that it matches in some small measure their grit and passion.

There have been other people whose enthusiasm and interest have been a constant support, sometimes more than they may realize. This book belongs to them too: Laurie Edwards, Susan G. Cole, Sandy Duncan, Lynne Fernie, Kate Hamilton, Barbara Hehner, Carol McIntyre, Susan Rockman, Dell Texmo, Eve Zaremba, Arnold Rockman, Keith Maillard, Ed Carson, the *This Magazine* editorial collective, and Peter Wilson. And Giorgio Vasari (1511-1574), whose book *The Lives of the Most Eminent Painters, Sculptors and Architects* I read in Florence, Italy, in 1965, and who gave me a model to work from.

Susan Crean

INTRODUCTION

The Second Barrier

ON JANUARY 11, 1982, the CBC's brand new, seven-million-dollar flagship, *The Journal,* sailed out of port and onto the nation's television screens. According to the hype and hyperbole of normally taciturn network executives, this was an historic event. The news was being shifted back to 10 P.M. from 11 P.M. and a half hour of current affairs created to follow it, reclaiming one full hour of prime-time television for Canadian content. *The Journal,* moreover, was to be anchored by two women, and things would never be quite the same again.

Once the confetti had settled and the public had had time to recover from its initial shock, *The Journal* and its audience settled down to reality. While it was not, in truth, the reinvention of the picture tube, the show was solid current affairs and from its very first week exceeded the producers' wildest predictions by attracting well over a million viewers each evening. *The Journal* was a huge gamble for the CBC, which had been rifling every region, budget, and broom closet for close to three years to find enough eggs for this one gigantic basket. And it had paid off, proving that there is a demand for original Canadian programming at that time of night; that some Canadians would rather watch a review of the day's news with Knowlton Nash, Barbara Frum, Mary Lou Finlay, and company than *Falcon Crest*. What, however, did *The Journal* signify for women? Was it a sign that Barbara Frum had succeeded Patrick Watson as the network's premier political interviewer? Was it a signal that women had finally arrived at a position of equality in television? Were Frum and Finlay tokens or were they leading a parade?

In the late seventies, it was rumoured in the media that the feminist movement was a spent force; that, like the student revolution of the sixties, it had blown itself out. The few charitable male critics who had been willing to concede women's rights now pronounced that feminism had achieved its goals and the world had obligingly changed. Robert Fulford claimed in *Saturday Night* magazine that women had "reached down to the patriarchal roots of society and yanked them up," transforming everything — economics, politics, and culture.

The perception gathered momentum. Women weren't just doing well, they were making it straight into the power structure, and all the way to the top in some professions. Articles on the first woman jockey or fire chief or roughneck gave way to ones on women in the boardroom and the executive suite. By 1983, enough women had made it to the senior echelons of the media to provide stories on the new women television executives; journalism students were writing essays on topics like "The takeover of the magazine industry by women"; and any hermit in the country could name three female media stars without thinking. Over at the CBC, where an equal opportunity office had been set up in 1975, head-office executives were patting each other on the back for having so effectively taken care of the issue.

Is it possible that media women have actually made suffi-cient inroads to be deemed, as the sociologists say, fully integrated? Are women in television, radio, and the news-papers pulling the same weight as the men, holding down the same jobs, and commanding the same salaries? The answers to such questions are, as usual, a mixture of yes and no. Some women have achieved great distinction and are doing as well as any male journalist, but most media women aren't. We do not need Statistics Canada to tell us that there are a great many more women involved in journalism than there were ten years ago. We also know, however, that the presence of women in a profession, even in impressive numbers, does not mean they have achieved equality in terms of power.

The mass media are such a familiar part of daily existence that it is hard to imagine life without them. Yet, as viewers/readers/listeners, we know very little about how they are organized, how they function as institutions, how the technology works, and why things are done the way they are. One reason we know so little is that journalists themselves have a distaste for reporting on their own industry. They say it feels too much like navel-gazing and might be perceived by the public as self-serving.

Although it may seem to outsiders that journalists travel in packs, they don't actually work that way. Journalism is a very solitary profession; most of the writing and creative work such as editing is mental activity that has to be done alone or in close collaboration with one or two others at most. Moreover, because everyone is constantly on the road, switching beats, and hopping to other media, it is difficult to get a sense of the profession as a whole. It is a polyglot, peripatetic occupation that does not encourage introspection or self-analysis. So it is that journalists have reported indignantly on discrimination in banks, business, and government while overlooking conditions in their own newsrooms.

So it is also that many people have assumed that women in the media are doing a lot better as a group than they really are. The presence and high visibility of women on the editorial and production side of journalism have obscured the fact that advances on the technical side and in management have been negligible. Even where policies of affirmative action and equal pay exist, they are not practised; even where efforts are made to provide maternity benefits for working journalists, it is no easier for women to run their careers and raise children in tandem. Many have to choose between the two, and those who do try to do both are often penalized for their efforts and their careers put on hold.

It took eighty years for women to make it past the threshold and through the first barrier into the profession, to establish themselves and gain acceptance as regular members of the press corps. It took three generations to consolidate the achievements of the pioneers of the 1880s and 1890s, during which time new media — first radio and then television — were being introduced. With each new invention, new organizations were set up and new standards were devised, by men. Each time, women had to start over again at the bottom.

Perhaps in the mid-1980s, we can finally say with some assurance that women have arrived in the media to stay. The foothold is secure enough this time that the danger of slipping back into oblivion seems remote. We should not, however, forget that the power women have attained is limited. It is just as true as it ever was to state that the media are owned and operated by men, and that the field of journalism is dominated by them. What may appear to be a dramatic change over the past twenty years only amounts to a qualifying clause on that statement: it is no longer invariable that *all* decision-making positions are occupied by men; now, about fifteen percent of the time, they are held by women.

Getting through the first barrier and filling the ranks of the profession has taken courage, strength, and, above all, endurance. But, as women are beginning to understand, this is only phase one. Breaking in and accumulating the numbers may be the easier step. For beyond lies a second barrier, a shifting barrier of subtler prejudice. And moving past the twenty percent mark may require a revolution far more radical than the one which brought women this far.

Three years after the launching, we can appreciate just how apt a symbol *The Journal* is for the status women have achieved after a hundred years in journalism. We can appreciate that Barbara Frum and Mary Lou Finlay are not token women by any means, but the parade they are leading is a parade of foot soldiers — researchers, assistants, and secretaries. Even on *The Journal*, where women constitute half the production team, work is divided into male and female spheres, with the lion's share of the pay, the prestige, and the promotions going to men and the lioness's share of the anonymous, routine work being handled by women. Barbara Frum's power may be awesome, but it is not the power of direction. Within the hierarchy of the CBC, she has no authority. Hers is the power of influence, a power she shares with other journalists who not only tell us the news but decide what the news is. They are mediators in the democratic process and instrumental in shaping our awareness of ourselves as a society. And that, of course, is an extraordinary privilege.

ONE

Rebels and Adventurers

THE PICTURE is growing faint, the details blurring with age and repeated reproduction. But she stands there, feet firmly planted on the earth, a magnificent figure in beaded buckskins and breeches, with a cane in her hand and a large hat upon her head. This is E. Cora Hind, circa 1911. The picture shows only the cutout figure (original photograph lost?) and we have to imagine the rest for ourselves. Cora with a group of dignitaries at the opening of the Calgary Stampede? Cora with a committee of cattle experts, judges at the Royal Agricultural Winter Fair in Toronto?

The second photo is a picture of the great woman at work. A closeup, in profile, of Hind examining a huge sheaf of wheat, which she has clutched in her left hand. She is much older here — in her sixties or seventies — and she wears steel-rimmed granny glasses and a very broad brimmed hat. She is studying the grain, feeling it through her cotton gloves, turning it over in her hands. A study in brown concentration. Her face is turned away, and you can't see much of its expression, only the square set of the jaw, the steady gaze, and the soft lines covering her cheek like feather quilting. This is Cora Hind in her prime: the international celebrity, first among her peers in the fourth estate, first among her sex to achieve such high honour in journalism.

The sharp increase in the numbers of women journalists, on air and in print, over the last two decades sometimes gives people the impression that their appearance was sudden. Perhaps we have been paying more careful attention to the achievements of women recently. Perhaps, having just passed through a couple of decades of firsts, breakthroughs, and new records for media women, we assume that such major advances have been packed into our own time. We forget that women have been practising journalism in Canada for almost a century.

What were they like, these women who were the fore-mothers of today's media women? They were rebels and adventurers: independent, curious, and fired with ambition to act on a wider stage than the one home and custom had allotted them. Feeling stifled, yet knowing somehow that their instincts were right, they abandoned convention and set out to find a way to accommodate their talents and realize their dreams. Sara Jeannette Duncan, Kathleen Blake Coleman, Gaëtane de Montreuil, and E. Cora Hind were four of the first, all of them born in the decade of Confederation. All four were determined that they would write for the newspapers whether the newspapers were willing to have them or not; all pursued that purpose with cunning and courage; and among them their careers spanned six decades and three continents.

Sara Jeannette Duncan — Redney, as she was called all her life by everyone who knew her — was born and brought up in Brantford, Ontario, the eldest surviving child among eleven in a large and well-to-do family. Even as a child she had one great desire and special purpose, which was to write. She longed to travel among the literary lights of her time and to experience that world of passion and colour which she somehow knew was where she belonged. She was a restless romantic: stubborn, superbly gifted, and very easily bored.

When she was seventeen, Duncan announced to her startled parents that she planned to become a journalist. It wasn't news that she wanted to write, of course — her father had especially encouraged her efforts — but he drew the line at journalism. Marian Fowler writes, in her wonderful biography called *Redney*, "Journalism wasn't at all a suitable occupation for a gently reared young lady, working in a smoky office full of shirt-sleeved men, spitoons, and smutty jokes. It was quite as improper as going on the stage." Besides, there were taboos no woman had yet defied in 1879. "No woman had ever worked in the office of a major Canadian newspaper. A few gentle ladies scribbled columns in the safe sanctuary of their plush parlours, but a woman working in an office? Never." Never, that is, until Redney.

For five years, Duncan schooled herself, carefully honing her skills by working for a local paper, probably the Brantford *Courier* since it was "kindly disposed" to women journalists and had had a couple of women writing for it in the past. One day in 1884 she saw an advertisement for the New Orleans World Fair and, in a flash of inspiration, realized that she was looking at her golden opportunity. With splendid aplomb, she took herself to Toronto, talked the editor of the *Globe* into accepting her as a special correspondent, and left for the United States. Redney was a brilliant success in New Orleans. She was immediately taken up by local society and joined the swirl of visiting celebrities; she also became something of a literary sensation herself, as she quickly began contributing to American newspapers as well as the *Globe*.

This expedition concluded, Duncan set her sights on her next conquest: the *Washington Post*. One of the most widely read papers in the United States, the *Post* was also a fairly good bet, since women had worked there before. Duncan was hired immediately, not as a reporter but a cut above, as an editorial writer. She was only twenty-four at the time. Twenty-four, and charged with more energy and ambition than Washington could contain. After a few months, the novelty of the job and the excitement of the American capital waned, and a sudden attack of homesickness brought Redney back home again.

Now that she was resplendent with American laurels, Canadian doors swept open at her approach. The *Globe* hired her immediately to write a daily column called "Women's World." This daily column kept her on the move, tramping through the muddy streets of Toronto, searching for material — people and places to describe, human foibles to satirize. Still she had time to keep up two columns in the Toronto *Week*, where she'd been writing for some time. To "Saunterings" she now added "Afternoon Tea," covering social and cultural events. Her writing style was well established by this time, as was her journalistic "persona," described by Fowler as amusing, opinionated, and steely. The range of her subject matter was broad, her tone cosmopolitan, and though she was politically rather conservative, on the subject of female self-sufficiency she was thoroughly modern and adamant. She herself was the embodiment of the New Woman of the 1880s who wanted to vote, pursue a career, smoke, ride a bicycle, talk politics, and play golf.

In the winter of 1888, Duncan moved in quick succession to Montreal and then Ottawa, clearly driven by restless ambition. She wrote a column called "Bric-a-brac" for the Montreal *Star*, and then went on to the capital as the paper's parliamentary correspondent (one of two women in the Press Gallery at the time), on the lookout for new subjects, new people, and excitement. She traded in the artistic milieu she had found in Montreal for the formalities of official Ottawa. To her chagrin, however, Duncan found that rigid custom barred her from participating in many important events, first because she was writing for a Liberal newspaper (when the Conservatives were in power), and second because she was unmarried. In the end, it didn't much matter. Ottawa, like Toronto, Montreal, and Washington, could not quell her wanderlust.

Duncan set off on a trip around the world, accompanied by a contemporary from Montreal named Lily Lewis. Scandalous! Two unchaperoned women who, furthermore, had the audacity to reverse the approved order for such grand tours by travelling backwards; that is, westward. As if trying to guarantee that she would have the adventures she craved, Duncan made a point of travelling without guidebooks or firm plans, deliberately staying off the tourist track and inviting the unexpected to happen. At the end of it all she had plenty of material for her first book, *A Social Departure*, and a marriage proposal from a dashing young English entomologist who was working at the Calcutta museum.

Duncan's marriage to Everard Cotes and her life in India did not bring her much happiness (her only child died a few days after birth), but they did afford her a home base and the opportunity to write. Her books appeared at regular intervals: more books of travel impressions, essays about life in colonial India, and the life work of her soul, the novels. Her masterpiece, *The Imperialist*, was published in 1904 and with it Duncan artistically and spiritually came home. The novel is set in a small town called Elgin (aka Brantford) and is a story of politics, community, and the maturing idealism of youth in a young country. In scope and depth, it was extremely ambitious, and its lukewarm reception stung Duncan. The reviewer in the *Canadian Magazine* was condescending as well as cool, warning readers to "kindly remember that a woman attempting politics must be judged leniently."

Kit Coleman, another pioneering Canadian newspaper woman, was born in Ireland. She emigrated to Canada in 1884, when she was twenty, gratefully leaving a bad marriage behind. She had no special training for journalism and no previous leanings in that direction, but somehow she managed to land a job with the Toronto *Mail* (before it amalgamated with the *Empire*) to edit a weekly women's page that she impudently called her "Woman's Kingdom." Coleman was to rule from this roost for the next twenty-one years; she was the first woman ever employed by a Canadian newspaper in such an editorial capacity and she was one of the very best. At first the "page" was only half a page that didn't stray much beyond the "Fashion Notes and Fancies for the Fair Sex" announced in the heading. Soon, however, Coleman was allotted a full page and, with that expansion, began to broaden her horizons, throwing in items about her travelling experiences and other adventures. She introduced "Potpourri," in which she wrote eye-witness reports of momentous events of the day, including the Klondike Gold Rush and Queen Victoria's Diamond Jubilee. Coleman's "Kingdom" became one of the most distinctive sections of the newspaper and was read avidly by men as well as women.

The climax of Coleman's journalistic career came in 1898, when she caught the scent of battle and decided, against the advice of everyone (including the *Mail and Empire*), to go to Cuba as a correspondent and cover the Spanish-American War. Getting there was the most arduous part of the adventure. First she had to convince the American Secretary of War to permit her to follow the troops with the other journalists; then she had to get a ship to take her there. Kit watched as the newspapermen departed with the troops from Port Tampa, realizing that she had been left behind deliberately. On the fourth try she made it, arriving in Cuba three weeks before Santiago surrendered. On the return voyage, she accompanied a shipload of wounded soldiers, with no doctor or medical supplies on board. Using her own small supply of drugs, Kit did her best to help the worst cases. The story of the "lady war correspondent" was sensational news. The British played it up in the press, and the Americans were equally enchanted, wanting Coleman to go on a nation-wide lecture tour. (She would have been delighted, except that she thought the war had been woefully mismanaged by the Americans from start to finish, and wasn't prepared to tell American audiences that.)

That same year, Coleman married and moved to Northern Ontario. In 1904, she joined a party of women journalists travelling to the St. Louis Exposition. The women had had to petition the CPR for the same courtesy passes that had been given to the men. Instead of complying graciously, the railway had issued a snide challenge to the women to produce a dozen paid writers of their sex — if they could. They came up with thirteen, and it was on the journey to the fair that the need for a women's press club was first discussed. The Canadian Woman's Press Club was founded in 1906, with Kit as its first president. In 1911, Coleman gave up her "Woman's Kingdom," which she had been editing from a distance for over a decade, and resigned from journalism. She was already in failing health, and in 1915 she died at the age of fifty-one.

Coleman reigned over her "Kingdom" for twenty short

years; Duncan, though she wrote all her life, was a journalist for only ten. Gaëtane de Montreuil's career lasted longer, but it too suffered interruptions, absences, and ups and downs. It was marked by a couple of exhilarating high points, interspersed with deep troughs of difficulty and disappointment. Gaëtane was not a prodigy like Redney or Kit, and she was well into her twenties before she began publishing. Her breakthrough came in 1898, when she was hired by the publisher of *La Presse* in Montreal to supervise the paper's "page féminine." The section was called *Pour Vous Mesdames* and consisted of her "chronique" touching on diverse subjects, literary reviews and essays, poetry, and her letters column, *La Petite Correspondence*. This was a genre that de Montreuil made famous in French-Canadian journalism and it was she who devised the format. Her objective was to engage readers in a dialogue through an exchange of views, and she considered it part of her "mission" as a journalist to forge new ideas. Ever cool and self-assured, in the delivery of her own opinions she seems to modern eyes quite condescending in style, but that didn't deter readers from writing in. Eighty-five hundred did, in one year alone.

De Montreuil remained at *La Presse* until 1903. She was then thirty-five and the previous year had married the poet Charles Gill. The next ten years were spent in semi-retirement, though she continued to write poetry, short stories, and even an historical novel, published in 1912.

From all accounts, including her own, Gaëtane de Montreuil was not an easy person to get along with. She had a troubled life and bore the scars of personal disappointment with some bitterness. Although she was a fervent believer in marriage and motherhood, her own marriage failed, and only one of the two children born to her survived infancy. A single mother and financially on her own by 1913, she somehow managed to make a living and keep writing through a long lifetime. In 1925, she was briefly rehired by *La Presse*, but by then she was a confirmed loner and didn't fit in well. She was fired after a few months. For all that, she was a courageous woman, blessed with a vivacious spirit and an armour-plated sense of purpose. She wrote continuously and abundantly into the 1930s, and published her last novel in 1946.

Another child of the 1860s, Cora Hind, had two abiding passions in her long life: prairie agriculture in the great unfolding Canadian West that was her adopted home — and writing about it. She was forty years old, though, before she got the chance to combine the two, by which time she was already a legend in the West. Almost twenty years had passed since the day Cora and her Aunt Alice had arrived from Ontario and Cora had applied directly to the editor of the *Manitoba Free Press* for a job. Perhaps she had heard of women working on newspapers (in 1882 there could only have been a handful in all of Canada); perhaps it was her own idea. Either way, the editor was having none of it. Cora was allowed to fill in an application and then was shown the door.

In 1882, the biggest thing going for the bustling town of Winnipeg was its promise. The first shipment of seed wheat to the East had been made only seven years before, the plains resounded with the thunder of the last buffalo hunts, and Louis Riel was still alive. What work could a young woman, orphaned at five and raised on a relative's farm in Ontario, possibly do for a living? Well, she figured she could always type. In 1882, that was a brilliant and original idea. The first typewriting machines had just arrived in Winnipeg, and Cora discovered that no one knew how to operate them. In short order she rented one, taught herself to type, and got a job with the law firm of MacDonald, Tupper, Tupper and Dexter. For the next ten years, Cora Hind worked in that office, chatting with all the farmers, cattlemen, merchants, and businessmen who came for appointments. In 1893, she opened her own bureau, becoming the first public stenographer west of the Great Lakes. Here she was even better placed to pursue her real interest, agriculture. At first, Cora picked the brains of clients who dropped by, but before long she was sharing information and knowledge of her own. Her bureau became a well-known meeting place for all sorts of people passing through town and Cora was the resident font of news, gossip, and intelligence. Dairy farmers' and cattlemen's associations invited her to their gatherings, not only because of what she could contribute but also because she would write up the reports of the meetings — which the *Free Press* would usually publish.

In 1898, Hind got her first opportunity to do a crop inspection, a profession which was to make her world famous. Old Col. J.B. Maclean, the business publisher from Toronto, had visited Cora in her office and seen her in action, so when news came that wet weather was preventing the crop from ripening, he wired asking her to make a survey.

Cora took the train west that night and, in the ensuing days, devised a system for surveying that she was to use for the rest of her career. It involved closely scrutinizing the landscape through the windows of the train as it edged west and talking with railwaymen, farmers, and townspeople along the way who were knowledgeable about conditions. She would arrive in a town, hire a team and driver, and head out across the prairie, carefully noting the fields and the conditions, and taking samples here and there.

Cora Hind was a diminutive woman but stoutly built and more than up to the physical demands of her work. What made the going difficult was not the terrain so much as the attire convention forced upon her — long skirts, tweed jackets, a decorous hat, and button boots. These she soon discarded in favour of breeches, high boots, gaiters, and a broad-brimmed felt hat. This was an extraordinary get-up for a female in those days, when farm women struggled through their chores in long, voluminous skirts. Once she got used to it, Cora Hind rather delighted in making a feature of her odd outfit. For special occasions, especially trips to Toronto, she added the beaded buckskin jacket presented to her by the Calgary Stampede and sported a gold-handled cane she was given by the Winnipeg Stocker and Feeder Show.

By 1901, the *Winnipeg Free Press* had acquired a new name and a new editor, J.W. Dafoe, who invited Cora Hind to join his staff, unaware at first that she had once applied and been rejected. She became the first woman agricultural editor in Canada and probably in North America — and one of the few women doing editorial work of any kind. She had an office, a space of her own in the paper, and a free hand with her department. Then, in 1904, the wheat crop again looked like it was in trouble, threatened this time by black rust. Experts in Canada and the U.S. were predicting ruin: a harvest of maybe 34 million bushels.

Cora wasn't prepared to have the West so easily written off by Eastern and American speculators. She proposed doing a survey and Dafoe agreed. Her estimate, laboriously tabulated, came in at 55 million bushels. Dafoe published her report and it caused a sensation. Other papers picked it up and it was headline news everywhere. The *Free Press* was putting itself out on a limb for Hind, backing her and supporting her point of view. When the actual yield for that year was finally announced, they were vindicated. The wheat harvest came in at 54 million bushels and Cora Hind was a hero.

From then on, Cora Hind's survey of the wheat crop was an annual event. Year after year, her estimates were more accurate than anybody's, more accurate than any government or other official prediction. And each summer, when Cora was preparing her survey, everyone waited and watched. The newspapers, the farmers, governments, grain exchanges, and banks — the entire country waited. Her report was always a carefully guarded secret that no one, not even her publisher, could see until it was ready for typesetting. For the size of the crop determined the price of wheat, and on the success of the wheat crop turned the fortunes of the entire West.

During her years as a journalist, Hind was always more than a reporter. She was a hands-on expert. She knew the business, understood the intricacies of the market, and was familiar with agricultural research. Governments called her in for consultation, and farmers' groups eagerly enlisted her interest in their activities. She was respected and revered around the world in a way no other woman has ever been in the field of agriculture. She was, however, never a disengaged expert. She was partisan and passionate about the West and about agriculture, and was never shy about defending either. In 1917, when businessmen were carping about the low forecast they expected her to make that year, wailing that Calamity Cora was about to savage the prestige of the West, she snapped back, "No one loves the West more than I do. I have seen it grow up but very early in my newspaper career I learned that the West was big enough and strong enough to have the truth told about it on all occasions."

In 1922, Cora travelled to England, where she took the opportunity to do a little politicking over the heads of state on behalf of Western cattle ranchers. She was concerned about the cattle embargo that Britain had promised to lift but hadn't because of false rumours of diseased Canadian herds. Cora had her facts; she also had her reputation with the British press, which turned out en masse to interview her. Several London papers, including the *Times*, took up the cause, pressuring Whitehall to lift the embargo. With a few well-planted words, Cora accomplished what the Canadian government and fleets of diplomats hadn't been able to do in thirty years.

Ten years later, Hind was on another voyage to England, this time in the first cargo ship carrying grain out of the port of Churchill. Hind had applied to all the proper authorities for permission to sail on this ship and had repeatedly been turned down: it was too dangerous and difficult a passage and ships often foundered in the fog and ice. Hardly one to be deterred by such fears, Hind took the train to Churchill anyway and tried to talk the captain into letting her go. His first answer was no. There were no facilities for a woman on board. But he must have been persuaded by Hind's disappointment and, realizing he would be spending most of his time on the bridge anyway, let her have his own cabin. She was on deck when the ship steamed into port in Britain. The ship had been christened *Youth*, and Cora Hind, at age seventy-one, was as young as any of them.

During the madcap early years at the *Free Press*, when the West was growing so fast you could hear it, Cora Hind must have felt she was standing right in the centre of the world, where the forces of technical and social progress met and exploded into the future. As might be expected, she was a feminist and a suffragist. She helped found the Winnipeg Political Equality League, which undertook one of the most enterprising and successful suffrage campaigns anywhere in the Dominion. Cora, along with Nellie McClung, was an active member of the League, and she surely must have been present on that famous evening in 1914 when crowds packed the Walker Theatre for the mock parliament in which Nellie played the "premier" receiving a delegation of supplicant men asking for the vote. Her devastating take-off of Premier Rodmond Roblin's fatuous rejection of the women's vote brought the house down. Not too long after, the Roblin government fell, the Liberals took office, and, in 1916, Manitoba was the first province in the country to pass legislation that gave women the vote.

Whether or not pioneer journalists like Duncan, de Montreuil, and Coleman were outspoken advocates for women's rights, they were certainly advertisements for the New Woman professional. But of the four, it is Cora Hind who seems most modern today, closer to our age than to the century she was born in. Because she was active until her death in 1942, memories of her are still vivid; because she was also part of a movement that reaches down into our own time, her presence seems immediate. She died at eighty-one, a celebrity who was honoured, awarded, and beloved. The Hind legend has waxed not only because of what she did as a newspaperwoman, but because of what she believed in and stood for. The pictures of Cora Hind decked out in her surveying finery hardly seem out of place in an era that has challenged every dress code known to fashion and tradition. Her breeches would be considered no more eccentric today than Farley Mowat's kilt.

Cora Hind's achievements remain unmatched. As a journalist with a rare gift for a field which to this day cultivates a certain air of machismo, she more than held her own. She became a leading expert in the growth industry of the day, and consequently became more influential, politically and economically, than any of her colleagues. Today, it would be like having the world authority on oil and gas production and the most accurate predictor of energy reserves in the West writing for the *Edmonton Journal*.

In yet another way, Cora Hind's life seems different from those of her sisters in journalism, who for all their independence of spirit were conventional in their personal lives and still firmly ensconced in the nineteenth century. Cora was the only one who never married and, moreover, did not regret it. She once said that she never envied other women their husbands, though she often did their sons. Being single may have spared her energy for her work and enthusiasm for her causes. For Kit, Redney, and Gaëtane, marriage was not on the whole helpful to their careers, although in Redney's case at least it didn't actually impede her writing. One suspects that for Coleman and de Montreuil, who married late in life, it was something of a deliverance (both financial and social) from an ambiguous status. Perhaps because she was living so close to the frontier, spinsterhood was less threatening to Hind.

Women journalists are still rebels and adventurers; they are still motivated by intense curiosity and the desire to find things out, to see the world and how other people live. They are still fascinated by power and the people who wield it, and are drawn by the action and the thrill of being there as the great events of our times unfold. They are often, still, breaking old moulds, defying the expectations family and society have of them as women/wives/mothers.

In a hundred years, though, the media have also changed; they have become institutionalized and bureaucratized. Women are no longer considered freaks if they choose a career in journalism and stick with it through a lifetime. Acceptance has come, but bringing with it the drawbacks of rules, regulations, and procedures. It is harder now to take matters into individual hands, to break step with tradition and prejudice by simply disregarding it. The escapades of a Kit Coleman or Sara Jeannette Duncan would be nigh-on impossible to pull off today. But then, they were alone and had no choice but to act alone. Women journalists today have each other's company, and there is uncommon strength, daring, and delight in those numbers.

TWO

Gentlewomen of the Press

TUCKED AWAY in an unremarkable corner of suburban Toronto, in a green-painted clapboard house, live June Callwood and her husband Trent Frayne. They have lived here together for most of their married life and the house has altered with the ebb and flow of four children growing up, leaving home, and returning with grandchildren. The trees have grown tall in the garden. It is February, but an early break in the weather hints of spring, and some neighbourhood boys are out practising minute shots in the basketball hoop over the garage. Callwood sticks her head out the door. "Boy, have you two grown over the winter!" she calls out cheerfully.

June Callwood's workspace is in an open nook a few steps above the livingroom area and just off the kitchen. She likes to be in the middle of things, with a good view. Her desk sits in a window overlooking the garden where the ashes of her youngest, Casey — just nineteen when he was killed in a highway accident — are buried. Life renews itself and there, propped up in the window, is a photo of two happy, laughing baby girls, her daughter Jessie's children, who catch her eye whenever she gazes out.

June turned sixty this year. She has been writing for magazines and newspapers for forty years and married almost as long. She and Frayne met at the *Globe and Mail* and in 1984 they both rejoined the paper as columnists (he, sports; she, City Living). Life for them has come full circle. The Callwood—Frayne marriage, almost as well-known as they are, has carried on through troubles and triumphs, and hinges on a deep and lively friendship that people around them can feel. It seems to be everything marriage was once cracked up to be: warm, open, affectionate. From the bedrock of family and friends, Callwood draws strength and support around her like a handwoven shawl, radiating generosity and welcome back out to everyone she meets. She's approachable and caring, always listens, and usually finds time to help.

Callwood began working during World War II, when women journalists had already become a regular feature in Canadian newspapers — not normally as part of the general news staff but on the women's page. They were "lady" journalists, whose columns were familiar fixtures in daily newspapers. It was standard practice then for a good paper to cover social news, providing readers with colourful accounts of the glittering highlights of the season. (In those days Society had a season the way baseball and television have now.) It was also de rigueur for ladies to correspond in a more personal and literary vein about their travels, their gardens, and their encounters with the wider world of ideas. Many of them wove politics and talk of women's rights into their writings, threading news of the New Woman through their flowery prose.

By the late 1930s, when June Callwood left high school and took a job with the *Brantford Expositor*, a handful of women were doing general news reporting, working with the men in the newsroom. Some papers simply refused to accept applications from women for these jobs. Others would hire women reporters only if they remained single. So secure were publishers about their preserve, so sure of its propriety and permanence, that none of the dailies young Lotta Dempsey worked on in the late 1920s and the 1930s bothered to install a women's washroom on the editorial floor. In her autobiography, *No Life For A Lady*, Dempsey wrote:

> The social editors and the managing editor's secretary tended to be the sole skirted inhabitants of the otherwise

all-male bastion. The social editor was out a lot, attending such affairs as pink teas. So, when not at her typewriter, she could use the facilities of some of the town's most prestigious bathrooms. At the office, with the managing editor's secretary, she would make the trip upstairs or down to the advertising, want ad, circulation or business offices. That's where the women were, in low-pay service jobs, and that, naturally, was where the women's wash-rooms were.

Ah! The social editor, doyenne of the ladies' press, mistress of her domain, discreetly removed from the crudities of the newsroom. Callwood remembers them as terribly respectable, impeccably dressed women who always wore hats and gloves and had three names. Most of them were married, which was quite the expected thing for society reporters and editors, and they wore the three names as a badge of their station in private life. They thought of their newspaper work as something they did on the side, as a hobby rather than a career, and though many worked full-time it was rather like doing community volunteer work.

Even newspaperwomen who were serious professionals and thought of themselves first and foremost as journalists were segregated from the men. Marjorie Earl, who joined the *Toronto Star* in 1942 as a rookie newshen, was not allowed to sit with the newsmen in the city department but was given a desk in the women's department instead. "J.E. Atkinson [the *Star's* publisher] insisted. He thought my presence would demoralize the men, so they went to great expense to run a phone line from the news department."

June Callwood went to work at sixteen because she had to. Hard times, an unhappy home life, and a mother who was anxious to see her beautiful elder daughter out earning her own keep were persuasive reasons to leave school early. The *Expositor* had its share of hats with three names then, and two female news reporters: Isobel Plant and Miss Ethel Raymond. "Miss Raymond was a perfect character. She wore gloves and I think sometimes typed with them on, and she always kept her hat on in the office. She was a stoutly corseted woman who couldn't spell, and the managing editor, who had an accent I later learned from Professor Higgins was British working-class, hated her with a passion and he then concluded he hated all women." But he was fond of June because, she surmises, she looked so young and brought out his paternal instinct. He worried about her and "he taught me how to write a lead and initiated my education as a journalist."

For Callwood and other women, the war provided an unexpected advantage. Towns like Brantford were bustling with activity and there weren't enough men left on the paper to cover everything. The big city dailies were forced to hire women too, though short supply sent them out beating the bush leagues for recruits. Which is how it happened that, after two years on the *Expositor*, Callwood found herself talking on the phone to an editor from the *Toronto Star*, who was offering her a job at $25 per week — twice what she was making. She may have been an ingenue, but Callwood had figured out that the *Brantford Expositor* was not the ultimate challenge, even though it was a great start. She had begun editing the country news, which came in late in the day from rural stringers, scribbled in pencil. She had learned to type and to be a photographer, and when she graduated to general news she was assigned stories considered a bit too rugged for Miss Raymond, such as being a "war correspondent" covering activities at the local army and airforce base.

Happy to be leaving home, Callwood set off for Toronto in high spirits and reported bright and early for work at the *Star* on the appointed day. The man in charge took one look at her eager young face and demoted her on the spot.

> They made me a secretary in the rotogravure section. I didn't even realize what that was, I was so optimistic and such a fool! I did cutlines for the pictures and answered all the mail. Within two weeks I had written an army sergeant at Camp Borden (who had criticized the caption under the picture of a tank) to say that I was really amazed to learn that sergeants could read. My father was a sergeant and I thought he'd see it as a joke. He didn't. Neither did the *Star*, and I was fired.
>
> So I went to the *Telegram* to see if they had openings and was told they weren't hiring women except as

secretaries. I then stopped off at a recruiting station to join the airforce, which was how I found out they didn't train women pilots — only men — and I wasn't going to join up if I couldn't be a pilot, so I went on to the *Globe*. It was in the same situation as other papers, frantic for reporters, so they took me on a three-day trial.

The *Globe and Mail* gave Callwood an apprenticeship in the big leagues. Years later, she would talk about the enormous importance of having a comfortable place to learn as a young person starting out, where mistakes are permitted. She was probably remembering her shy and unworldly young self, working alongside the hard-bitten old news pros in the rough world of journalism. She made it because she was clever, absorbing the lessons as fast as they came, and because she ran into some generous souls who saved her bacon more than once. Perhaps it was out of concern for an eighteen-year-old kid alone in the big city; perhaps it was Callwood's sunny nature. In any case, during her three-day trial she was sent to cover meetings of the Ontario Medical Association and walked into a situation she didn't know how to handle. Confronted with a bewildering agenda that defied any logic of reporting that she understood, Callwood stumbled around until the *Star*'s Don Carlson took her under his wing and helped her write her pieces, even though he was scooping himself in the process, since the *Globe* was a morning paper.

Once on staff, Callwood was assigned suitably "soft" assignments like the Board of Education meetings, the Miss Toronto Pageant, or Eaton's and Simpson's splashy fashion shows. Sometimes she was sent to the courts, where she caught glimpses of worlds she'd never seen before. On one occasion she covered the trial of a woman who was up on a manslaughter charge for aborting herself with Lysol. The woman already had ten children, but the law was firm. To convent-educated June, it was a shocking revelation. She got a crash course in the politics of reproduction that made a lasting impression. "I think a lot of my position on abortion stems from that time."

On another case, being female proved to be an advantage that backfired. It was a series of trials in which a single prosti-

tute was the key prosecution witness against eighteen defend-
ants. The prosecutor was extremely helpful, "much more so
than if I had been a man," Callwood recollects. She was
allowed to hang around the witness, and so discovered that
the woman was a heroin addict whom the police were keeping supplied so that she could testify. Callwood reported the
fact, the *Globe and Mail* printed it, and the following afternoon
the judge threw all eighteen cases out of court and rapped
the paper's knuckles for sending such a green reporter to
cover the case.

That situation, however, was not the one which imperiled
Callwood's job. Reporting on the seamy side of life as it
trailed through the justice system was considerably less
alarming than her lengthy ordeal at the hands of the *Globe*'s
boss:

> I had a very serious problem with George McCullagh
> who owned the *Globe and Mail*. Very serious. He was
> only in his thirties, a very fit and handsome man and
> enjoyed the company of young women. He asked me up to
> his office one day shortly after my arrival and talked to
> me about my future as a writer. At first I was delighted;
> McCullagh often fraternized with staff. I'd seen him
> hanging round the cafeteria chatting with them. I was
> stunned to be in his office with its stately panelling and
> adjoining dining room. He told me he had a suite at the
> Royal York Hotel and asked if I would like to have
> dinner with him. I knew I wouldn't get out of that hotel
> room with my hymen, but I didn't want to lose my job
> either. So I said that I was busy. He kept on asking and I
> kept on being busy. Well, after a while, I'd been called
> upstairs to his office so often that all my protectors
> downstairs on the editorial floor knew about it and were
> horrified. Bob Farquharson, The Managing Editor, on
> occasion would give me an assignment and leave orders
> that under no circumstances could I be taken off it. The
> woman on the switchboard would cover for me when
> McCullagh called: she'd tell him she was looking for me
> and then tip me off so I could hide in the ladies' room in
> case he came down.

Once McCullagh asked me out to his house and, thinking everybody was going, I agreed and found myself alone in his chauffeured car. He thought it would be much more convenient if I just stayed the night; his wife wasn't home so I could have the room down the hall, and the chauffeur would take me back in the morning. I invented some reason why I absolutely had to be back at my apartment and fled. But the day finally came when there were no more places to hide from George McCullagh. I told him I had a date with a man. "I'll give you a lot more fun than he will!" was his response. I reminded him that he was the same age as my mother. He called me a fool and instructed Bob Farquharson to fire me.

Farquharson, to his great credit, dug in his heels and adamantly refused. But that confrontation didn't quite put an end to the harassment:

Finally, I told McCullagh I was going to be married and when he wanted to know if I had slept with Bill [Trent] yet, I said yes, figuring it might put him off. "Well," he said, "I want to be the one who gives you away." We fixed a wedding date and then as soon as McCullagh had gone off on one of his trips to England we moved the date up so I didn't have George McCullagh take me down the aisle. Bob Farquharson did.

It reads like the script of a tawdry melodrama, but what if Callwood *had* been fired? What if there hadn't been responsible men around to intercede? Would her career, hardly begun, have foundered? What if she hadn't found Trent Frayne, the man she's been married to these forty years, a man she says she loved before she met him, having once spied his picture in the newspaper? At that stage in her life, Callwood's thoughts were squarely on marriage and children, and when the first was born in 1945 she was elated: "I figured my real life had finally begun."

This was not exactly an auspicious beginning for someone who was going to become one of the star journalists of her generation. But even then, there were those who could see the sparkle of promise. Ross McLean, who knew Callwood first in the Brantford days, remembers her "landing among us with an impact you could measure on the Richter scale." That energy has since touched many lives and spanned many media. Callwood is a remarkable woman — one of our best-known journalists, and also one of the best-loved women in the country. She is respected and admired by people all across the political spectrum and is habitually asked to run for office by everybody. She is also one of the very few writers (Germaine Greer is another) who can turn motherhood into a controversial issue. June has been doing that since the mid-sixties.

Children are Callwood's great joy and lifelong cause. She worries about the life and health of babies and, time and again, the distress of children has moved her to action. In the late 1960s, it was Digger House, a relief centre for drop-outs, runaways, and kids in trouble with drugs. She teamed up with David DePoe and other hippie community workers in Toronto's Yorkville area, where the "flower children" were hanging out, to the great annoyance of local merchants, the city fathers, and the police. In the 1970s, it was Nellie's, a shelter for battered and indigent women and their children; in the 1980s, Jessie's, a centre for teenage mothers. Callwood is no chequebook philanthropist; she's a social activist who still does a regular night shift at Nellie's.

The list of June's causes, committees, and chairships is lengthy, and what she stands for is very much a part of who she is and what makes her tick as a writer. She is what the French would call a *journaliste engagé*, a writer who is openly involved in social reform. Some would call it advocacy journalism, but Callwood has not often been stuck with that label; partly, she thinks, because the position she speaks from is unassailable. "I do not have to go and interview people about battered wives. I have firsthand information. No one can call me on the facts, or the issues I talk about. As for speaking out personally, I have the right." And, as a veteran vice-president of the Canadian Civil Liberties Association, she knows what she's talking about.

It may be that Callwood's secret lies in her openness and

her capacity to empathize, to sense the psychological dimensions of human behaviour and capture those truths with words. These were not qualities she knew she had at the outset, and, in fact, it was some time before she fully realized that writing was to be her life's work. Bored and restless at home with a toddler, she turned to freelancing for the *Globe*, and then decided to take flying lessons. Her instructor was a woman. "Violet Millstaed was her name and *she* had gotten herself into the airforce as a pilot — albeit for non-combat duty, delivering aircraft. But she flew Spitfires."

It was still a few more years before Callwood was to write the piece which she describes as the first real writing of her life. "I finally learned how to do it when Jill was three or four. I started doing articles for *Maclean's* and for the first time pushed myself to see how well I could write — I had been playing games all that time. And I found I had something." The "moment" was an article about a child prodigy named Patsy Parr who played the piano. It was to be an easy little upbeat piece, only this time Callwood saw something more:

> Previously I would have written about the clever little eleven-year-old girl and her nice mother. But this time I saw the relationship and heard a click. I saw a child being pushed to the edge by a mother who was living through her. I was careful not to do damage; so I wrote about the long hours of practicing which meant the little girl couldn't go outside to play with her friends. She performed with the Toronto Symphony Orchestra, had a short career, and then she broke. She was a teenage failure and it was all there when she was eleven.

Through the 1950s, Callwood wrote regularly for *Maclean's* and other publications, establishing herself as one of the top magazine writers in the country. She was certainly one of the most prolific and versatile, writing more than sixty pieces over the decade. Once, in the space of five months in 1958, Callwood had three articles published in *Maclean's* on three very difficult scientific subjects: the universe, the birth control pill, and the Orenda engine that was then being built for the Avro Arrow, the Canadian-designed supersonic jet interceptor. The editor of *Maclean's* during this period was Ralph Allen, a great Callwood fan who handed her some of the best assignments. But that was only the magazine articles. Callwood also began writing books, and in three decades has produced about twenty, including several ghosted autobiographies (of Barbara Walters, Otto Preminger, and Helen Gahagan Douglas). Two books were special labours of love, one on the human emotions called *Love, Hate, Fear and Anger*, and the other her history book, *A Portrait of Canada*. Both were milestones in her life and career.

Always the swift learner, Callwood was rarely daunted by any subject, no matter how complex or high-tech, be it astronomy, medicine, or aerospace engineering. But of all the tough subjects she has had to bone up on, she is proudest of her research into psychiatry and psychology for *Love, Hate, Fear and Anger:*

> That year I was pregnant with Casey; it was a late pregnancy, I was thirty-eight and we'd been wanting another child and had assumed we were not going to be able to have one. I was warned that I might have some difficulty and not to be too active, so I spent almost the whole nine months in the University of Toronto Library, reading. The book idea came about because of what I call The Larry Mann Phenomenon. I had just finished a piece on character actor Larry Mann. It was one of those sensitive pieces about his relationship with his brother and his weight problem, his lack of confidence and his professionalism and all that feely stuff. I thought to myself one fine day, "Am I going to spend the rest of my life writing about Larry Mann?" I knew that I was getting a reputation for "psychological insights." People would exclaim, "Imagine, your understanding that my mother didn't love me." So I began to wonder what the emotions really were, how do they develop, and why do some devlop more than others? I asked Ralph Allen if I could do a series, and worked out a package deal that was the highest on record ($1,000 a piece when they were normally paying around $500 or $600). Then I got a stack pass to the library and went around asking

experts, "What are the human emotions?" which was a very dumb-sounding question.

The experts recovered; Callwood's book was a resounding success, hailed by professionals and the general public alike, and it found its way into first-year psychology courses all over North America.

Reaching a position where she could marshall the time and the resources to prepare such a book was an achievement — it is for any Canadian writer. You have to be very productive, very good, and in Callwood's case, with three children at home, extremely well organized. On that score, she claims it was an advantage to have apprenticed in a noisy newsroom, which gave her a high tolerance for the chaos and confusion of kids underfoot. (Such tolerance, in fact, that one day when they were very little, she completely forgot whether she had fed them lunch or not and only the dirty dishes in the sink could tell her.) Long-term projects require enough money not only to pay expenses but also to buy peace of mind for the high degree of concentration longer and more complex writing projects require. Modestly, Callwood reveals the secret. "I am one of the highest-paid freelance magazine writers around because I have a husband. Had I been alone, I wouldn't have been able to hold out for higher fees, which I do every time, pushing up the limit." She considers it her responsibility to let others know what she is getting for her labours, and she did religiously for years until there was a Periodical Writers' Association to negotiate fair minimums with publishers. Though she says, "I am subsidized by a forty-year marriage, which is a little like being a millionaire socialist," her own husband has occasionally benefited from her tough stand.

If *Love, Hate, Fear and Anger* was a book about individuals coping with the world, *Portrait of Canada* was a history of a people coping with nationhood. It was a very ambitious book, grand in scope and detail, which took a great deal of courage to tackle, knowing that generations of historians have picked over every inch of the field. What makes *Portrait of Canada* important and memorable is not any reinterpretation of the principal facts of Canadian history, but Callwood's unique way of relating them. Her interest focuses on flesh-and-blood people rather than historical personages; she thinks about things like how old an individual was when making his or her mark on history and she is ever curious about the silent majority whose lives were seldom considered at all. So the reader is treated to more biography and social comment than academics tend to feel is seemly. Predictably, some of them were furious about the book and one or two said so in hairsplitting reviews.

Although Callwood is a success, she is very hard on her own work. It is a common complaint among the creative — the realization failing to live up to the conceptualization. The right word, the perfect structure, and the best metaphor always seem to be one draft away. Looking back on her career, Callwood recognizes that the biggest struggle has been the artistic one. Once launched as a freelance writer, she was spared the difficulty that some have had getting recognition and getting work. "I had a good reputation and I don't remember having to earn that against hostility." Initially, she was blessed with protective innocence. She smiles, "I suffered from a tremendous lack of awareness. I'm hyper-aware now, but then I lived in a great bubble of confidence that was almost certifiable. I assumed I could learn about heart surgery by watching operations at the Hospital for Sick Children, reading the literature, and asking questions. Although all the surgeons were men, I saw no reason why I couldn't understand it."

But there were times when she was sharply reminded that she was an interloper in a man's world:

> Two awkward things happened during the Orenda engine story; I wanted to fly the test bed B-47 at the SAC base in the U.S. It took six months to get clearance and permission and I was only the second woman to do it. The embarrassing moment (which I was warned about in advance) came when there were no washrooms aboard and the men had to urinate into bottles. The other was my moment of triumph. I was at the Orenda plant and being shown around by a man who kept me at a distance from the engine and kept insinuating there

wasn't much point in answering my questions since I wouldn't understand anyway. I knew a good deal about jets by this time and finally at one point I stopped, looked at the engine carefully, and said something about it looking as if it were capable of 20,000 pounds of thrust, easy. You should have seen his face! Then he unbuckled and had lots to say.

Slowly, her perspective on the world, and women's place in it, shifted and matured until the proverbial click:

Kate Millett, who wrote *Sexual Politics*, had introduced her editor at Doubleday to the term Ms., and subsequently my editor at Doubleday wrote me a letter addressed to Ms. June Callwood. I had never seen it before and I had to figure out what they were doing. When I did, I saw the whole feminist world in that microcosm. I could see that Mrs. and Miss (and I was entitled to use both) gave out information which is nobody's business. Originally I kept Callwood, you see, not because of feminism but because of sexism. A married woman who worked in the forties was considered a bad reflection on her husband and after I married, the *Globe* did not want its readers to know that a married woman was working as a news reporter and so they insisted I not use Frayne. When I saw Ms., everything unfolded for me. It was like I was on the road to Damascus and the goddamn light shone!

Not long after, Callwood wrote an article for *Maclean's*, entitled "Is There Radicalization after 40?," in which she talks with great amusement of her own recently raised consciousness:

Formal weddings used to make me ache with the poignancy of all that stylized show of trust and commitment. The last one I attended, however, I kept wondering why the bride had that dumb curtain on her head and why her father was leading her down the aisle to hand her over to the groom — *a man-to-man mediaeval transfer of rights*. Why was her mother relegated to a seat in the bleachers? Why didn't the bride speak up when the clergyman asked "Who gives this woman in holy matrimony?" — *is she a fully consenting adult or a warm Barbie Doll?*'

"That article," says Callwood, grinning with pleasure, "gave me a handle on everything. I took off my brassiere and haven't worn one since." She also stopped wearing make-up, even on television, and insists on presenting her face — grey hair, wrinkles, hot flashes, and all — to the public, as it comes, without artifice. Her feminism has been worked into her general philosophy of life and is expressed with clarity:

> Feminism is really my highest ideal for human conduct. Life should be as fair as we can possibly make it, given how unfair fate is. It should not be made worse for some people for reasons that are irrelevant. By regarding the relationship between men and women, we are moving towards the possibility of a fair society, where people could deal with what happens to them, and things are not so unconscionably unjust that they collapse and lose their own sense of importance and worth. I can then see children being released to achieve their potential, parents getting rid of the games and the power struggles which in turn warp children.

Christina McCall belongs to the generation that followed June Callwood into journalism. She was one of a coterie of extremely bright women who began to work as journalists in the mid-1950s, equipped with university degrees and a solid grounding in the humanities — not a background that had ever before been commonplace in newspapers. While still a student, McCall landed a summer job with *Maclean's*, helping out with their annual fiction contest. Though she had her fantasies about New York and writing for the *New Yorker*, she loved the job, the place, and the people. By chance, there was a job opening when she graduated and she happily grabbed it, starting at the step-and-fetch-it level, but progressing within a few months to research. "In those days,

Maclean's published everything: all the artists in town, all the writers in the country, and most of the political figures congregated in its pages. Next to CBC Radio, it was the centre of communication."

Very quickly, McCall decided to try her hand at writing. She wanted to do an article on a woman prospector named Viola MacMillan, who had amassed $10 million in mining interests and was president of the major association of miners on the continent. MacMillan shuttled between a Miami apartment, a mansion north of Toronto, and a downtown penthouse decorated completely in pink. McCall worked on the piece on her own time and with the rather tepid blessing of the managing editor at the time, Pierre Berton. "I was quite shy and I remember Berton's response was along the lines of 'Well, let her have a try.' He was probably thinking I'd never manage it. But I did and it was good enough for them to run it without any changes, which was pretty remarkable." It made McCall the youngest writer who had ever published an article in *Maclean's*. Berton and editor Ralph Allen recognized her talent, and when she announced that she was going to leave the magazine to marry Peter Newman, they tried hard to dissuade her. Newman was *Maclean's* Ottawa correspondent at the time, and it was he who decided that McCall ought to leave *Maclean's*. "Peter felt it would somehow be detrimental to his career if I stayed. Though it was essentially his decision, it was my choice too and I take responsibility for that. Nevertheless, it was conditioning that made me think his job was automatically more important than mine."

The only place to go from *Maclean's* was *Chatelaine*, a thought that filled her with despair. "I was pretty intellectual and I thought women's magazines were the pits. Oddly, though, *Chatelaine* was a good thing to do, for what women usually wrote about in *Maclean's* was health and welfare stuff or entertainment and I would have been stuck with that too." Instead she got Doris Anderson (editor of *Chatelaine*) who let McCall spread her wings and write on subjects of her own choosing. She wrote a major piece on the divorce laws and had a column, "It's Your World," of potted news for women, which gave her license to travel all over the political map, dealing with, for example, foreign policy and immigration.

Over the next several years, McCall worked on a number of Peter Newman's projects, helping him with his *Toronto Star* column and his books on Prime Ministers Pearson and Diefenbaker, at times working full-time on his research. Her daughter was born in 1964 and, though McCall never disappeared into the role of housewife-mother, she did at various intervals put her own ambitions aside while she tended her child and supported her husband's career. It was an arrangement that led to a lot of depression:

> Peter still didn't want me writing about politics myself. He found it threatening and disturbing. So I suppose the deal was that we needed the money. He would say that he could earn more than I could, which was true: he did usually earn twice what I did. But then I discovered, before leaving *Maclean's*, that Peter Gzowski, who came from the Chatham *Daily News* to replace me as researcher, was going to be making $7,200 where I'd earned $4,800.

In exchange for her self-effacing efforts, she got an unusual education, accompanying Newman to his interviews, on election campaigns, and on cross-country trips. But her work didn't get any credit — other than a terse and romantic dedication "to my Christina" in *Renegade in Power.* All the same, she knew she was contributing more than leg work. "I had perceptions and a response to politicians that was very fresh and very much my own and the exchange worked in a curious way because no woman on her own could get that close to politics and politicians in those days. Maybe they do now but they didn't then. Sitting like a mouse in a corner while those guys talked was a very valuable experience."

By 1967, the life of the quiet, loyal wife had palled. McCall realized she had to return to her own work. She wrote a piece for *Saturday Night* on the centennial summer, whereupon she was offered the job of Ottawa editor. "Peter found that very upsetting, but I told him I had to take it." Later on, there was a move to Toronto and the beginning of a book that was then called *The Anatomy of Canada*, in which McCall's collaboration was to get equal billing. "The book brought about the end of my marriage."

No one has the formula, of course; some media marriages thrive with both partners working in the same area, complementing each other. But the Newmans' union didn't survive the blossoming of McCall's career or her sense of being used as an unpaid, live-in researcher. Nevertheless she looks upon marriage to Newman as having been as advantageous as it was detrimental. She is, after all, the only woman who has been observing national politics at such close quarters for twenty years. There was the day, however, in 1974, when she heard her "click." Eight years later, she described it in *Chatelaine*.

It happened at a dinner party at the home of Brigadier Malone, the publisher of the *Globe and Mail*. Bruce Hutchison, the famous editor and reporter, was the guest of honour. After the meal, while the host was seeing some other guests out, Hutchison turned to Peter Newman and asked what was going on in the Canadian capital "with the particularly avid interest of an old Ottawa hand," wrote McCall:

> My husband murmured that he hadn't been in Ottawa for months but that I had spent the previous week there doing research for a book we had contracted to co-author. "Ah, gathering 'the colour,' I suppose," said the older man, who had grown up in an era when women journalists were either sob sisters or society columnists and "colour" writing was all they were thought fit for. I shrugged off the patronizing tone and, warming quickly to my subject, began to talk, describing the internecine conflicts between Pierre Trudeau and his Minister of Finance, John Turner. Just as I got to a particularly affecting piece of news about what Turner's deputy minister thought of Lalonde's social welfare ideas, our host came back in the room. The old journalist, eyes bright with interest, turned to him and called out, "Dick, come quick and sit down. *Peter* is telling me some fascinating stuff about what's going on in Ottawa.

Significantly, Newman said nothing, and in that moment McCall knew it was time to leave the marriage.

Thirty-nine years old and a single mother, McCall found herself out looking for a job. Though she had never been drawn to newspapers, that is where she now went. The *Globe and Mail* hired her as their national reporter, with a mandate to cover the country, looking at people in power and those without it, at provincial governments as well as small towns. How could you complain? This was a senior position on a paper that had the reputation of being a writer's newspaper. "To the people at the *Globe*, I had the best job on the paper. My work was never tampered with and I was allowed to take whatever time I needed to work up stories. I wrote 100,000 words during the first year, of magazine quality material, and still I always felt I wasn't writing enough. I'd be hysterical with fear and worry if I wasn't producing and my byline wasn't appearing." But McCall herself was applying the pressure, not Clark Davey or Richard Doyle, the editor and managing editor who hired her.

For all her privileges as a senior writer, McCall found the atmosphere at the *Globe* dreadful. The hierarchy of the place was mid-Victorian. "A management chart was tacked up on one of the pillars in the newsroom and there was one woman on it, the women's editor, who accounted for a single desk." The near-total absence of women was jarring, compared to her experience on magazines, but she also felt that, despite the lip service, reporters of either sex didn't really count for much at the *Globe*.

If life was strange in the newsroom, it was positively absurd on the road. It was also arduous. "It's a life with no dignity and no matter how long you do it nothing much accrues. The same energy has to be expended each time out and though I suppose you do acquire knowledge and access to people, the job itself doesn't get easier." Although McCall was never in the position where she had to jockey for position or go into head-to-head competition with other reporters, she did travel with the press corps on occasion and saw what went on. "Those men are *very* tough with each other and, my God, are they rough with women; verbally and in every other way they are obnoxious. During the Trudeau regime they were treated like zoo animals and they behaved like zoo animals, spraying each other with beer, indulging in macho talk so that it was like being on one long football weekend."

McCall's experience of the press gallery in Edmonton was equally uncivilized:

> I went to Alberta to find out who the men were around Peter Lougheed. I didn't know the province well, but I decided to begin in Calgary, where he had been a lawyer, and while I was there — through hard work and some luck — I found out what I needed to know. But because I know how politicians behave, I also got the strange feeling that Lougheed was on the verge of calling an early election. When I went to Edmonton, I was barred from the press gallery, and although friends assured me any Eastern journalist would have been treated thus, I am sure it was because I was a woman. I have a hard time believing that a man from the press gallery in Ottawa would have been relegated to the visitors' gallery, where you were not allowed to take notes. Anyway, I told them my hunch about the election, which they thought was a terrific joke.

Then she drifted off to observe the proceedings on her own. "I sat there through the day and sure enough an election *was* called. That left me in the very awkward position of having to persuade the commissionaire to let me use his telephone so that I could call Toronto!"

It wasn't too long before McCall was fed up with newspaper journalism, at least as a steady diet. Deliverance arrived in the form of an offer from *Saturday Night* to be associate editor. Even though it entailed a cut in salary, she was delighted. Moreover, McCall had finally realized that the field of politics was her forte and writing books was where she could make her best contribution, because she would be able to take a large chunk of material and develop and shape it without glossing over the complexities.

I love politics for particular kinds of reasons which I think are a woman's reasons. They have to do with the relationships of people who get themselves into an extreme state of ambition. It exists elsewhere, of course, but is very clear in politics, where you have the right to ask questions about it. I find it fascinating to see what that does to people and it definitely has had an effect on just about everyone I've ever watched. In some ways I think I find it so interesting because women, by comparison, do not yet understand how those political interchanges work. Writing about it gives me a front-row seat in the most wonderful and absorbing human drama.

In twenty years, manners and mores have changed enough that it is possible for McCall to practise her métier:

Men now talk to me as if I were a man. They will even say antiwoman things to me, which I find bizarre. Politicians will badmouth Margaret Thatcher and go on about how desperate the British are to have allowed a woman to take over their country. They will say absolutely terrible things about Monique Bégin and Iona Campagnolo and others and do not seem aware who they are talking to. At the same time, they talk to me absolutely seriously, without giving me a lot of nonsense, which is a good thing.

Despite her solid credentials, McCall was extremely nervous about *Grits*, her contemporary history of the Liberal Party in power, published in 1982. She was fearful that it would be dismissed: discounted by academics and ignored by other political journalists. She laboured over the manuscript, delaying publication, double-checking facts, agonizing over her interpretations, and scrutinizing her arguments. There would be no chances taken. As it turned out, the book was extremely well received, one of the hits of the season, and the reviews were often effusive. Still, McCall does not believe that her fears were unfounded. She knows that women have something unique to contribute to political writing but she also knows that men (and sometimes other women) can be blind to those qualities.

> Women have a completely different view of politics and bring to it a different education. People who usually write about politics or history do not bring to it much knowledge of human behaviour and I think you miss the essence of politics when you miss that. I think I notice different things; for instance, how a deputy minister relates to a minister. That can be a very volatile relationship and crucial to the making of a ministerial career.
>
> Men, I think, are oblivious to some aspects of the workings of the power structure. They know if a person is useful but will not notice the emotional exchange taking place. Why, for example, does a deputy minister with a particular temperament derive tremendous satisfaction from backing a man who has an entirely different make-up? Men don't think about those exchanges and I'm not even sure they understand the terrific kick they get from "their guy's" power, which is to say, the emotional content of their pleasure.
>
> My models are writers like Rebecca West and her book *The Meaning of Treason* — about the Soviet treason trials — in which she responded to the protagonists on both a literary and psychological level. That book was thought of as being highly subjective — too subjective. To men it is the gloss on analytic journalism. They call it "colour." To me it is the actuality. The real life.

A few months after *Grits* was published, McCall got a call from Richard Doyle, asking her to lunch with the *Globe*'s publisher, Roy Megarry, in his private dining room. It's a time-honoured, rather formal tradition for publishers to summon politicos and pundits to brief them on the state of the nation and the directions in which the political winds are blowing. "I had the sense," smiles McCall, "that I was the only

woman ever to have done that. It was an important day for
me and a good day for women too. Megarry was listening
attentively and really wanted to know what I was thinking. I
realize I probably could have had any job I wanted that
winter; and perhaps it's an instance of a woman backing away
from power. But the truth is, I don't really want to suffer that
life of the newspaper journalist. I want to write books.

Some people, including some women, suffer the life gladly.
Lysiane Gagnon is one. A columnist for *La Presse* and one of
the best-known political writers in Quebec, Gagnon has been
working for newspapers all her adult life, beginning as an
eighteen-year-old reporter for a popular weekly tabloid, *Le
Petit Journal*. She had then just completed her *cours classiques*
and, unlike most of her school friends who were heading for
university, Gagnon didn't want to continue studying, she
wanted to work. With only a vague idea of what she wanted
to do, she set out to see if she could make a living by writing.
   After a few days on the job at *Le Petit Journal*, she realized
that it wasn't just the writing she liked, it was everything: "the
editing, the newsroom, meeting people, and discovering the
curious things you do in the daily course of being a reporter."
Somehow she had landed in the right profession and there
she has stayed, working without leave and often without
holiday, engrossed. She did not, however, stay long at *Le Petit
Journal*. Once she had mastered the basics, she realized that
her prospects were limited at a small weekly that was sensa-
tionalist and, if not actually a "yellow" tabloid, was certainly
borderline. The obvious place to go was Montreal's largest
French-language daily, *La Presse*. By chance, *La Presse* had
just undergone a major internal upheaval when Gagnon
arrived with a portfolio of her best articles, carefully chosen
to impress the new editor-in-chief, Gérard Pelletier. Pelletier's
predecessor and a group of *La Presse* reporters had defected
to a rival paper (the short-lived *Le Nouveau Journal*) and
Pelletier was in a hiring mood. Gagnon got the job.
   Gagnon has worked at *La Presse* for the better part of
twenty years, following an uninterrupted trajectory from
general news to education and on to politics, as the paper's

Quebec City correspondent. In the late 1960s, she was the first woman to get the education beat, which was blistering with the heat of student unrest, government reform, teachers' strikes, and incipient language conflict. Still, she recalls that a well-known male journalist expressed surprise about a woman applying for such a job. On second thought, he mused, perhaps there were feminine aspects to the field — pedagogy, child rearing, and so on. Gagnon was aghast. Certainly that was not what intrigued her, and she told him so.

While still on the education beat, Gagnon made the political scoop of a lifetime. It was 1968. The Royal Commission on Bilingualism and Biculturalism was still in session, producing its long series of reports.

> I got my hands on one of the most explosive reports, the one which dealt with ethnic minorities and showed, among other things, that French Canadians ranked at the bottom of the socio/economic scale, just above Indians and Italians. At that moment, the Commission was deliberating about whether or not to publish it. The independence movement was very militant at the time; it was after the visit of de Gaulle, the FLQ was active, and some people were advising them not to release it. *La Presse* ran a huge series over a week and it was a tremendous event. The RCMP conducted an investigation to find out how the documents had been leaked. I was interrogated, but they never did find out.

It was a magnificent coup for Gagnon, a journalist still in her twenties. Hers became a byline to watch.

Gagnon has always worked in a predominantly male environment. In her first ten years at *La Presse*, there were rarely more than four or five women on the newsroom staff, and even today women constitute roughly twenty percent of the staff. In the Quebec City press gallery, Gagnon was again one of only three women journalists who'd found their way there. However, she has never felt isolated. On the contrary, she counts many of her colleagues as good friends. The differences she has noticed pertain less to her treatment at the hands of men than to her own work ethic. As a woman, and for a long time the youngest in the newsroom, she did feel obliged to work harder and to be more conscientious.

The Bilingualism and Biculturalism Commission coup was a turning point for Gagnon, not only because it established her as a rising star but because it boosted her self-confidence. From there, it was a natural progression to political reporting and eventually a column of her own. Confidence gave her the courage to extend her reach; her lifestyle made it possible. No children and minimal familial obligations freed her for the demands of that very taxing and time-hungry profession. Political reporting is not a job that submits to office hours or respects holidays (let alone the needs of a sick child). For that reason, Gagnon maintains, it is not the job for everyone, and she is not anxious to see it made more accessible by securing special professional concessions. She makes it sound as if it is an obsession as much as a profession. If so, it is an adored obsession, for you do not get the impression she is a self-sacrificing person, but rather one whose work and personal interests are so well-meshed that they form a seamless fabric of daily life. Moreover, political commentary takes that kind of concentrated effort to produce; it is a mature journalist's vocation, something which requires a decade or so to develop the background for, which needs practice. This may be why so few women, thus far, have entered the field, and why even fewer have stayed.

Gagnon would agree with Christina McCall that women bring a different sensibility to the task of pol-watching:

> Women are culturally conditioned to listen, to be attentive and to feel things, to negotiate rather than confront. Women are therefore less threatening to others. Men, on the other hand, are taught to suppress their emotions. If something emotional happens, say in the middle of an interview, men, even sensitive men, can be thrown off. Having been taught to handle our emotions, we are not so frightened when emotions surface — whether they are our own emotions or other people's.
>
> There is another advantage. Women are not culturally conditioned to seek out power; rather the reverse. We

shy away from it or at least from the outward manifesta-
tions of it. So, you see, women are in a very different
position in relation to men in power; we are not assumed
to be vying with them for position or even aspiring to do
so, and this means we can cover politics with a detachment and distance that is impossible for men.

Marjorie Nichols arrived in Ottawa to work for the *Ottawa
Journal* about the same time that Lysiane Gagnon was breaking into *La Presse*. As Nichols tells it, she was hired sight
unseen from Missoula, Montana on the strength of a single
letter — the only application she sent out. Having decided to
return to Canada, and knowing the nation's capital was
where she wanted to be, she simply picked the name out of
The Editor and Publisher; "I guess I liked the sound of it," she
chuckles at her youthful spunk. She had been to university in
Montana and had then got a job writing and reading the
news for an FM radio station. She was happy enough with the
work until the day someone bluntly informed her that the
highest she could ever go in broadcasting would be to write
Walter Cronkite's news for him.

At the *Journal*, Nichols started at the bottom — on the
night shift, covering the police beat. Then she began working
her way up what she calls the toothpaste tube system (i.e.
squeezed from the bottom) to better shifts and better beats,
her gaze firmly fixed on political reporting. "I can't explain
why I made a beeline for that, but sitting as a reporter doing
nightside police and Saturday morning weather, you do see
there is a pecking order and that at the very top of the heap
are the reporters on Parliament Hill." Chance came along
and gave Nichols a shove up the tube. "One of the guys on
the Hill had a heart attack and another got a Southam
fellowship (meaning he'd be away for a year) so I was sent
over to the Hill, temporarily, and stayed."

Some people would say Nichols was born with ink in her
veins. From childhood she burned with a passion for news
reporting and she knew exactly what she wanted to do in life.
She made it to the Hill in a record one year and five months.
It was 1967, and she was twenty-three years old, the youngest

reporter in the press gallery and one of four women. The others — Joyce Fairbairn, Frances Russell, and Brenda Large — had all come from the wire services; Nichols was the first woman to make it from a newspaper. Back then, wire services were the poor cousins of the newspapers (in reputation as well as salaries) and so were more likely to hire the occasional woman. "In those days women had a choice between welfare or working for UPI. Joyce [Fairbairn] went there and lived in penury, there is no other word to describe it. So if you were willing to work like a trooper with no overtime pay and no time off, like Joyce, you had a chance."

If women found it difficult to make it to Parliament Hill in those days, a lot of men did too. For one thing, the press gallery was much smaller; radio and television journalists had only been accredited in 1959, and when Nichols first arrived there were only about seventy or eighty members. Today there are more than 300. Then, too, parliamentary reporting has changed drastically, and not necessarily for the better, in Nichols' view:

> I know I'm going to sound like an old frump but I totally disagree with today's approach. Parliament used to be the genuine focus of political reporting and the debates were a major dimension of it. I remember the late shift of the *Globe and Mail* used to file running copy of the debates on the front page of the second edition. Today's reporters scarcely deign to cross the street to the House; they prefer to watch proceedings on a TV monitor in the press building. Nowadays they will send the most junior reporter to the Hill along with a tape recorder to ask some questions. But there was a time when only the select made it as parliamentary reporters and when it was a very senior, very prestigious posting. The median age of the gallery was probably over fifty.

Once Nichols got to the Hill, she was there to stay:

> I knew they could never blast me out of there because — well, I'll tell you what I did. I was given the dregs of the stories, as you can imagine, and I knew the only way I

was going to get major ones was to get them myself. So I waited around until after everyone else had gone home and then I'd comb the corridors of Parliament. I'd stay every night until eleven or midnight and I always got something. I didn't know the significance of what I was doing at the time but I met every backbencher, every messenger, every secretary, every clerk and all of the guards.

In Nichols' opinion, the real difficulty facing women is getting to Parliament Hill in the first place. A short detour after high school into an accountant's training course at the Royal Bank had taught her about discrimination and pecking orders. "Banks at that time were hiring the smartest women and the dumbest men. The men became accountants and the women became clerks." Newspapers, she reflects, were marginally less hidebound than banks, the difference being that through sheer force of talent and hard work it was possible for a woman to prevail in journalism. Nichols could supply both ingredients, in quantity. Once she had been accepted in the press corps she didn't encounter any barriers of prejudice. Yes, there was "non-support" from colleagues, but only from people she discounts as "neither intelligent nor enlightened." The rest were rather gallant. "Not that we women didn't pull our weight, but the Charlie Lynches would open the door for you rather than trample on you or elbow you in the eye, as they do these days."

For a long time, she enjoyed her special perch. "My thinking has become clearer on that. I had made it and I didn't know if I wanted to be crowded. I knew I was in a unique position then and I simply wouldn't be honest if I said that when I was twenty-five and one of the few women in the press gallery, I would have encouraged someone to open the floodgates and let in a whole lot of other women."

After six years or so on the Hill, Nichols was lured to the West Coast by the Vancouver *Sun*. Later, the FP chain sent her to Washington and her reports were syndicated in its papers. But for the past ten years she has been a political columnist for the *Sun*, conducting her nomadic life from a home base in Vancouver. She hasn't the national exposure of comrade-

in-print Allan Fotheringham, though she's equally renowned, respected, and occasionally feared in the business.

Nichols is the quintessential newspaperwoman. She loves
the rush of current affairs, pacing life to deadlines and
writing in a white heat to catch them. Forever fascinated by
the machinations of politics and power her pulse quickens at
the scent of a good story. And five days a week she reports
back to her readers. Like Lysiane Gagnon, she has by now
written hundreds, if not thousands, of articles, becoming
recognized as one of the best in the business. Like Lysiane
Gagnon, Nichols is also a happy workaholic and without
children. "It would have been absolutely out of the question
with kids. In the last two months I've been in New York,
Japan, China, Toronto, Ottawa, and next week I leave for
San Francisco. How could you do that with kids?"

When Nichols was originally hired by Bill Metcalfe at the
Ottawa Journal, he made a comment to her that stuck in her
mind. "He told me he hoped I was a country girl (which I
was, having grown up in Red Deer, Alberta) because he
figured that a farm kid from the prairies was about the most
resourceful sort of person you could find anywhere." Thinking back over the careers of those women she knew in the
early days, Nichols detects a pattern in the influence of R.S.
Malone and Bill Metcalfe, who were Publisher and Managing
Editor of the *Winnipeg Free Press* together in the 1950s. They
seem to have had a hand in advancing most women she
encountered in Ottawa in her early days. Nichols connects
that to their prairie background: first, prairie women, especially farm women, contributed to everyday work on a more
equal footing than elsewhere in the country, and second, the
legacy of Cora Hind persists. "Those men had most probably
known Hind, may even have worked with her as young
reporters."

The June 25, 1984 issue of *Maclean's* covering the Liberal
leadership victory of John Turner. Inside are four cover
story articles, three of them written by women. Another
milestone reached and passed without fanfare in the
Ottawa bureau where two of the three, Carol Goar and Mary

Janigan, are stationed. Goar has been Ottawa bureau chief for *Maclean's* since October 1982, when she was plucked from the *Toronto Star* by editor Kevin Doyle. She had been a newspaper reporter since graduating from journalism school in 1975, working successively for the *Ottawa Citizen*, Canadian Press, FP news service (where she and Janigan first met), and then the *Star*. Goar felt that her newspaper background made her a less than obvious candidate for a senior position on a magazine. But there she sits, the first woman commanding *Maclean's* Ottawa operation; a small, wiry person who dominates the room with a clear, strong voice and the force of her sharp-edged intellect.

Goar is one of those blessed individuals who has known all her life what she wanted to do. As a kid she got a thrill when *The Hamilton Spectator* arrived with a thud on the family doorstep in Burlington, and she would look through its pages thinking to herself "I'm going to write for newspapers like these someday." She wasn't the sort of kid who liked the Triple Triangle Club activities at the local Y, where you learned to make piggy banks out of old Javex bottles; so when her mother signed her up, Goar would slip off to the library next door and lose herself in books, especially the one about the amazing adventures of the American pioneer woman journalist, Nellie Bly.

At university, Goar selected her courses carefully. She realized that if she were planning to be a first-rate commentator in public affairs she had better learn what makes the economy tick. "Possibly I thought there were not too many people writing well on the subject, so it was something I could do." When she was at Canadian Press later on she asked to cover economics, only to be informed that "there were procedures." To get economics, one first had to go to Parliament Hill. Dutifully, Goar went off to spend a year on the Hill, which is how she fell, quite by accident, into political reporting. Eventually she did get to write about economics; when she left CP, she was one of their top business reporters.

When Kevin Doyle of *Maclean's* asked her to be bureau chief, Goar's first response was to accuse him of joking: "I've never run anything in my life but a typewriter," she told him. Moving into a management position was not something she had contemplated and, she says, "Frankly, I don't know if

I ever would have pushed myself in that direction." In the end, the proposal did make sense to her; knowing that her old friend Mary Janigan was already part of the Ottawa team helped persuade her.

For Goar and Janigan and their generation of the seventies, it has not seemed to be a disadvantage to be a woman and a journalist. Not only have the opportunities been there; opportunities have occasionally been thrust upon them. Explains Janigan:

> By the time we hit journalism, newspaper editors were becoming conscious that they had better Do Something. And Doing Something consisted of getting A Woman. A number of organizations hit on Carol and me as the tokens, which is why it raised eyebrows when *Maclean's* put two and then three women in Ottawa (Susan Riley being the third woman in a bureau staff of five). That was going beyond the realm of Doing Something. I think it was being gender blind.

A few people, however, as Janigan recalls, made irritating remarks:

> It was stupid. People started coming up to Carol and me to ask how the two of us were going to get along. The assumption seemed to be that two women cannot get along; a bunch of men can, but not a bunch of women. In 1982, imagine! I wonder what they expected would happen — that we would be consumed with jealousy and our friendship would go down the tubes? It hasn't been that way at all, of course. In fact, it is the easiest thing in the world to work with one of your best friends!

But what about working on Parliament Hill in the press gallery, covering one male bastion from deep within the ranks of yet another male bastion? Janigan recalls she had some trouble at the beginning, when she first arrived in 1974:

> I remember it so vividly because I took it so badly. I had been reporting since 1971 and no one had ever given me

trouble — either inside the newsroom or outside. I
came to the Hill and found that if I asked a question in
the scrum [the huddle of reporters who ply the politicians for comments in the House of Commons corridors]
it wasn't answered. If I got a man to ask it for me, it was.
That shook me up. It was a short-lived phenomenon,
but it depressed me enough to consider resigning; I very
nearly did. There was not yet a great deal of consciousness about women's role so I'd assumed *I* had done
something wrong. Also I had been raised by a very
independent-minded father and I could not compre-
hend why on earth I had to put up with such silliness. I
remember thinking at the time that if women in the past
had to put up with a steady stream of that sort of thing,
it was a wonder they weren't all jailed for assault.

Goar found that being female offered an interesting but
short-lived advantage when she was first doing interviews
with businessmen:

I found they would assume, "Ah, a woman. She's not
going to ask tough questions." So you could catch them
off-guard. You would ask an innocent first question and
follow up with a hard-hitting second and catch them
staring at you, visibly thinking "She can't possibly be
asking me this!" And then they would say something
remarkably candid and you would go back and write it
up. It was wonderful, though it didn't last long.

Possibly this is where some male journalists get the idea
that women have an unfair advantage. "They believe," says
Christina McCall, "that women journalists get material from
male politicians because they are women, which of course
isn't true. The way information is exchanged is by way of an
exchange of power, between male politicians, male bureaucrats, and male journalists. It is all part of a network of
power exchanges which they all understand perfectly." The
suggestion is, then, that women trade in something other
than power: flattery and ego stroking, with or without the
sexual innuendo. The fact is, however, that no serious

journalist could hope to build a lasting career by handing out candyfloss. In Janigan's judgement, "If you are frivolous, the crunch comes when the politician (or whoever) has six calls on his desk; he is not going to call you first."

Goar cannot recount any moment when she felt discrimination within the profession. She does admit to a sense of obligation to the women who preceded her, carefully noting, "I want to say to those women, thank you for getting us this far; but now people like me are going to react as ordinary human beings in this business." Which is to say, she sees herself as an individual, as a reporter, as an employee of *Maclean's*, and as the Ottawa bureau chief, rather than as a woman, when she approaches a story. She brings along her own personality, talents, and traits, and if gender is one of them, "so be it." But she doesn't approach her work with her female consciousness flipped on. Still, there are times when she wonders. "There are not many women's issues which come our way as political reporters, and I wonder how much of that is choice. Perhaps we are blind to them. Do we have to wait until the MPs laugh in the House when the issue of wife-beating is raised? I was appalled when that happened, and it caused me to stop for a moment and think — are we doing a good enough job here?"

If the job isn't done well, Goar is the woman responsible, at least at *Maclean's*. She does not soft-pedal the fact that she is the one who decides what will be covered; and for her it is the most tangible aspect of the power she has acquired with the bureau. "In other jobs, I could listen to the radio and wonder whether we were covering a story; now I listen and the buck stops here. I was a cog in the machine at the *Star* and CP. Here it is my job to make sure we cover everything that needs to be covered."

On a mundane level, Goar also has to keep the office in supplies and the xerox machine running. When labour difficulties arise, her job has meant crossing a picket line: "one of the hardest things I have ever done. I've always been a member of the Guild." She acknowledges that power does alter a person's self-image in subtle ways. "I have the power of hiring and firing — which I have used so far to hire one receptionist — and I sense power in ways that you would not notice in the day-to-day operation of this office but which figure in my perception of myself."

At thirty-two, Goar has done exceedingly well; she has speeded through the ranks at a rate worthy of Marjorie Nichols. In early 1985 she made another spectacular leap — back to the *Toronto Star* as National Affairs columnist. Christina McCall is right in saying that we have passed the stage of thinking "how delicious" when a woman writes about sports or politics or any of other traditionally masculine subjects. Nowadays, no one notices when another woman journalist appears on Parliament Hill. But, say Goar and Janigan, the MPs still make an enormous fuss when a woman is elected to their midst, usually for the wrong reasons. Goar complains, "All those snide remarks about Lynn McDonald when she was first elected, about the hat she wore in the Commons. No one even mentioned what she was *saying*." After ten years in the business, Janigan finds herself becoming impatient with the politicians' excuses for the paucity of women in Parliament. "Political parties are a good decade behind the news media and for them it is still a question of tokenism. Perhaps politicians accept women as journalists and yet cannot accept them as colleagues, because as reporters, women can still be cast in the handmaiden role."

There are other women journalists who, like Goar and Janigan, have established themselves in the profession in recent years without encountering massive barriers. They have written well, landed stories, broken others, outfoxed the competition, and won awards with ingenuity, determination, and extremely hard work. They have not felt the sharp edge of discrimination slicing into their ambition, nor have they sensed the gentle undertow of prejudice depressing their talent. Goar grows hesitant, though, when the conversation turns to the success of women as journalists. "As an individual journalist compared to any other male journalist operating on Parliament Hill, I don't feel any handicap. But women as a group — well, I don't see many women who are editing newspapers; I don't see many women in the executive suite in this business; I don't know any other women bureau chiefs on Parliament Hill. So the signals would say to me that we haven't got there yet."

Other women will tell you that newsrooms are dens of entrenched chauvinism, "the most sexist places in the world." Feminism, they say, has only motivated the profession to apply a polish of liberal respectability, which wears thin in strategic areas like the promotion and appointment of women to senior positions. Newsrooms provide lead aprons for women working on VDTs (video display terminals), and men get a day's paternity leave. But there isn't a single paper in the country with a female managing editor or publisher. On this subject, Marjorie Nichols has a few bon mots:

> In my view, the Catholic Church will allow a woman pope before there will be a woman newspaper publisher. We [journalists] presume to be the guardians of the public mores and codes and issues. Just look back and see how indignantly we reported on discrimination in the boardroom. Good God! I remember the discussion that went on for about ten years over whether in a second reference a woman could be referred to by her surname or, heaven knows, by Ms! Those debates shook journalism to its foundations. I'm not being cynical at all when I say that. I know exactly what news institutions are and they are of necessity bound by tradition and by some Absolute Rules. There is no difference today in the way a managing editor thinks, the way he analyses things, or what his considerations are, from his behaviour twenty-five years ago.

In 1984 there were two women editing Canadian newspapers: Barbara Amiel of the *Toronto Sun* and Lise Bissonnette of *Le Devoir*. There are two ways of reading this record. Two women editors in a field of fifty daily newspapers may not sound impressive but, when you are coming up from zero in a period of three or four years, that is a great leap. The other view is not so charitable. Bissonnette and Amiel are not editors of lucrative major city dailies, but of what can be characterized as marginal enterprises. This is not to take anything away from the significance of their appointments, but to understand that the *Toronto Sun* (the "little paper that grew") is no match for the *Toronto Star* in its circulation (235,000 to the *Star*'s 490,000), or in its editorial cachet.

Within the profession, the *Sun* has a reputation for beer-barreling right-wingism that borders on the sensational. With its coarse "tits and ass" approach to the news, the paper is hardly a high-watermark of journalistic excellence, and much less a place where you might expect to find a woman in charge. Improbable though the appointment was, Amiel was not battling entrenched tradition (the *Sun* is barely a decade old), nor was she competing with long line-ups of senior journalists vying for the job. The circumstances were special, and Amiel was offered the job on a platter when no one else with the right qualifications could be found.

As for *Le Devoir*, it is in a class by itself; it is the little paper that didn't grow but whose influence far outstrips its tiny circulation of under 45,000. Everyone who is anyone in political, professional, and intellectual circles in Quebec — or who aspires to be — reads *Le Devoir*. Since it was founded by Henri Bourassa in 1910 as a vehicle for his ideas about French-Canadian nationalism, it has been a forum of political debate in Quebec or, as former publisher Claude Ryan styled it, "the place where opinion leaders of Quebec come to dialogue." The editorial pages are the heart of *Le Devoir*. Here the pros and cons of issues are laid out in detail and at length, often in two or more installments. More essays than articles, they come from academics, labour leaders, students, poets, ministers, and even prime ministers. Pierre Trudeau himself occasionally descended to the op.ed. pages of *Le Devoir* to engage in some intellectual fisticuffs with Quebec nationalists. And during the fiercest fighting between federalism and independence, leading up to the referendum in 1980, Lise Bissonnette was in charge of the Editorial section, which routinely ran to two or three pages.

There is nothing to compare with *Le Devoir* in English Canada; no paper that has such an intense relationship with its readers or the desire to participate in that sort of political and ideological debate. That reputation has won *Le Devoir* accolades, along with accusations of elitism. Pierre Bourgault, who after twenty years is still a fiery spokesman for independence and one of René Lévesque's most acerbic critics, scoffs at it, calling it "nothing more than a letterbox for Quebec's intelligentsia." Montreal journalist Dominique Clift, who is also a well-known analyst of Quebec politics, was more scathing in an article about *Le Devoir* that he published in 1983. At this time *Le Devoir* was in the midst of an economic crisis that had been building for years. The paper's readership had remained stagnant through the seventies, Clift noted, although the number of people graduating from universities and entering managerial and professional jobs was skyrocketing. He alleged that its audience hadn't expanded because the traditional elite "to which *Le Devoir*'s staff certainly belong" was obsolete and out of touch with the rest of Quebec's population.

Bissonnette was heartily annoyed by Clift's notion that *Le Devoir* was a haven for scions of the establishment. She points to herself as a counter example. The sixth of seven children and the first to get a university degree, she was brought up in the northern mining town of Rouyn-Noranda. Her father was a modest shopkeeper, and the family income rose and fell with the fortunes of the miners. She came from the lower-middle-class, and though she has achieved prominence among the Quebec political intelligentsia, she wasn't born to it. As a woman, moreover, she certainly wasn't a member of any traditional elite.

Bissonnette often talks about how, as a teenager, she dreamt of writing someday for *Le Devoir*. She recalls the glamour of rubbing shoulders with the paper's educational correspondent at a conference she was covering for her school paper when she was just sixteen. "I learned from my educational studies later that people from my kind of background do have higher aspirations than their parents — but not that high. I could get a university degree, but working for *Le Devoir* was something I couldn't even think about."

But think of it she did, a dozen years later, when she had been specializing in the field of higher education for some time, had almost completed a Ph.D., and was working at the University of Quebec at Montreal (UQAM), in the first planning office established by a Quebec university. She heard there was an opening for an educational reporter at *Le Devoir* and knew that she was ideal for it. At twenty-eight, she had been intimately involved in education policy and politics for ten years — and she could write.

But getting hired by Claude Ryan was not easy. "I called and called for three or four months and finally after a couple of interviews he said yes. I am sure he thought I was just the person he was looking for, that is, on paper, but the fact that I was a woman was something new for him. He had never hired one before, and he did, after all, have the same biases as other people of his era. So he didn't give me a big salary or take me on a permanent basis."

When Ryan was publisher of *Le Devoir*, he was known as the Pope of Saint-Sacrement, the back street in old Montreal where the paper has its offices. He was a towering presence in Quebec through the sixties and seventies; the anointed confessor, confidant, and consultant to a succession of Quebec premiers. Under him, *Le Devoir* enhanced its reputation for thoughtful opinion, independent journalism, and, since the paper is not governed by the commercial imperative to the extent most dailies are, for its openness to a broad spectrum of ideas and political attitudes. All the same, with its aura of old tradition and heavy intellectualism, one would not expect *Le Devoir* to have the welcome mat out for women. However, Ryan mellowed quickly upon Bissonnette's arrival. Once he saw she could produce the goods, "he accepted me and played fairly."

After about eighteen months of covering education, Bissonnette heard that the correspondent's job in Quebec City was available. With the encouragement of a close friend, she decided to go for it. It meant a major promotion in status, a switch to political reporting, and moving to the press gallery in Quebec City. The reaction of her colleagues was strange:

> The all-male executive of the union (which regulates the procedures governing advancements) was stunned. I'll remember it all my life, because the president was my own brother-in-law. He was the one who warned me it was a very difficult job, where you are right in the firing line, and that it would be hard for me as a woman. The union guys wanted to plan a strategy for the application,

to put it in at the eleventh hour so that Ryan couldn't block it as they expected he surely would. But I thought that was silly. I decided to play it straight and fair and clean and so submitted my application on the first day of the competition. When it closed, Ryan came into the newsroom and I will never forget it. He stood in front of my desk with everyone there and said it was a very good idea; he never would have thought of it himself but he expected I was going to be great in Quebec City.

The incident taught Bissonnette something about prejudice. "I am not saying that Ryan doesn't look upon women with all the biases of his own generation. But the union was just as prejudiced in its way as he was. The way it planned and plotted seemed to imply it also thought the idea was extremely special."

Bissonnette went to Quebec City and, ten months later, to Ottawa as parliamentary correspondent. In Quebec City, the atmosphere reminded her of nothing so much as a boys' boarding school:

The press gallery is more of a man's world than the newsroom, where at least you don't have to deal with your colleagues all the time. In political reporting, you are together constantly and, as a group, I found them to be full of themselves and their own importance. They behaved as if they thought being aggressive and getting the prime minister in a corner and pinning him with a question — aha! — is what journalism is all about. I never felt at ease in the Ottawa press gallery either.

As a method of gathering news, Bissonnette found the press conferences and the scrum fairly useless and annoying exercises. Conventional wisdom has it that a good reporter never goes home; he is constantly out cruising the bars and clubs and press corps hang-outs, hoping for stray leads, leaks, or casual comments which will lead to a story. Bissonnette never did that. She went to her office to work, refused to become a member of the press club, and does not believe she ever suffered for it or missed any important gossip. "In Ottawa you have to use the phone; you call people to get your story. That's the way it really works. Political reporting is not a shooting match, although that is the way it is practised."

Uncomfortable though she felt at times, Bissonnette does not think that the sexist attitudes of male journalists cramped her style or inhibited her performance. She ran into the usual situation in which as a woman she was watched and kept track of more closely than a man, and in which double standards still held sway. "When a woman goes to dinner with a politician, there is gossip. When a bunch of reporters went to the Yukon for a three-week canoe trip with Pierre Trudeau no one called foul, though for sure they would get some privileged information."

Generalizing, one can say that there are two kinds of women journalists: those like Marjorie Nichols, who are hard-news hounds attracted by the intrigue and the action, and the more contemplative types, the people like Christina McCall who are writers attracted by the contradictions and paradoxes in people's behaviour and by the tragi-comic poignancy of the drama.

Bissonnette belongs with the latter group. Her chief ambition and delight is writing, though she has little time for it now. She is also driven by the desire to master complex topics and to understand the world through the exercise of her intellect. She is a thinking woman's journalist and her life has been geared to her métier. She has never married nor had children and has lived much of her life alone, which she has not considered to be a hardship. She has been able to put in the hours and the concentration necessary to acquire the background and experience for editorial writing. As always, that freedom was purchased at a price, though a price that was neither consciously negotiated nor unwillingly paid. Like many women, Bissonnette has followed her own rising star, never stinting on enthusiasm or effort because overall she is captivated by her work. For all that, she is not one-sided; she is worldly, well read, witty in both official languages, and a lover and collector of art. She speaks with quiet assurance in a voice that is full of the authority of knowledge, a voice which, like her appearance, is never loud or ostentatious but compelling nevertheless.

Before returning to Montreal, Bissonnette became an editorial writer for *Le Devoir* and during the period following Ryan's departure (for the Quebec Liberal leadership) when the paper was limping along without a publisher. She crossed the corridor to the management side, in order to help editor-in-chief Michel Roy with administration. In the spring of 1982, she became editor-in-chief. The appointment was received with surprise and delight — a great deal of surprise from those in the profession who don't read the paper often and think of it as staid and old-fashioned. Some of *Le Devoir*'s readership, too, was muted in its enthusiasm. As Bissonnette says, it is a readership which takes a proprietorial interest in all the paper's affairs — financial, editorial, and political — and many had already pronounced their disapproval of her presence on the editorial page. She was criticized for the usual things — spelling, grammar, her opinions — but also for daring to bring up certain subjects, like abortion, in public. But the biggest hurdle to clear was not the chauvinism of the readers; it was the reaction of other journalists to the editorial changes she introduced soon after she took over.

Le Devoir was in deep financial trouble and everyone knew it could not survive by standing still. "The challenge is to become more modern without abandoning the old spirit," Bissonnette announced. With the publisher, Jean-Louis Roy, and the paper's executive, Bissonnette decided that the newsroom had to be overhauled and the beats reshuffled. The editor-in-chief has the power to do this but had rarely exercised it in the past. There had been only a perfunctory annual effort to persuade people to shift places, which usually left things more or less the same:

> We decided we ought to be strong enough to insist, and I said that I would do it. And I did. I talked to everyone and explained that even if they didn't think it was right, we were going to try it. In some cases it was very easy; others were terribly hurt and thought it unjust. I had people crying in my office and people resisting. We

pushed and pushed and it got to the point where people had to work or leave, because as Jean-Louis said, though *Le Devoir*'s productivity was higher than any other paper's, it was not acceptable any more. Some people took that very badly and some people left.

This, of course, gave Bissonnette the opportunity to bring in new blood and shape the paper further. Among the changes last year was the introduction of a daily economics section and more cultural coverage. The restructuring, however, also led to some public displays of ill-humour.

One Saturday, Bissonnette opened *La Presse* to find an article about *Le Devoir*'s troubles by Daniel Marsolais, which boldly declared that the "real problem" at *Le Devoir* was not financial instability but Lise Bissonnette herself. "She is accused of being intransigent, of operating informally and in secret, and of not having confidence in her journal-ists....Everyone agrees that *Le Devoir* is in the throes of an unprecedented leadership crisis," he trumpeted.

Bissonnette had had an inkling something was coming, because there had been a phone call from someone at *La Presse* asking general questions. But she was not at all prepared for the anonymous quotations from people in *Le Devoir*'s newsroom, who were "fearful of eventual reprisals" should they go on the record. Or for the comments attri-buted to a colleague and former *Le Devoir* correspondent, Michel Vastel, whom she had considered a good friend, and who had never before so much as registered his disagree-ment with her: "Within six months of her appointment, she has already annoyed the mainstays of the editorial floor, people who have given their life for the paper. That is inadmissible and abnormal."

You learn two things from such an experience, Bissonnette declares ruefully, "that there is no such thing as a friendship that remains untouched in such a situation, and that some people will come into your office and chit-chat, telling you all sorts of nice things but *not* telling you what they really think." She did think women were more open in voicing their disagreements with her and in presenting arguments, "maybe because they felt they could tell me more than they would have told a man." Perhaps, by the same principle, the men felt they could not be frank with her — so they talked to Marsolais instead.

Bissonnette admits that she has had a great deal of adjusting to do. Never before in her life has she had responsibility for managing people.

> It is something, to go from writing editorials to being responsible for the whole thing. I'm not saying that as a woman, but as someone who has never taken a course in management. Saying no to the expenditures of money was not the hard part, but rather making the decisions that directly affect people. It is not that women can't cope with power, it is that we are not prepared for it; and to be frank, I wasn't.

Unlike Lise Bissonnette, Barbara Amiel did not apprentice in newspapers before assuming the editorship of the *Toronto Sun*. In fact, she was never drawn to news, much less to newspapers, and through most of her career has written for magazines. Her first jobs were in television, where she quickly recognized that she was primarily interested in current affairs. In the back of her mind, she had always planned to write. She had written as a child, in high school, and at university, but for a long while didn't try to pursue it professionally: "I didn't think I had anything to say."

When she finally did take the plunge, it turned out that she had plenty to say. Her first major article was an exposé on the firing of Dr. Andrew Malcolm from the Addiction Research Centre in Toronto, published in *Saturday Night* magazine. It was vintage Amiel, argumentative and cheeky, and deliberately controversial.

The decision to drop everything in order to concentrate on her own writing coincided with her marriage to George Jonas (author, playwright, and fellow-traveller on the right). Amiel had been making good money writing for television, but she was writing things like game shows for CTV. Was

this what she burned to do with her life? With Jonas'
encouragement and financial backing, she began freelancing magazine articles.

> I was late starting — I was thirty-two — and so I decided
> to begin with the tough stuff, to write for *Saturday Night*,
> which I judged to be the toughest market where I could
> establish some credentials. The Malcolm piece took God
> knows how long to write and two complete rewrites.
> I told Fulford [Robert Fulford, editor of the magazine] I
> would keep doing it until it satisfied him. Previously my
> only published articles were a couple of guest columns in
> *Toronto Life* and a piece for the back pages of *Maclean's*
> called "Let's Reinstate Debtors' Prison." You should see
> *that* one for "right wing."

Maclean's then asked her to try out book reviewing, which
she loved. Peter Newman was not terribly enthusiastic about
her efforts, according to Amiel, but was persuaded to accept
her as a contributing editor anyway. In due course she was
promoted to full-time staff writer, though technically she did
avoid going on staff. (Another facet of her pragmatic "right-
of-centre" bias is her disapproval of employers and employees "being forced to go through the Labour Relations Act if
they want to terminate a relationship," so she opted for a
loose letter of agreement — no company benefits or UIC —
and still found the fit uncomfortably confining.) "Newman
suggested the column, which was initially to alternate between
myself and Mordecai Richler, and was supposed to be on
culture. Fine, I said, having no intention of making it a
'culture' column, for as far as I could see culture is the air we
breath and the ideas we think and I thus felt I could write
about anything."
   In time, the uncomfortable fit became unbearable:

> The column was fine but I had to fight tooth and nail
> because my ideas did not fit with theirs. If you belong to
> one school of thought you can identify something as an
> oppressive act and you don't have to prove it to a
> researcher. If you belong to another school of thought

you literally have to prove two plus two equals four. I got tired of that. But why whine? How many other people have columns? I was also having difficulty with the assignments. I was perceived as having a bias and therefore not given the kind of articles I really wanted, and I wasn't much good at those Peter Newman was coming up with either. For example, the one on the jet set. That was a very good idea but I loathed doing it. The curious thing was that I had no idea who the jet set was; it may have looked as if I should have, but I didn't. In any case, *Maclean's* was becoming more of a news magazine and less of a place for writers.

It was high time to leave. Coincidentally, Douglas Creighton and Peter Worthington, publisher and editor of the *Sun*, who had been talking to Amiel for some time about writing for the paper, now came up with an offer. They wanted her to join them as assistant editor and heir-apparent to Worthington. "I told them I knew nothing about newspapers and they said I would learn. I thought and thought about it, and gradually what had seemed ludicrous became a challenge."

It seemed to Amiel that she had scarcely arrived when Worthington was leaving. By the end of her first full year he had quit to run for Parliament and she had inherited his job. Her situation was the exact opposite of Bissonnette's. Coming from the newsroom, Bissonnette outdistanced several individuals who had once been senior to her, and two or three perhaps who also had claims on the editor's job. She thoroughly understood the resentment, yet, she suspects, had she come into the position from the outside it would have been easier for her. That, of course, was precisely Amiel's situation, but for her it only altered the complexion of the problems slightly. There were still many disjointed noses in the *Sun's* newsroom:

I had trouble on two levels, both of them probably legitimate. Quite rightly, I was perceived as someone with no newspaper experience. Had I been a man and been catapulted into the job, there would have been resentment from people already here who had been

working for a decade towards the job themselves. Add to
that the fact that I am a woman, and resentment reaches
a very high peak. One thing that worked in my favour is
that the job has traditionally been held by a high-profile
person. The *Sun* is not like other papers; it is a personality paper. We promote our people as stars, or try to in
our own little way. And so I think that took some of the
edge off the resentment, because people could rational-
ize to themselves that, well, yes, she's a woman, and sure
she doesn't know anything about newspapers, but she is
on *Front Page Challenge* and magazines write articles
about her and she does television and she writes books.

That she was female and glamorous and Barbara Amiel
was all the encouragement people needed to leap to the conclusion that Amiel had auditioned for the job in someone's bed:

I didn't know at the time how rampant the rumours
were. I thought people were joking. It wasn't until I
heard the fourth version, which had me running off with
virtually the entire board of directors, that I realized
people actually thought it might have been a possibility.
Now, I think, there is a general awareness that this is not
what happened, so the resentment remaining is what is
endemic to any top job. People resent me because I don't
know enough about newspapers, or because I appear to
be disorganized, or to have the wrong ideas, or because I
don't understand who the *Sun*'s readership is, or because I'm too intellectual, or because I'm not good at
second base. But I don't think it's because I'm a woman
any more.

Still, you have to wonder why a newspaper would gamble
on someone so inexperienced.

I think if they had found a giraffe with the right ideas
they would have taken it. Now that I'm sitting in this
chair looking for an assistant, I see how difficult it is to
find journalists of a similar conservative persuasion in
Canada — it isn't in England or the States, but it is in

Canada. The fact that I was a woman was probably a handicap in their eyes. But they had been looking for so long without success that they were prepared to overlook it.

It is instructive to realize that both Amiel and Bissonnette got their top jobs because of their ideas. They are both ideologues, although their outlooks are profoundly different; both are intensely interested in politics, not simply for its own sake but because of its relationship to a broader theory of society and the role of the state.

In some quarters — including, no doubt, the newsroom of the *Toronto Sun* — *Le Devoir* is not thought of as being a "real" newspaper, because it does not address a mass audience, and worse, it wanders into the realm of abstract ideas. The *Sun* has no such identity problems and is far more likely to be accused of gorging on trivia than of indulging in too much intellectualism. Yet Amiel was hired for her intellectual qualifications. It is one of many contradictions in her story. She is absolutely right about the fact that she is a personality: someone who is known as much because of who she is as what she writes. With Amiel, who is dead serious about her beliefs, it is hard to determine how much of her notoriety is due to her outrageous political statements and how much to her outrageous good looks. For in print, as in life, she tends to colourful extremes.

She writes with passion but seldom with compassion, in a style which is arch, clever, and comes at you straight from the lip: arch in revealing conflicts and character; sharp for the purpose of carving up the enemy, which includes the left, the state, and bleeding-heart liberals. She often serves up ideas with anecdotes in a manner that strays into tabloidism, as in her incredible-but-true confessions about her addiction to prescription drugs and 222's, her abortion, and her incarceration in Mozambique. It is terribly risky, though, inviting accusations of exaggeration, and it often has the effect of distracting readers from her other arguments. But there is one quality her critics should never forget: Amiel's admirable steadfastness, her uncompromising commitment to her own convictions.

Amiel arrived on the set at Global TV for a live discussion following the airing of *The Day After*, a television drama about the devastation of Kansas by nuclear missiles, clad in magnificent pink ruffles. The only woman on the panel, she proceeded to deliver an anti-Soviet, pro-nuclear defence position that would warm the hearts of the most hawkish crewcut generals in the Pentagon. Of course, it is a person's politics that matter and not her clothes, but Amiel does manage to make her looks part of her politics. She is a remarkably beautiful woman and, as they say, she flaunts it.

The pros and cons of good looks and how to use them is something every woman thinks about. Early on, Amiel concluded that in the long run hers could be more of a help than a hindrance. On her first job, as clerk typist in CBC TV Variety, she made a deal with her boss to enter the Miss CBC beauty contest as his department's nominee, in return for a recommendation for a transfer to Current Affairs. (She won both the contest and the transfer.) "The irritant is, though, that later on if you become involved in an area that requires intellectual muscle, people do have trouble reconciling style and content. Looks can be used to dismiss the quality of your thought. Instead of attacking your arguments, critics talk about the fact that you wear Saint Laurent dresses and have your nails done."

Amiel takes this risk, too, one which very few women journalists would dare. Some people do indeed dismiss her as a result, saying that all that high fashion and "those bosoms" get in the way of serious journalism. But there is no denying that extraordinary beauty and brains are a powerful combination when the mix is just right — the impact of each is multiplied exponentially.

The evolution of an image, Amiel suggests, is imperceptible. It's hard to pin down the moment when "it" takes on an existence of its own (she thinks around the time she and ex-husband Jonas published their book about the Demeter murder trial); and it is hard to know how much of a hand others in the media had in its fabrication. Amiel, however, does not seem at all preoccupied with the effect of her persona. "Look. It's fun and it's interesting and if you want to be listened to, and if you're running a minor theme but not a major one in the *zeitgeist*, you do sometimes have to act like a performing bear. Being a woman helps, because people happen to be more interested in women now."

Reconciling the form and content of Barbara Amiel is not quite as simple as Amiel would have it, however. It is not difficult to reconcile being an ideologue and having champagne tastes; that description fits most political leaders, from Pierre Trudeau to Fidel Castro to Ronald Reagan. Amiel's basic contradiction is more subtle: it lies somewhere between the style of her persona and her political message, between a personal life that screams mainstream and a political stance that bemoans its underdog marginality. She looks like someone who is making it with the establishment and talks like someone who is defending an oppressed minority. "No one will ever believe it. I am a zealot. It is hard for people to grasp that zealots can also like good food and nice clothes. More than anything else in this world, you see, I think that North America — and Canada, in particular — is the last refuge of liberty. This country is worth fighting for and I want to go down fighting, go down with my boots on."

Amiel wrote her book *Confessions* with her boots on, but as she feared, few people noticed or debated her ideas. It is an autobiographical account of her pilgrimage from the political left (of the soggy, soft-headed liberal variety, not the NDP or socialist left) to the eccentric position she now occupies on the right. Gradually she fell out with former friends and colleagues in the media (the "gliblibs") and her sense of alienation may well come from the oddity of her political attitudes within that special milieu. Though she has often claimed that the mainstream media are full of far-leftists who abhor their right-wing equivalents (herself included), she rather disproves her own point when she delivers it from a column in *Maclean's*.

When you set her in a broader picture, her ideas are not all that marginal or even unusual. The views that abortion is morally wrong, that socialized medicine is an unhealthy invitation to public abuse, are fairly widely held opinions in Canadian society. And very probably she could find goodly numbers of *Sun* readers who would agree with her that the women's movement has constructed a false version of history by alleging that there has been a male conspiracy to oppress women, and who would go all the way with her to conclude that feminists "want to justify the abandonment of justice and equality in the marketplace in order to make up for the past wrongs."

When it comes to feminism, Amiel is ever the rugged individualist. While rejecting the historical and philosophical analysis of feminist thinkers like Simone de Beauvoir, she concedes that "the women's liberation movement has done a helluva thing for us. It has finally made businessmen realize what an important market we are and that women want to see women in important places." But, she warns, "The power of the dollar and the power of success will break down the doors of the boardroom more effectively than any government can."

While she has never felt that her sex has been a barrier to advancement in her career, Amiel does acknowledge its effect.

> I still find myself ill at ease working with the men here [at the *Sun*]. I shouldn't feel that way, but I do. Men's attitudes change very slowly, as do mine, and it's hard for them. My publisher deals very fair and square with me but still I can't go drinking with him because I don't drink, I don't know jokes, and I'm not really interested in the Blue Jays. There's a whole range of things that separate us. Moreover, I don't deal with him in business terms because I'm an editorial person and media people don't deal with the business end. I'll tell you, it is women like Sonja Bata [vice-president of Bata shoes] and Bette Stephenson [Ontario Minister of Education] who are probably doing more for women than anyone else. When Creighton runs into either of them, he will be dealing with tough seasoned ladies who speak his language.

In a chapter in *Confessions* called "Cows, Sacred and Liberated," Amiel pretty well dismissed the women's movement as an agency of thought control. She still sees feminists as women who would have "the CBC cast female hunchbacks in lead roles intead of white males and would make it illegal to show happy housewives washing dishes in films." Yet she doesn't deny the title feminist; she takes it over and redefines it for herself. "In terms of helping other women into the mainstream of life, it is a natural thing to do; in terms of being proud of women achieving, how could you not be?" She accepts being criticized and being called names like "fascist bitch" and "sexist," though it isn't pleasant being hated, for she seems to relish being the odd-woman-out, even while she directs herself and her energies towards the mainstream.

Given all this (plus a new publisher — Toronto's ex-Metro Chairman Paul Godfrey), perhaps no one should have been surprised at the news of Amiel's resignation in the fall of 1984. Even "real" feminists can find a militantly macho environment debilitating after a while. She left to marry, and moved to England.

Lise Bissonnette has also had a collision or two with feminists. She has never been an activist or a militant either, but she has been a feminist most of her life. "Reading *The Second Sex* was like drinking milk. I kept thinking, 'this is right, this is right' from beginning to end." Among feminists in the media, however, there has been a debate, going on for some time now, about the responsibilities of women who "make it" in the mainstream media.

Three years ago, the Fédération professionnelle des journalistes de Québec organized a gigantic conference of media women. Bissonnette was there and was delighted to see about six hundred women gathered together.

> One workshop in the schedule was on *la femme alibi* ["the alibi woman" or token woman] which I walked into by accident. Then I was prevailed upon to stay by the participants because, as one of them said, "You are one of those!" I was almost assaulted by people who asked me if I hadn't "crossed over," and I must say it was a lively discussion and not at all one-sided. There was what I would call the traditional view that women should not be part of any kind of masculine power structure, so that

if you do go in now before the values are changed, you will become part of the system. Not that people were saying you should absolutely not go, only that when you do go, you inevitably accept some rules. It is a fact; we do. There is no doubt in my mind about that. The other view says that if we don't go, things will never change. And that debate has not yet been settled.

THREE

Women on the Airwaves

MILLIONS OF CANADIANS know Betty Kennedy. For twenty-five years, they have been watching her on *Front Page Challenge* and listening to her in the afternoons on CFRB. Thousands read the candid account she wrote about the death of her first husband Gerhard in 1975 and were moved to tears. Kennedy was a cohort of the late Gordon Sinclair on *Front Page Challenge* and on the airwaves of "Ontario's family station," and like Sinclair she's become over the years a household name and a media institution. Unlike Sinclair, however, she did not do it by being flamboyant, opinionated, or loud.

Contrary to the convention that stars are those who blaze trails, smash icons, or break records, Kennedy's fame is based on uncontroversial competence. She's a journeyman journalist, a middle-of-the-road wife/mother/broadcaster who inspires people to write articles about her entitled "Nice Girls Finish First." Yet it is precisely her quality of personable politesse that has worked so well on *Front Page Challenge* (CBC television's long-running success), balanced between Sinclair, who liked to ask rude questions, and Pierre Berton, who likes to ask rough ones, smoothing the edges off both. On air and in person she's the quintessence of calm, cool, and understated control, and except for the hint of merriment in her voice, which deepens into a hearty chuckle when she laughs, she seems very reserved. That, however, may owe as much to style as temperament.

The style is basic businesswoman with just a *soupçon* of upper crust affluence, which suits CFRB's audience like a pair of Gucci shoes. Kennedy's office in the Standard Broadcasting building at the corner of Yonge Street and St. Clair Avenue (where Rosedale and Forest Hill meet to shop and play tennis) is immaculate. It is easily the neatest of any working journalist in radiodom, and definitely the only one that has been "decorated" by someone who knows her chintzes and the subtleties of beige. Paintings, not posters and bulletin boards, hang on the walls; upholstered furniture and a wooden chest replace regulation metal filing cabinets and old swivel chairs. Everything is arranged to make the best of a small space and none of it would be out of place in a den at Limestone Hall, the thirteen-room Georgian country mansion owned by her second husband, G. Allan Burton.

Kennedy matches the decor of her office perfectly. She is smartly dressed, superbly well-groomed; there is not a single discordant note to disrupt the symphony of creamy colours and softly tailored lines. She exudes the kind of confidence that comes from years of managing a bulging schedule with a minimum of fuss and a maximum of efficiency. Like the skater who makes a triple salchow look easy, Kennedy makes her balancing act — involving radio, television, writing, directorships, a family of twelve mostly grown children (four of her own and eight acquired through marriage), volunteer work, and social engagements — seem effortless. Yet you do not get the impression of someone hurtling along in the fast lane; this is a steady pacer, the kind who wins the race.

When Betty Kennedy was a teenager in Ottawa, there were two things she dreamt of doing someday: flying an airplane and writing for newspapers. She was mad about aviation — kept a scrapbook and read everything she could on the subject — but never learned to fly. When the opportunity did finally present itself in adult life, the dream had lost its lustre. Not so with newspaper writing. At sixteen, when she had completed grade ten, she decided to get a job. It wasn't a surprising thing to do in the 1940s. The war was on, and the Depression was still a vivid memory. In her own family, she had aunts who worked, and her mother was employed at Bell Telephone. So young Kennedy went down to the *Ottawa Citizen* and presented herself. "I told them I wanted to work on a newspaper and wanted to write. Within a day or two, I got a call telling me to come in and start work. When I look back it does seem surprising; I don't think it could happen today."

The job was, of course, a modest one, "answering phones, writing obits, and taking last-minute changes down to the composing room where the Scottish foreman was less likely to chew my head off than someone else's." She was also detailed to print up the news bulletins that were posted outside the *Citizen* offices on Sparks Street, which she did by hand with rubber stamps. Kennedy remained at the *Citizen* for over four years, getting basic training as a reporter "on the — guess what — education beat" but also covering Diplomatic Row.

Kennedy had her first taste of radio while working on the paper.

> The *Citizen* was part of the Southam chain, and there was a strike in the composing room in Winnipeg, which meant that the *Citizen* couldn't publish either for a period. We'd come into work and in addition to our usual beat would check the assignment book for special duties. Since we didn't have a paper to get out, I came in one day and found I'd been assigned to do a fifteen-minute daily radio show.
>
> Nobody told me how to do it or gave me instructions about what to do. I was just sent over to the radio station. Well, for the first week I wrote the whole thing and rapidly discovered that I couldn't write fifteen minutes worth of material every day that anybody would want to listen to. So I decided to handle it the same way I would a beat. I began to go after stories and guests, interviews and commentaries on all sorts of things that were happening. I guess I did that for a couple of months and then the radio station offered me a job, because somehow that show had built an audience, though to this day, I have no idea why. I certainly hadn't a clue what I was

doing. There was nobody around to tell you, so I'd go in and someone would tell me when I was on and yell "cut" at the end. Curiously enough, it never occurred to me to leave the newspaper for radio.

There were several moves over the next decade: a period in Montreal in the fashion industry, marriage, the arrival of children, a stint in Calgary with a radio discussion show there called *State Your Case*, and then back to Montreal where the chance to try television came her way.

Kennedy had called up CBC's programme director with an idea and went down to discuss it with him. They needed a host for the locally-produced Saturday edition of a public affairs show called *Tabloid*, and, as a result of that conversation, Kennedy was asked (it was a Thursday or Friday, she recalls) if she would be free the following Saturday to do the show.

> I had never been in a TV studio before in my life. I did know how to conduct an interview, since that is a journalist's stock-in-trade, but they gave me no instruction whatsoever. I suppose one characteristic of television in that era was spontaneity. Can you imagine just calling someone up and suggesting they take over a television show on such-and-such a date when you've never really seen them work? I can remember wondering what in the world one was supposed to wear and whether there were any rules. They had said nothing to me; hadn't even given me the location of the studios.

Nineteen fifty-nine was a turning point, the year Kennedy moved to Toronto. She had been living in Ottawa again, doing a regular afternoon television show for the local CBC station — the result of another of her programme ideas — and she was doing all the research, writing, and performing herself, "for I hate to tell you how much money." Her concept was to bring on a variety of articulate guests who were doing interesting things, "not so different from *Take 30*, but with the advantage of being in Ottawa and being local." It was the first time such a show had been done by CBOT, and at the end of the first year the show was renewed. But the producers, to Kennedy's horror, hired someone else the following season. "That's the business, I guess. I wasn't fired, because you only had a contract for one season, but it certainly was a blow. I hadn't had words with the producer or anything like that at all. It came as a bolt out of the blue." And it had the effect of resetting her course.

She had also been working on another idea with CBC people in Ottawa for some time, with lots of encouragement and no success. She wanted to do a radio programme for teenagers that would offer an alternative to rock and roll music and dance shows, and would eventually go to television. It was a great idea. Friends, however, suggested to Kennedy that she was wasting time on it in Ottawa; she should take it to Toronto. Someone else advised her to take it to the advertising agencies, for if she managed to attract a sponsor for it she'd have no trouble selling it to a radio station.

Kennedy took both pieces of advice. At the first ad agency, she was told that only one radio station in Toronto was doing any "programming," and that was CFRB. Off she went to talk to the programme director there, with her proposal tucked under her arm. Like everyone else, he thought it had merit:

> But he said it didn't particularly fit what CFRB was doing. He also told me that the station had been on the lookout for a female broadcaster for several years and asked if I would mind doing a tape for him. So I sat down and did a tape and they gave me a job.
>
> For the first week or so, I did a ten-minute slot in the morning. Then they came to me and said that actually what they wanted was to put me on for an hour in the afternoon where they needed to build an audience. So I moved there and have been there ever since. I do remember being told that since Kate Aitken had left they had auditioned 200 women for that job. I have no idea what it was they were looking for and I suspect that they would have been hard-pressed to spell out what exactly they had in mind.

They might not have known what they wanted, but when

Kennedy appeared they knew what they liked, even though she was very different from Mrs. Aitken.

For two-and-a-half decades, Kate Aitken was the reigning First Lady of Canadian radio. She was here, there, everywhere: a one-woman marching band and a treasure trove of information. For most of those years, she broadcast over CFRB in Toronto, CJAD in Montreal, and the CBC Radio network, while also acting as women's editor of the weekly *Montreal Standard* and director of women's activities for the Canadian National Exhibition in Toronto. She split her week (the first six days of it) between offices in Toronto and Montreal, and handled a correspondence that averaged 360,000 letters a year from listeners and fans, all of which were answered and signed (no rubber stamps as a matter of pride), keeping twenty-one secretaries going full tilt. In spare moments she gave speeches (about 150 a year), lectured on cooking, and served on committees and boards such as the publicity committee for the Kiwanis Music Festival.

Kate Aitken was a food consultant, world traveller, etiquette expert, hostess, author, and housewife extraordinaire. People said she could make scouring pots seem glamorous. She began with cooking lessons and lecture tours, and in 1923 she was asked to run the CNE's first cooking school. She immediately set to work turning a few home-baking exhibits and a collection of handicrafts into the largest section of the fair. Then she filled in for a CFRB broadcaster who'd fallen ill, and was an immediate hit. It was radio that made Kate Aitken famous and piped her cheery voice and commonsense advice into one-and-a-half million households every week. That was six hundred broadcasts a year; and she also found time to write books, fifty of them over her career, mostly cookbooks and travel and etiquette guides. *Never a Day So Bright*, her reminiscences of childhood in Beeton, Ontario, was a bestseller, and her steady stream of newspaper and magazine articles was equally popular. She had a column in the *Globe and Mail Magazine* called "In Your Mirror" until 1962.

Kate Aitken travelled to exotic places all over the globe: Europe several times a year, South America, the Far East;

fifty-four countries and two million miles over a lifetime. In 1949, she circled the world by plane, covering 25,000 miles in seventeen days. People were always keeping count of Kate's exploits, the better to marvel at her breathtaking energy. Kate Aitken also met the rich, the powerful, and the royal. She had tea with Churchill, was presented to numerous reigning monarchs, and was invited to Princess Elizabeth's wedding. She interviewed Mussolini, and, in 1953, Canadian troops in Korea. She went on missions abroad to collect stories, went to food and economic conferences, peace conferences, and fashion shows in Paris. Everything she did, everywhere she went, was grist for a voracious mill.

Aitken was also a successful businesswoman. Early in her marriage, when she and husband Henry owned a poultry farm near Beeton, she won prizes for her flock of white Wyandotte hens. That venture was followed by a home canning scheme, which produced 12,000 jars of fruits and vegetables that she supplied to private customers and exclusive food shops in Toronto. Much later, in 1953, she opened a luxurious health spa where "Canadian and American gals can get a solid weekend of health and beauty aids, pampering, exercise, and rest."

Kate Aitken was a petite woman who was always dressed for action and fashion in a natty tailored suit, hat, and gloves; a "feminine dynamo" and, as Gordon Sinclair dubbed her in 1950, "The Busiest Woman in the World." (And probably the only one who could pack everything she needed for a world trip — camera, typewriter, supplies, and clothes — into 59 pounds of luggage.) She amazed people with such feats; became famous just for doing what she did and sharing it with an audience. The audience responded with love and admiration and letters asking for recipes, help in raising the children and organizing the meals, tips on running the household, and advice for the lovelorn.

It's doubtful that Aitken's Superwoman record has ever been matched. When she "retired" from radio in 1957 — a decision she never explained — she kept right on writing and organizing until she died in 1971. Her broadcasts always seemed informal and folksy, although they were entirely scripted. The secret she discovered early in her radio career was that listeners were curious about the world at large, and thrilled at the chance to live adventures vicariously through Mrs. A. She brought the outside world to stay-at-home wives and mothers and even the occasional man. (About 18 percent of her audience was male.) The mixture was all her own: current affairs of a kind we would today call personal journalism and consumer information. The practical and the fanciful were woven together in Kate's inimitable style. She was slotted in among the soap operas like "Ma Perkins" and "The Guiding Light," and was "brought to you" by Tamblyn's drug store and Good Luck Margarine. On air she could be commanding or comical but never controversial. She may have been an exotic figure in real life, but on the radio, her message to women was safe, clean, and one hundred percent supportive of traditional female roles.

Still, being a celebrity of her time and something of a contradiction, Aitken was the subject of gossip. People were intensely curious about her marriage and the fact that this champion of the housewifely arts didn't appear to be living with her husband. While she was out girdling the globe, Henry, a practising accountant, was off for long stretches in northern Ontario towns. Throughout Aitken's public career, he carefully guarded his anonymity; indeed, it was said that people closely associated with Mrs. Aitken wouldn't have recognized Henry had he appeared wearing a name tag. "I've heard the talk and some of it hurts," wrote Kate finally. "It grieves me when people say that Henry and I are separated, divorced, or unhappily married. We've been so happily married for so many years that I think we are one of Canada's most devoted families." But the speculation continued. Aitken would sometimes point out that lots of families could not be together as much as they liked. In a 1951 issue of *Chatelaine*, she reiterated all that, yet partly undid her case while commenting on a rumour that her daughter Mary was being groomed to take over her job. "She's too happily married to want it," trumpeted Kate.

In the 1950s, even Kate Aitken couldn't square working and travelling, apart from her husband most of the time, with the contemporary ideal of marriage. She clearly was breaking some of the rules, and was quite defensive about it, protesting that her family got together every Sunday on the telephone. The public never quite accepted that, secretly suspicious that Aitken, for all her public success, was shirking her matrimonial duty.

Kate Aitken probably was the busiest woman in Canada; possibly the busiest *person* in all of Canada. Although she claimed she worked because the family was not well-to-do, she obviously got a lot more than money out of it. However, she also disclaimed being ambitious. "I have no desire to be a world beater — never have," she'd say. Yet she can't have denied her own enormous influence. Certainly the Canadian government didn't overlook it, when they drafted Aitken's energies to serve the war effort.

Kate Aitken was one of a kind. Not because she was the only woman doing daytime radio from the 1930s to the 1950s — she wasn't. But she had few rivals. The one woman always presumed to be her closest rival and therefore her archest of enemies was Claire Wallace, who also could be heard on CFRB for a while in the 1930s, on *Tea Time Topics*.

Claire Wallace began freelance writing for the *Toronto Star* in the early 1930s. She was divorced (and her ex-husband had died shortly after the split) with a small son to raise; work for her was no hobby. She was born into a newspaper family and had gone to private schools, so working for a newspaper made sense to her. It didn't make sense to H.C. Hindmarsh, though, when she applied to him for a job.

"Why don't you open a gift shop?" he helpfully suggested. She didn't, of course, but kept on badgering him and other publishers for work and finally got a column, "Over the Teacups," which she wrote for a year before leaving to seek her fortune in England. It was when she returned from London that she made the move to radio, with her suppertime show *They Tell Me* on CBC. This was the programme that Claire Wallace rode to fame. It became tremendously popular, second in the ratings only to *The Happy Gang* during the day, and it lasted for eighteen years. These were thrice-weekly fifteen-minute shows, fully scripted, with five to six items a show.

Wallace's approach was a bit different from Kate Aitken's.

Her specialty was current affairs and human interest stories. She went after the personalities behind the news, "the story behind the story," as she always put it. And she'd do crazy things to get these items. She loved, for instance, to go undercover: as a store detective; as a maid, "to learn the truth about domestic work conditions"; and once she spent a night alone in Casa Loma (Toronto's "authentic mediaeval" castle, reputed to have ghosts). On another occasion she put an advertisement in the paper for a gigolo and got 300 replies. Wallace was known as a "news snooper and story scooper" and like Aitken travelled incessantly. She was always on the lookout for material, and nothing was too local or too trivial (which is to say gossipy) for her. Listeners were often her best tipsters.

Wallace was also a confirmed daredevil and obviously liked the thrill of taking risks. She was the first Canadian to fly by Clipper across the Atlantic, the first woman to fly TCA across Canada, and the first woman broadcaster to learn to fly. Once, she broadcast from an airplane five thousand feet above Niagara Falls. Her press releases were forever recounting the lengths and depths Claire Wallace would go to get a broadcast. She climbed to the top of Mount Paricutin, a volcano in Mexico, walked on the ocean floor in diving gear in the West Indies, and descended three thousand feet to the bottom of a gold mine. Everyone was amazed, the more so as Wallace was a tall, beautiful, willowy blonde, hardly the rough-and-ready athletic type. The publicity writers were careful to reassure the public that, for all her antics, Wallace was still every inch a wife and mother. In private life, they would say, she is Mrs. James Stutt (she remarried in 1942), mother to young Wally, a wonderful cook, and an ordinary housewife whose hobbies include collecting china cats.

Betty Kennedy does not see herself as part of the Aitken-Wallace tradition of broadcasting. "They did a lot of cooking, fashion, and very personal topics. I think of myself as a journalist primarily, but they thought of themselves very differently, primarily as personalities. Aitken built her shows around whatever she was doing and made it very interesting.

It really was sort of 'Kate Aitken's Adventures in Wonderland' and she was a fantastic character."

Only once has Kennedy let her journalistic guard down and strayed into personal journalism. When she wrote *Gerhard, A Love Story*, an account of her first husband's death from cancer, she allowed her private life to stray into the public realm and caught some people by surprise. "I wrote the book honestly. It was something I felt very deeply about and, yes, I guess it was a departure. Of course, I don't go on the air every day and bare my soul. I'm sure people would not be interested, to start with!" But once she let the public have a peek, they didn't want to leave it at that. Ten months after Gerhard died, following a couple of months of rumours and denials, she married Allan Burton (whose first wife had died of cancer within a week of Gerhard). Kennedy's fans were stunned. The book was still selling in large numbers and many were still grieving in sympathy when the news of her remarriage broke. So readers wrote her critical letters berating her for "remarrying so soon." To this day Kennedy finds their interest inappropriate and a trifle annoying.

Not long after the wedding, Margaret Dury Gane wrote a rather unflattering profile of Kennedy for *Weekend Magazine*, suggesting that she was cold and aloof even among her colleagues, and that her circumspect "cookie cutter" image was the despair of the media. "It's likely Kennedy still hasn't accepted the fact that what really attracted the readers was the book's revelation of her as a sensitive, suffering human being." There are still people wondering why she made that sudden step out of character and then an equally quick retreat.

Of course, Kennedy did not make a name for herself with personal journalism or displays of passion. Her following, which includes many of the people she has interviewed, has been built on professionalism. Her style is easy-going, her focus general interest rather than hard-nosed investigative journalism. She rarely interrupts and avoids putting people on the spot. For this reason, politicians don't avoid her. When journalists all over town were getting the cold shoulder from Prime Minister Trudeau, Kennedy would get calls requesting an interview.

There are many sides to Betty Kennedy, not all of them hidden. Very much in the Aitken tradition, for instance, Kennedy is an accomplished businesswoman. She has been invited to join the boards of numerous companies and has selected a few (Simpsons until 1979, the Bank of Montreal, and an American multi-national, Akzona Inc.). She isn't an entrepreneur as Wallace and Aitken were (Wallace was a chinchilla rancher for a while, and when she retired from radio opened a travel agency that did very well), but she has ventured into some very high-powered boardrooms where very few women have trod before. When she was invited onto the board of the Bank of Montreal (an operation she deems to be quite progressive in these matters) only one other woman had ever been a director. That was Madame Vanier, who hadn't stayed long. "I was surprised by the invitation. But when they put the idea to me, they also said they were asking another woman from Quebec at the same time, because they felt Madame Vanier as the single woman on a board of fifty-three had not been comfortable."

Meanwhile, Kennedy has married into the Canadian Establishment. Her husband's family has since lost control of Simpsons, but Allan Burton is still a very wealthy man and a member emeritus of the business elite. Kennedy has become used to chauffeured limousines, stately homes, and regular mentions in Zena Cherry's society column. She is, all the same, a self-made woman. She is one of the very few women who entered the Establishment as much on merit as through marriage. So nowadays, the articles on Women in the Boardroom invariably include Kennedy in the roundup. She has acquired great influence through her work as a broadcaster and now adds to that the power of her business connections. Like Aitken's, her influence reaches far beyond her audience.

On air, Kennedy does not confine herself to "women's interests" as Aitken did, but neither has she championed women's rights or espoused feminist causes. This is not to say that Kennedy is oblivious to the existence of discrimination. Although she has not experienced it herself, she has certainly observed prejudice in action and has had to overcome some confining aspects of the Aitken legacy herself:

If there was a setback for women in private radio in the

sixties, don't you think part of that had to do with the concept of the kind of broadcasting women did? The "women's show" had been dead as a doornail for twenty years or more. Yet if you were a station manager or programme director and a woman came to you saying she wanted to do a show, the red light flashed "women's show" and the reaction would be "sorry, we don't have any place for that." Part of it also may be that neither those doing the hiring nor those seeking to be hired were visualizing women's role as simply that of a broadcaster. That makes an awful difference. I don't think anyone wants to hear endless decorating hints any more, or any of those topics that used to be lumped together as "women's interests."

In general, Kennedy, like Aitken, has not been given to wielding her influence in defence of any cause or idea that involved social change. Kennedy, like Aitken, is comfortable with the right-of-centre conservatism of CFRB. Both women have been "improvers," believers in hard work, perseverance, and individual initiative. Kennedy, in the Aitken tradition, has played the role of Exceptional Woman with panache and to rave reviews.

Ten years ago, Valerie Pringle joined the staff of CFRB. At age twenty she was an eager rookie, just graduating from Ryerson Polytechnical Institute's course in television and radio arts. In her second year, she signed on as a summer student, as the Good News Reporter. "I was very keen and quite aggressive about getting that job, which I thought was a bit of a plum. I thought it would be fun to do feature reports round the city, you know, weddings in streetcars and Grey Cup parades." She kept on doing features through her third year at Ryerson, and for several years after coming on full-time staff. Everything went swimmingly, until one fine day she was told that she wasn't really working out and was pulled off the air. Her voice was "too shrill," and listeners were complaining.

With that she retired behind the scenes, wondering if the criticism was justified. She took some voice lessons and never gave up on the idea of on-air work, for this was what she had always enjoyed most. She was assigned to work with host Andy Barry on the 7 to 8 P.M. shift. With his support, she slipped back behind the mike when he was sick or on holiday. In 1981, when Barry left the station, Pringle was offered the show. Despite the long apprenticeship she had served, she felt as if she were being thrown in cold. "I thought I would die, I was so terrified. There I was, opposite Barbara Frum and *As It Happens*, replacing Andy Barry in the biggest station in the country. I just didn't know if I would be able to sustain it."

But sustain it she did. With Pringle, the legacy of Kate Aitken and Claire Wallace reached into a third generation. The genre of broadcasts, of course, had changed a good deal, moving into the mainstream of current affairs journalism. Yet Pringle's approach has always been her own. She is hesitant about calling herself a journalist:

> That title has such weight, I'd almost think it presumptuous to call myself that. I guess I am a journalist when I'm doing shows on the shooting down of the Korean airliner (and I think we outstripped *As It Happens* on that one) or the Pope or Reagan. Yet I feel I didn't properly earn my stripes, not having come out of a strong news background. So I vacillate between being a journalist and an interviewer.

On air, Pringle is chatty and relaxed. She sounds just like she looks: bright-eyed and ebullient, a younger version of Betty Kennedy, with the same wholesome good looks and casual elegance. But her style as a broadcaster is quite different from Aitken's discipline or Kennedy's cool. She gets further on *gemutlichkeit* than she ever would on grammar, which is exactly what charms listeners. She does sound like your next-door neighbour having a try on radio; she does make it sound tremendously easy.

Married the year she went to work at CFRB, and now the mother of two babies, her life has until very recently revolved around family, squash games at the club, lunch with friends, and her job at the station, just four blocks from home. "I've lived my whole life around Yonge and St. Clair," she chuckles, amused at the ring of stability in that admission.

Valerie Pringle is a success story, and when Bishop Strachan School, the private girls' school from which she graduated in 1971, trots out the names of old girls who've done well, her name is up there along with Veronica Tennant and Zena Cherry. Still, if she hasn't broken with her background, she is a bit unusual. Not too many BSS old girls go to technical schools. Not many of them continue working once they are married and mothers. Pringle has managed to combine both job and family without visibly straining either. It helps that her husband is an investment dealer with Dominion Securities Ames, meaning "a lot more is possible that wouldn't be as easy on my salary alone."

She has help living in, because she is away most of the day.

> Sometimes I wonder who I'm warping. I'm not warped and my mummy was at home. Attitudes are changing though. It never occurred to me to stay at home, really; it never occurred to me, either, not to have kids. I know women without children who thought they would be married by the end of their twenties and who therefore have to keep working. At a certain point they've had to do a turnaround in their heads and make peace with the possibility that they may never marry. They are going to have to continue working, so they had better be more systematic about getting on with it.

Pringle is quite cautious about commenting on the choice of other women to stay home; she recognizes that her job seems glamorous to others but she keeps her own ego in check and tries to avoid name-dropping.

> Sometimes people make excuses for me because I have this demanding job. I don't think it is any more demanding, say, than being a manager for Bell Canada. I never know when a hot story may come up and that seems exciting — phoning Granada or Lebanon, wow! — as if that's really important. All I'm doing is dialling. It requires no brain power. It doesn't make me more im-

portant or significant. It just seems that way. Still, you can be silly and never mention your work. But sometimes I have caught myself casually talking about what Lucille Ball said and I tell myself to stop being obnoxious. So it is hard to keep a balance because the job does seem so overpowering.

Late in 1984, Pringle left all hesitation behind and accepted a job hosting CBC television's new daytime programme, *Midday* (the replacement for *Take 30*). *Midday*, a daily current affairs magazine, was not, however, created with a predominantly female audience in mind, but was, instead, directed to a general, lunch-hour audience.

In a curious way, the tradition has come full circle, from Kate Aitken, who made women's interests her medium and whose work was an elaboration of the housewife role, to Betty Kennedy, the complete professional who lives her private life very much apart from her broadcasting career, to Valerie Pringle, who seemed not to have chosen a profession in radio so much as found a great job that fit her family lifestyle. With *Midday*, she crosses the street to work in public television, joining the premier mass medium of the age. In so doing, she updates the tradition and turns a corner in her own career.

Between Betty Kennedy's debut and Valerie Pringle's, the world of private radio underwent an astonishing transformation, and it is something of a miracle that there is room today for either of them. The station Kennedy joined in 1959 was a fixture on the AM dial, serving comfortable middle-class Toronto. That hasn't changed much. The audience has grown to the near-million mark, making CFRB the front-running station in its market, which is by far the biggest and the wealthiest in the country. In the fifties, however, it wasn't at all clear that radio had much of a future, or if it did, what that future could be. As television took greater hold of the public's imagination and leisure time, it was obvious that radio had to redefine itself if it were to hold its audience and advertisers.

In the late fifties, commercial radio arrived at the cross-roads and, almost without thinking, headed off down the road of "theme" (or special interest) broadcasting. The programming mix offered by individual stations narrowed, as they set about cornering a particular market, trying to please a particular crowd or age group with country and western, folk, rock, classical, jazz, or, as in CFRB's case, with easy-going middle-of-the-road music.

In a contracting market, competition was fierce, and yet there was very little room in the recorded music format for variation or distinction. The main difference, beyond the style of music, was the personality of the disc jockeys, hired to give the time and the temperature between records. The concept of "the show" was abandoned; the jockeys, more-over, lost creative control. They had (and have) no input into the station's programming, which is basically a matter decided by marketing consultants. DJs are handed a play list from which they cannot deviate, because each station is licensed to play a certain kind of music, a certain proportion of which must be Canadian.

In many ways, the late 1950s and early 1960s period was radio's bleakest hour and certainly its least imaginative. But one original invention will undoubtedly be remembered, although it has all but joined the dodo bird in heaven: the radio hotline show. Typically, these were broadcast during the daytime and typically, they were hosted by fast-tongued, quick-witted characters who loved being provocative and would rather be rude to callers than risk a dull show. Guests were brought into the studio, too, for hosts and callers to grill. Often they were politicians or officials with a policy to defend, and then hosts had a field day, keeping them hooked and squirming in the hotseat between calls and during commercials. It was exciting and outrageous radio.

Precious few of the hotline hosts were women; even fewer women were drafted into the ranks of the DJs. Without doubt women suffered a major setback during this period and were effectively banished from the airwaves except as recording artists.

In fact, it was to be years before women got back in front of the microphones in anything like the numbers or the authority they had had in the 1940s and 1950s. Only in the last five years has private radio finally allowed women back on the air with shows of their own. Not surprisingly, the comeback, when it did occur, was on FM radio and in the dead of night. Stereo still is AM radio's junior partner; a place where the audiences, the ad revenues, and therefore the risks, are modest — a good place to "let the ladies do their thing." Women who got it into their heads to apply for on-air jobs on AM were routinely told that the radio audience wasn't yet ready for a female voice.

That answer, almost verbatim, was given to a very talented woman when she came to Toronto to audition for CHUM news in 1977. The absurdity of Jane Hawtin's position was that she had actually been called in from Kingston to apply for the job. She had been doing a daily show, *Kingston Today*, on CKLC for six months or so. She had been hired by the station manager, whose father, Allan Waters, also owned CHUM.

> I did a really good audition and we talked salary and starting date, the whole bit. Then upper management decided Toronto wasn't ready for a woman doing the news on AM. They don't remember the story but I remember it *very* clearly. The person who wanted to hire me was so furious he actually came downstairs and told me what had been said. Of course, I had been doing an interview programme with a two-minute newscast off the top. So I was in no position to compete with newscasters with ten years' experience (which is what CHUM usually hires). Still, he was prepared to hire me.
>
> Then a secretary at CHUM, who had seen the whole episode and was disgusted, phoned up someone she knew at Q-107, which was just going on the air, and told them my story. I got a call from the news director at Q, who told me they had filled pretty well everything but would I take the weekend news? Of course, no one works for six months in a small radio station and moves immediately to a major city station, but I didn't know that at the time.

She also didn't realize how lucky her first break in

Kingston had been. She had originally gone there to get a university degree at Queen's, planning to go on to law school. On the way, she discovered the theatre. Jimmy Waters of CKLC, who saw her acting, offered her the full-time job on air.

Hawtin at thirty is very much a woman in charge of her life and work. She's a grande dame of Rock Radio, big-hearted, witty, and wise; a statuesque figure with her own New Wave chic, strikingly dressed in a black satin bomber jacket with Q-107 screeching off the back. She's a woman at ease with herself despite the hoopla and hype of showbiz, and she suffers fools with sarcasm. An audition at CITY-TV a while back landed her the unsolicited advice to lose twenty pounds and Hawtin was infuriated. "Fuck you," she hurls at the memory of their infantile attitudes. "Call me when you've grown up. I'd lose twenty pounds for me, but *not* for them." Hawtin more than survives in an environment she calls openly sexist. She has prospered, found a niche, and moved in with the plants. Being a feminist and very down-to-earth, she meets the machismo head on.

Picture this: a Loni Anderson look-alike contest, with the winner getting the receptionist's job at Toronto's raciest rock station. Or this: an early morning jockey who invites listeners to call in and tell people what they are doing or wearing "between the sheets."

The boys love their old tricks, says Hawtin — even when they backfire, as the beauty contest approach to hiring did, and even though they have to admit it offends a lot of people. Two years ago, when Q lost two of its on-air women, the ratings took a dive. It seemed obvious that women were tuning out. When Hawtin returned from a four-month maternity leave, management was in a flap:

> I was told there was an active campaign to cut out the cutesy jokes on-air and to curb sexist features like "Between the Sheets" which used to make me vomit. We do it to ourselves, though, because some women took the bait and called in. Other women did the right thing by changing the dial. There could have been other reasons why they stopped listening. The heavy male nature of rock music for one. There has to be a blend of hard rock

and something with feeling in it to soften it up or women go away. Of course, I laughed. I loved it! "The women are gone and we need to get them back," wailed Gary, the programme director. I wonder why, Gary. I wonder why.

And imagine this: Hawtin being instructed, shortly after her arrival, to stop referring on air to her husband as her husband. "Your lover or main man is okay; but not husband or boyfriend. Please." Husband didn't fit the Q image of singleness, going out every night and living the rock lifestyle. Hawtin, new mother in 1983, is back at work while her "main man" has taken a sabbatical from the recording industry to stay home with Amber. Once a day, he makes a trip to Q's offices on the thirtieth floor of a high-rise at Yonge and Bloor, taking the baby to her mother for a midday feeding.

Gary came in once when I was feeding her and launched into something, and then realized what was going on. He just couldn't do it. He backed out the door and fled. No one else reacted that way. In fact, it was terrific to have a baby around the place. It rather changed people's attitudes when they found she wasn't imposing, that you could still get things together without her disrupting everything.

Hawtin's own attitude about these things is uncomplicated and commonsense. She realizes, though, that there have been tremendous changes in seven years. "When I started in radio, there was still no recognition that women had any right to be there. Now they know that they need us in order to have a balance. A radio station with no women on it sounds funny. To go from not needing or wanting women on air, to believing a station sounds funny without them, I think, is a monumental change."

And perhaps, Hawtin muses, it was just as well that she started with the worst experience in her professional life, co-hosting the Kingston show with a "super chauvinist who was mortified to have to work with a woman." Not only was the s.c. going to have to work with an inexperienced woman but, as he soon found out, a woman who was hip, smart, and hired to give the show some sparkle. Though just two years older than Jane, he seemed to come from another generation, "the kind of guy who at twenty-four, living in a university town, didn't own a pair of jeans. I actually accused him of wearing boxer shorts, one day. He was just old in his mind." He was also deadly serious about his career, and found it difficult to deal with the Hawtin phenomenon, a would-be actress who took to the airwaves like a duck to water, and who was doing better interviews than he was in no time.

> Because I had the voice control and a few brains I didn't find it that difficult. What was hard was keeping up the confidence. It was alright for a couple of months and. then I began believing him, that perhaps I shouldn't have been there. I remember one day running an interview the s.c. had taped, and after the first few minutes there was nothing, dead air, something had erased the rest. Instead of staying with me, he had a temper tantrum, picked up the tape, threw it across the room, and stalked out. I had to flip the mike on and extemporize for ten minutes until he decided to come back in. Meanwhile I could see him in the control room talking to the manager, who was yelling at him.
>
> At first I tried to win him over. Then I decided he was just a jerk and stopped bothering. I got on with my own work. He realized at some point that I did know what I was doing and I think he was intimidated.

What happened next is textbook — or maybe Harlequin Romance, where the guy falls for the girl who stole his thunder:

> Not only did we do the show together, we shared an office. We were together twenty-four hours a day. And he would do this strange high-school stuff, like coming over to me when I was doing an interview and putting me in a headlock. When I told the programme director he went into hysterics, because everyone knew the s.c. hated my guts. But it was true and eventually I had to take him aside and tell him I was married.

In the very late seventies, with the debut of FM rock radio, why were women suddenly invited to read the news? Had the female voice dropped, lost its alleged shrillness? Or had audiences just become accustomed to the sound, deciding that if a woman could be believed telling the time she could probably be believed reading the news. Q has had a fair number of female "jocks" — Dusty Shannon, Samantha Taylor, Kelly Rose — and from the outset had three women newscasters, including Jane Hawtin.

> I have always wondered why we were hired, so I called up the old news director and asked: "Was it tokenism or was it a gimmick?" "Neither," he said. Q was trying to do a totally different kind of news — a conversational style that everybody is doing now. Q went to a style that said "Here's what's happening, folks, and let me explain why it might be important to you." They were deliberately looking for people who didn't have mannerisms, who sounded the same way on air and off. Experience was irrelevant and possibly a drawback. He told me that it just turned out that most of the tapes they liked were by women. Not to deny the publicity value of three women doing the news — but it wasn't a premeditated gimmick. I'm not sure if his interpretation is true or not, but I don't think it was tokenism because they did not have to hire women. Not back then.

Hawtin got her foot firmly planted in the door with the weekend news, which she would write and read herself. Before long, she was doing interviews and contributing to a fifteen-minute current affairs show called *Barometer*. It is now on for an hour, between noon and 1 P.M. Hawtin produces it, chooses the guest and topics, does the research, and hosts it live with a co-host, Gene Valaitis. *Barometer* is her real delight and it also gives her special status in the business, because her show doesn't have the restrictions of the regular disc show. It has an open format and she has "total creative control," deciding what goes to air and what is covered. It's her show the way *The Betty Kennedy Show* is Betty Kennedy's. That's a rare form of power in radio.

Moreover, it is something of a coup to have an information

programme stuck in the middle of a rock radio day. "The general attitude in rock radio," says Hawtin, "is that talk is not important. They believe talk is for women and rock is for men. So the danger is that I might have ended up with only women listening and not maintained the numbers and mix of listeners. That hasn't happened. I've always kept sixty percent male and forty percent female." So she has earned her freedom.

Katie Malloch is another female exception: another woman with her own style, her own music, and her own way with an audience on late night radio. Her name has become synonymous with jazz on the CBC stereo network, where she has her own two-hour show on Saturday nights. As Malloch puts it, she got her break through affirmative action, when Johnny Yesno, who was the producer of CBC's *Our Native Land* in Winnipeg, decreed that all the stringers in the regions providing inserts for the programme had to be native. Malloch's grandfather was a full-blooded Mohawk, so she applied and got a job doing short weekly items. She was studying anthropology at McGill at the time and had already decided against the academic life: "The field was overrun with concerned people and there weren't any more tribes to study, anyway." She dropped out of an M.A. programme and went to work at the Rainbow Bar and Grill, picking up a freelance assignment as campus reporter for a local afternoon show, once again on the CBC. This gave her a chance to develop some editing skills and to learn something about how a show is put together. Then she tried commercial radio: two months with rock station CKGM, doing the news on the 4 A.M. to noon shift, a wretched job that meant getting up at three in the morning and living in the unpleasant hyped-up environment of eternally "with it" Top 40 radio.

> Within a month my face broke out in the worst case of acne I've ever seen. All the bosses I'd had at the CBC were female, and suddenly there I was working for a real jerk in a three-piece suit — a twenty-nine-year-old going on sixty-five — who said to me when I asked for a

daytime shift, "I don't think the city's ready for a woman's voice in the daytime."

That was 1975, almost twenty years since the same station had made headlines by hiring Marge Anthony as the first woman in English Canada to host an all-night show. For twenty years, audiences, very mysteriously, were ready to believe the news from the mouths of women at 5 A.M. but not 5 P.M.

After two months in purgatory, Malloch knew that private radio was never going to be a comfortable setting for her. Back at the CBC, the co-host job on the afternoon show *Sounds Unlikely* was open, and producer Ramona Randall urged Malloch to go for it. Two-and-a-half happy years followed, working with Wayne Grigsby. Then an outbreak of budget cuts (a chronic disease at the CBC) forced the producers to drop Grigsby, who was on contract and costing a lot. They kept Malloch, who was on the CBC's announcing staff and thus didn't cost the show anything directly. Malloch was on her own. In the meantime, she was developing a special passion on the side.

Since childhood, Malloch had been surrounded by music. "The stereo was a jewel box for me. You opened it to find magic" — the sounds of Billie Holliday, Sarah Vaughan, and Benny Goodman. Her parents were jazz aficionados. "They had good taste and introduced me to enough to let me know there was a lot of good music out there." It was the most natural thing in the world, really, for Katie to be given her own jazz show — *That Midnight Jazz* — for six years and *Jazz Beat*, now in its third season, which comes on Saturday nights at 8 P.M.

Doing these music shows was a different experience from the daily afternoon rolling home show.

For one thing, you get much more mail when you do a nighttime show. I don't know why. Perhaps people are sitting around listening to you at night with nothing else to do, and jazz audiences anyway seem to write a lot of letters. In any case, I started to get the feeling of broadcasting to the whole country, instead of just

Montreal. With the rolling home show, there are weather and traffic reports and the nuts and bolts to get through, so you don't ever get the chance to say, "Listen to this eighteen minutes of great music." During the day, they want a nice breezy, snappy personality, but at night I got to select my own music, so I felt it was much more my show.

Indeed it was. Malloch settled into late night jazz as if born to it and quickly acquired a devoted following of jazz buffs and people who just liked her enthusiasm, her gentle expressive voice, and the long stretches of undiluted music. CBC blurbs refer to Malloch's "warm candle-lit voice," which doesn't quite capture an approach as steamy and vivacious as hers. Although she is dealing with a subject she knows and cares deeply about, Malloch doesn't set herself up as an authority and disapproves of hosts who are out to prove how much they know, indulging in long-winded opinions and endless trivia:

> I always wanted them to shut up and play the music. So I was determined to keep the talk brief and make the bridges really nice, combining things so that the music wouldn't be all from one period or one style. I'd put something from 1938 up against something from 1972, things with completely different styles but which sounded musically (if not historically) really good together. It was like playing in a sandbox all by myself.
>
> Then too with the afternoon show I was talking to other people all the time: producers, guests, Wayne, technicians. You are surrounded by people. With the jazz show, I'd disappear with my little pile of records down to the studio where a nice dozy technician, grateful for a simple record show, would be the only other soul around, and the two of us would be like two contented cows munching happily in a field.

After leaving *Sounds Unlikely*, Malloch was immersed in music for a while. She teamed up with Gérard Lambert, Quebec's resident expert on French music, to present

Québécois and French-Canadian music to English-speaking listeners on the English service, on a show called *Radio Active*, heard on Saturday nights. They were "breaking the sound barrier between anglophone and francophone Canada," as CBC's *Radio Guide* claimed hopefully. Lambert would choose the music and then tell Malloch about it, so she could talk about it on-air. Though a native of Montreal, Malloch hadn't encountered Quebec music often. She was delighted to get into it, and also for a chance to polish up her French. (Lambert complained that his English did not improve at all while working with her.) The satisfactions of the show weren't simply linguistic and musical. As a Montreal "anglo," Malloch was faced with the change in Quebec society signaled by the Parti Québécois victory, and her response was to embrace the possibilities of cultural coexistence. Like many others living outside the designated production centre of English CBC, she has been invited to move down the road to Toronto, where the lights and the opportunities are alleged to be brighter. But she resists, determinedly: *"J'y suis; j'y reste."* (I'm here and I'm staying.)

A steady diet of music could not continue forever, though. Malloch knew that she would have to get back to "more populated shows." "Keeping a balance between getting lonely and getting overloaded" was the objective, and it was time to give up *That Midnight Jazz*. Now she turned to television, moving to a local entertainment programme and back behind the mike with her old friend Grigsby. *Stepping Out* is a local weekly show that loosely defines entertainment to include anything from Sarah Vaughan to the opera to the Danny Grossman dancers to the Théâtre de Variété. "Thankfully, it is not another talk show where an endless stream of guests file in to sit in uncomfortable chairs in a studio." Instead, it consists of interviews and reviews shot on location and presented by Malloch and Grigsby in the studio.

Television was not an experience that Malloch sought or looked forward to. Two seasons on *Stepping Out* have confirmed her suspicions about the medium:

> Television is essentially a dumb medium. There is a feeling that radio is where you begin and, if you are

smart, television is where you end up. Yet television is dumber than radio. Not the people working in it, necessarily, but the set of values you are judging it by. In television, you have to worry about things like the colour of the film and why it is too blue, and you can spend ten minutes or an hour discussing that when you could be discussing the content of the programme. As a woman, of course, you know that you will be judged physically and even if you don't want to be judged that way, you will be. You know that there will be some people sitting at home watching you because they think you are cute.

You can read Malloch's scepticism about television in the clothes she wears on the days she tapes the show. Silk blouse elegance from the waist up, jeans and cowboy boots below — urban chic for the camera, country casual for herself.

The relationship with the television audience feels odd and remote to Malloch, after the intense and personal connection with jazz radio listeners. *Stepping Out* generates no mail, and though it has made her recognizable in the streets of Montreal, it is that vague rather purposeless recognition typical of television. People come up to her in the métro and ask her if she isn't Kathy Keefler (CBC local's news anchor). If they do know her from *Stepping Out*, they almost never comment on items, but rather on her hair (better this year), or they want to know if there is real booze in the glasses she and Wayne sip from. This is what made her realize how much TV's message has to do with surfaces and how warped the attitude of television viewers is, in the sense of being critical about the least fundamental element of your work:

> You present an outstanding item and viewers are likely to come away not thinking about what you said but about whether you have put on weight. Radio and television seem to be there for different purposes — almost like two sexes — and within the traditional value system of the corporation all the attention goes to television. But in radio circles there are many devotées who would never work in television. And people notice there is a vastly different atmosphere in radio; that there is a

much higher proportion of women who have real input and are actually defining the sound of CBC Radio, or at least as much as the men are. In television, the men seem to be more the old-fashioned, hardbitten broadcasting types, pleasant enough, but from another decade — I'm not sure which one — somewhere between the forties and sixties. They are forever talking about "sexy shots."

Television, moreover, seems to grow bigger and less manageable egos:

There is something very strange about talking to a camera way across the room, while the guys are standing around reading newspapers or picking their noses. It is pretty silly sitting there talking to a piece of metal in the first place, but in radio at least the mike is up close and you are sitting in a low-ceilinged room with a mellow light and the producer and technician behind the glass a few feet away.

In radio, you have more control than in television, where the producers and directors and assistants are all off the floor and out of sight in a control room somewhere else. They operate the mike, not you, and you sit there like an idiot in a room the size of a parking lot with forty-foot ceilings, on a set pretending to be a cityscape behind something pretending to be a desk. It feels so phony and false and perhaps it just takes a bigger ego to bridge that gap.

It is not easy to specialize in radio as Katie Malloch has done. There just are not that many opportunities for solo flight. "I know if I were smart," Malloch says ruefully, "I'd leave the CBC and go to the private sector, where I would make a lot more money. But I also know that I'd go crazy doing what they do. I don't want to sell maxi-pads; I'd rather sell Duke Ellington. And I know that I couldn't do a jazz programme anywhere else in the country."

Not all hosts on radio are doing the same thing, and not all hosts have the same power. A privileged few have artistic control and create their show around themselves, as does

Malloch with *Jazz Beat*. Most programmes, especially on AM and in current affairs, have several producers, story editors, and reporters, all of whom have a hand in setting the content and style. Hosts can have more or less involvement: they can be straight announcers who come in to read a prepared script and whose major contribution is "a set of pipes," or they can be part journalist, part interviewer/host, and a legitimate part of the production unit. Traditionally, most CBC hosts belong to the announcing staff, a pool of men and women who are assigned to a variety of duties through the radio and TV schedule: announcing the news, giving station breaks, introducing programmes, and reading public announcements. Some of them do a little of everything; others are assigned exclusively to one programme.

Anne Budgell came by her specialty in quite a different way from Malloch, and her field is, to say the least, "non-traditional." Budgell is the agricultural and resources commentator for CBC in Newfoundland, and is host/producer (with Jim Wellman) of the daily half-hour *Fisherman's Broadcast*. "The only place I could be doing what I'm doing is here. A programme like this would sound ridiculous anywhere else, really — unimaginable. But when I think of it, the fishery in Newfoundland has more to do with what goes on in this province than any other single thing."

Budgell had several years' experience in radio and television news before she applied for her job in radio. Her previous contract had been in television with the local supperhour programme, *Here and Now*. On that show she had learned to heartily dislike the makeup (and the constant skin irritations), and the necessity of continually inconveniencing people by dragging lights and camera equipment into their offices or living rooms, disrupting their lives — all for a 40-second clip. She also disliked having to humour technicians: "I had to kiss ass and bite my tongue in order to get along with some very difficult people." Finally, she resented never having enough time to really learn about anything. "Every day I got a different assignment, and I had a feeling that I was doing nothing very well."

After a six month "time out" to think through whether she was where she really wanted to be, Budgell applied for the *Fisherman's Broadcast* job, along with about forty other people, mostly men. Though women have been general news reporters for some years, it hadn't dawned on the powers-that-were that a woman could also do this job. The men on the hiring committee who interviewed applicants asked what she knew about the fishery:

> I told them I knew more historical stuff from reading than I knew about the contemporary situation, but of course, I knew who the major personalities were. I said I figured I was a good reporter and had learned about off-shore drilling and iron-ore mining, and that fishery had as much to do with me as other fields do. They looked at me as if they had never thought of it before.

Moreover, she was convinced this was no fringe or minority interest, but "a subject that touches every life in the province." Far from restricting her horizons, she believed that the job would give her a chance to acquire some detailed knowledge about something, and to practise her profession with the advantage of that specialty.

There were a few jokes about changing the name of the show to "fisherpersons" or "fisherfolk," but there was no resistance from the people in the field or in the fisheries to a woman taking charge. In fact, she has considered it an asset that she doesn't come from the fishing community (her family comes from Labrador), because she takes nothing for granted and has no trouble asking the "dumb outsider's question."

Budgell's approach has also broadened the range of the programme a bit. It used to be thought of as rather folksy — ignored by the cbc higher-ups, but kept in the schedule because it still had the ratings. Budgell has turned it into a more solid current affairs show. Gone are "the Old Skipper interviews, where you call up a colourful character 'round the bay and let him speak his mind for a while" and where opinions are accepted without being challenged or explored. Predictably, she got a reputation for being tough, and a nickname — Anne Bludgeon — to go with it. (This was helped by erroneous rumours that she was fired from *Here and Now* for badgering Premier Moores during an interview.)

> It's not great having labels like aggressive and abrasive slapped on you; but women will be criticized for things that are expected of a male broadcaster. I'm not surprised by it. I've gotten used to it. But I do not think of myself that way. I know I'm polite, that I let people talk, and that I do not do any of the things people think I do.

It's not pleasant to experience this double standard, but it is a small irritation compared to the massive wall of thick-headed prejudice and social convention that E. Cora Hind had to breach. Like Hind, Budgell inspires respect and trust from the people who know her, and not long after she became the fisherman's broadcaster, the executive producer of current affairs admitted, "Hiring you, Anne, was the best thing we've done all year."

Margaret Pacsu is a familiar voice to anyone who listens to CBC Radio. After Jan Tennant made news by breaking the gender barrier in 1970 to become the first woman staff announcer in CBC history, it was several years before another woman was admitted. That was Pacsu, who was followed shortly by a flock of other women — Bronwyn Drainie, Shelagh Rogers, Barbara Smith, and Judy Maddren among them.

There is definitely something august about CBC announcers — it is partly a matter of tone and partly tradition. Some find the importance attached to the job exaggerated, but it has to do with the CBC's vaunted independence, the legacy of doing constant battle with outside interest groups, politicians, and advertisers, who all in one way or another have tried and continue to try to bend the public broadcaster to their particular will. The effort to keep the news impartial and the programming balanced is audible in the CBC's service. Announcers have to *sound* official: they are not hired for their sparkling personalities or their gift of the gab, as are their counterparts in private radio, but for clear, pleasant, and unaccented voices, good diction, and most important, an air of authority.

Margaret Pacsu is a most surprising woman. You would never take her for an American (which, by birth, she is); somehow she seems European, and she speaks with a lilting, mid-Atlantic accent. Blonde, with dark blue eyes, she has classic features and a classy style tending to eloquent under-statement. She is a delight to meet, charming, *very* funny, and fascinating to talk to. It doesn't take long to realize that she is a woman full of hidden (at least to the public) talents. She speaks beautiful Parisian French, has acted, has recorded a comedy album with Glen Gould, has knowledge of contem-porary French romantic music and a special interest in young classical musicians (who, she feels, don't get the attention and support they deserve), and for four years had a brilliant career in market research in France.

And all her life, Margaret Pacsu has wanted to sing. She is a singer/comedienne and would have liked to have had a career performing professionally. When she was very little, she dreamt of becoming a movie star, but as a young girl growing up in the lap of American luxury in Princeton, New Jersey, these ambitions seemed to her unattainable, not because they were impossible dreams, but because they were "not permitted."

"I wanted to sing in a nightclub or do musical comedy, but in 1960 nice girls didn't do that. My father certainly didn't want his beloved second daughter singing for a living on 52nd Street. So instead I got engaged." Which definitely was approved of, and Pacsu still has the monogrammed towels from the venture. She did not, however, go through with the marriage, though all the invitations were sent. Instead, she fled at the last moment to France, where she taught English in the lycée system for several years and existed on a Fulbright teaching scholarship.

Pacsu was a late bloomer, and she still has not struck exactly the right chord or hit her creative stride. However, she has reached a point in her life when she has gained some perspective on a career she sees as haphazard and unfocussed. She confesses to being envious of those people — the

Barbra Streisands of the world — who ignored the "not permitted" signs and went straight ahead, following their ambition come what may. Pacsu has defied the signs herself on occasion, but perhaps more out of desperation than conviction. She became a reluctant adventurer and kept running into challenges and remarkable opportunities, often in fields for which she felt little affinity but which certainly took her to some remarkable places.

Pacsu grew up modestly privileged. She went to the best schools and graduated from one of the most prestigious women's colleges. Her parents were Hungarian emigrés — her father a brilliant research chemist and her mother a concert pianist — who came to the United States in the thirties and decided to stay. Pacsu did well academically, went to Smith College in the fifties when the slogan was "rings by spring," and made a stab at graduating to middle-class wifehood but flunked the wedding. After her first sojourn in France, she returned to the United States and spent a desperate summer trying to find a job in New York ("the answering service used to call up to see if I was all right"). The one job that materialized was with a Cincinnati-based market research firm, and within a year she was back in Paris setting up an office for them.

When Pacsu finally returned to North America for good it was 1970 and she had spent most of the sixties in Europe. She felt out of sync with the social revolution going on at home. "I recall going to see two movies in the first weeks after I got back — *Bob & Carol & Ted & Alice* and *Midnight Cowboy* — and I thought I should get right on a plane and go straight back to France. I didn't understand what had happened. I was shocked beyond belief. First of all, what were all those people doing in bed together?" Her research firm was by this time getting ready to launch itself in Canada; Pacsu was more than happy to leave the United States and try out Toronto.

Once there, she spent two years in an office on Consumers' Road at Sheppard Avenue in the bleak nether reaches of suburbia.

I had a horrendous identity experience sitting in that

office overlooking a parking lot, looking at all those cars and traffic and the Red Baron restaurant. There was to be yet another focus group on yet another food product or feminine hygiene product and I thought, What am I doing in this business? I have to get out. This is not my skin anymore.

She had, in the meantime, been picking up some freelance work at the CBC, reading scripts of Québécois plays for drama producer John Reeves and doing a bit of acting. The more she did, the more unsettling it was and the more she realized it was time to stop avoiding her true aspirations. She applied for several host jobs, failed the auditions, but in the process learned a lot about television.

Her next move was to visit the executive producer of the CBC's local news show. The whole area of consumer reporting was being neglected by *Weekday* and, she informed him, she was the person who could set it right:

> I went in there and aced the interview. [Tim] Kotcheff gave me a job as a story editor and with a healthy cut in salary I left those housewives and detergents and was then somewhat closer to where I should have been. Of course, I've never ever done a consumer item in all the days I've been at the CBC. Instead I specialized in children, the arts, old people, and animals, which was great because the place was full of people with very strong personalities who wanted to do controversial heavy items all the time.

By 1972, Pacsu had done more than a hundred items and was running dry. A bad back was giving her problems and she was feeling the insecurities of working on contract. Kotcheff had been generous — giving her sick leave when he was not bound to — and it was he who proposed that she try for a staff announcer's position. Her first day on that job was trial by ordeal:

> I was ushered into a studio at four o'clock in the afternoon to host a live classical music show. Jan [Tennant]

was sitting next to me and I asked her what I should say. "You could begin by switching on the mike and saying your name," she whispered. Jan was filling in for Monty Tilden that day, but she had terrible laryngitis and couldn't do it either. It was two minutes to air and Fred Radigan, the producer, hadn't been told he'd have to do the show with a new chickie who knew nothing at all about the programme.

After two hours of live music, I then had a small break, taped an hour's worth of syndication — which I had never done before either — and then I had to do the 11 P.M., midnight, and 1 A.M. sign-off newscasts, which were eleven-minute broadcasts complete with cutaways (as Winnipeg left, and so on), all done to time! It was the most awful thing I've ever been through and I have never had another shift like it in my life. The music show was *Divertimento* and the story on that, of course, is that I have been doing it ever since, though it is now called *Listen to the Music*.

Announcing, Pacsu discovered quickly, requires great precision and a concentration on presentation. Though she had already won her spurs in television as a reporter, she has no desire, as Jan Tennant had, to anchor the news. "That is a horrible, dreary job. You have to have tremendous physical stamina. When I was doing *Weekday* I got nothing out of it. You get very tired, you get bad skin, and your private life goes down the toilet." Radio announcing was a welcome relief. It was varied and interesting and secure, even if the hours weren't regular. But she realized, security came with a price tag.

"Acting went out the window...and though I like the work enormously, it is still a second-choice career. I did always want to be an actress and comedienne and being a staff announcer is a cop-out." In a sense, it has been something of a trap. Pacsu's frustrations are perhaps more with herself than her job. They come from a sense of self-betrayal, for not having followed her original impulse and for taking detours instead. It took twenty years and the mastery of two careers before she felt secure enough to return to her real love and ambition, and she is now singing pop songs from the 1920s and 1930s on the amateur circuit around town.

Margaret Pacsu now feels settled in Canada and for the first time in her life, has planted some perennials in the garden. She and radio producer Robert Campbell live in a huge old Victorian house on a hill, on a dead-end street in midtown Toronto, and are patiently restoring the place room by room. The two have recently adopted a son, and she is thrilled with late motherhood. But she says, clenching a fist and grinning, "I swear I'll be a singer in a nightclub before I'm fifty!"

FOUR

The CBC and Radio Journalism

Or, Why You've Never Heard of Judith Jasmin and Helen James

IT WAS THE LATE 1960s on the West Coast when Madeleine Champagne began to freelance for Radio-Canada. Free love, folk festivals, feminism, and Zen Buddhism were on the minds of a generation of young people, the ragtag crew of activists, artists, and drop-outs who called themselves flower children. It was all happening in British Columbia and down the coast in San Francisco, but back in La Belle Province, where the independence movement was absorbing everybody's energy, it was still news.

Champagne was in her late twenties, living with an American draft-dodger, trekking up to the Queen Charlottes and down to California, taking in the times and living *à la vagabond*. For a time, the couple moved with their baby daughter into the B.C. interior, where you couldn't have flowers to wear year-round but where you could live as close to nature as you dared. It was a time for excursions into the cultural unknown, when people travelled to India looking for wisdom and tried psychedelics in the pursuit of insight. Young people didn't ask permission to make their experimental films or set up their communes, head shops, and health food restaurants. They just did it — on their own and with a little help from the occasional government grant.

Champagne was briefly a movie actress, drafted by her

friend Sylvia Spring into the title role in the pilot for her feature film *Madeleine is*. This is a vintage Early Women's Movement cautionary tale, about a woman's escape from the clutches of an archetypal male chauvinist. She plunges first into fantasy and then heads down reality road towards self-possession and liberation. The actual Madeleine was also busy launching herself independently in the world.

Champagne's particular gift, spotted by an astute radio producer at CBC Vancouver, was the way she wielded her pen. She began writing *reportages* on the Pacific hippie lifestyle, dealing with subjects like homosexuality, drugs, and the women's movement. During her sojourn in the interior, she wrote a series called *Pacific 2000*, which became a hit with the audiences in Quebec. It consisted of an exchange between two boys, one living in the city and the other in the country, counterposing the fast-paced city environment of rock concerts and demonstrations with the holistic life back on the land.

Eventually the party ended; Champagne returned home and began a career in radio journalism which has continued for thirteen years. She has tried production, done some hosting and writing (a kids' TV show called *Clak*), but mainly she has been a reporter for Radio-Canada's noontime current affairs programme *Présent*. She has always worked *à la pige*, as a freelancer on contract.

There are two schools of thought about the freelance broadcasting life. One view sees it as living dangerously — even irresponsibly, if one has dependents — close to the financial edge. There is no unemployment insurance, no maternity leave, no pension, no guarantee of work (except in the short term), and, of course, no regular paycheque to count on. Then there are the extra pressures — to produce quickly, to hustle your talents around town, to land a story before anyone else has it, and to keep your name fresh in the minds of producers and editors. To many people, that sounds too much like a recipe for ulcers.

However, the opposite view sees freelancing as a ticket to freedom, the perfect life for those who are most productive when they have control of their own projects and time. And for people who are highly motivated, self-disciplined, and full of ideas, it is a great way to work — no boss, no office hours, no committees. You could argue — and many free-lancers do — that there is safety in a multiplicity of skills and in spreading one's dependency through several sources of income. If you have one job, you only have one to lose; when you have five or six projects and several sidelines, you are not likely to lose all of them at once. Nonetheless, some of these professional nomads do seek out a favourite watering hole or two and will settle into what looks like a semi-permanent relationship. The CBC is without question the country's major source of freelance work, and a surprising number of people, including producers, executive producers, and on-air personalities, are self-employed and not on staff.

While she has been with the CBC as full-time freelancer, Champagne has continued to write for magazines and newspapers and to teach journalism. Her hectic pace is deliberate, part of a strategy for keeping several irons in the fire. "If everything fails or I have to move I'll be more likely to find work if I have recent experience teaching and writing. I am trying to protect myself, really, to ensure my economic independence." With that objective in mind, Champagne has also carefully cultivated a specialty in two areas of journalism: economics and Canadian affairs. Both carry a good deal of prestige within the profession and have won her recognition and interesting assignments for *Présent*. The fact is, however, that while she is fascinated with both, Champagne's special gift is for "softer" subjects. In 1980, she won the coveted Prix Judith Jasmin, awarded by the *Circle des femmes journalistes* for journalistic excellence, for a documentary she made on prostitution. The project took her a year to prepare, including extensive research and long interviews with street people in Vancouver, Toronto, and Montreal.

When talking about her approach to stories and people, Champagne becomes animated. Her dark eyes glint with the fervour of the radical-adventurer who is still there beneath the exterior of a young urban professional comfortably arrived in the eighties. "I'll tell you something very funny," she says:

> You know how grouchy and grim René Lévesque always
> looks? I remember seeing a huge publicity photograph

of him not long after the PQ was first elected, making a
presentation to Miss Alouette, or anyway to some beautiful young woman, and he had the radiant face of a
newborn. His emotional side was showing — that dimension which exists in all people and animals. We [women]
know it's there; men might know it too, but they tend to
forget it. I *never* forget it. Touching it, drawing on it,
may not pay off in journalism in terms of money, but it
certainly pays off in terms of your own satisfaction.

I don't usually say this; I am being very candid here,
but my own God-given talent is human interest stories.
That is what I do best and do extremely easily. I just lock
eyes and seem to enter people. When I did the documentary on prostitution, people went into such extremely
intimate detail that it was almost obscene to listen.
Although when I do such topics, I find twenty little notes
in my mail box at work the next day praising it, this is not
what gets you advancement and position in the profession. What brings recognition is "serious journalism."

Being good with human interest stories is a trap. It can
limit your chances to do other stories if you get "branded" as
someone who can handle the emotionally trying situations
like bereaved families or flood victims:

They know I can do these things. One day I was sent out
to cover a wildcat strike — the union guys were being
quite violent, brandishing things about, threatening to
kill everybody, and it was a fairly ugly situation. I
entered the place as if I were a queen and they all talked
to me. I got the comments I needed, came back, and put
it on the air. For me it seemed to be no problem. I don't
know why. But to protect myself I am trying to steer
away from those subjects and assignments.

All the same, the chances to do documentaries like hers on
prostitution are not frequent nor do they naturally occur to
assignment editors. They have to be lobbied for and defended.
The traditional concepts of what constitutes news, and thus
what is newsworthy, have changed little, even if the attitudes

of individual journalists have. "It might be," Champagne muses, "that men are becoming a little less shy about expressing humour and emotion. Around *Présent* I have heard them referring to that quality as the 'à la Madeleine' approach."

Champagne gives the impression of someone bristling with enough energy and curiosity to run an entire newsroom — someone who has probably never had a dull moment in her life, who is very self-directed and self-assured and, as she admits, ambitious.

> Not out of a desire for money or power within the hierarchy, but because there are things I know about that I want other people to know. I like economics, for instance. To me, it is like a good detective story, a puzzle; I think I am a good popularizer, or as we say in French, "vulgarizer." When I was young, I didn't think so much in terms of ambition as exploring. I wanted to see many countries, have many mates, and lead many lives.

She weighs and measures her life and career, arriving at the conclusion that were she a man "I'm sure I'd have my own show by now. I'm sure I'd be much higher; and given the fact that I never miss a deadline, am always on time, and invariably in a genial mood, I should be farther ahead." It does not really bother her, though, that she is not. For there are sacrifices she knows she is not prepared to make. She's reluctant to be away from her family (now numbering four, with the addition of another child three years ago) for any length of time. "I know very well that I am not willing to go to Lebanon for two months. A friend told me recently that his sixteen-year-old son said bluntly that he had no right to say anything because 'you were never around when I was young.' I am not willing to hear that from my children."

Champagne has not felt that she has been overtly discriminated against, though she's certainly aware of inequalities:

> I am the highest paid woman in this unit, but still I am paid at a lower rate than all the men. Moreover, since I

am on contract the union has no jurisdiction and we cannot take up certain issues such as child care as a travel expense.

Perhaps I have not paid enough attention. Perhaps it is because I have had a very long and happy relationship with the man I am with now, because I have two children, a nice house, a country place, lots of friends, and the opportunity to teach that I haven't taken the time to reflect on that.

In Champagne's unit, three out of twelve of the journalists are women, about par for the course at Radio-Canada. When the journalists' union counted heads for a brief it made to the 1983 Abella Commission (on employment opportunities in crown corporations), it found that twenty-three percent of the journalists working in news and current affairs were women, while eighty percent in the junior category of researcher were women. In television and radio, it uncovered a yawning income gap between male and female reporters (on the order of $4,000 to $5,000 per year), which is apparently growing wider. Even among researchers, the majority of whom are women, the income gap exists. The response of Radio-Canada's management to the charge of discrimination has been to deny it: they claimed that the union's figures matched the proportions of men and women applying for jobs in the first place and was, therefore, a matter of self-selection; they also said that if the pay differences between men and women were not because of seniority (the union's finding), then it must have to do with merit (women somehow being less deserving of merit pay increases than men).

In October 1981, six hundred women gathered at the Hotel Meridian in Montreal to talk about their lives and their careers in journalism. They came from broadcasting and newspapers; they were researchers, editors, writers, reporters, interviewers, and *animatrices* (hosts). They were young women just starting out, middle-aged women at the summit of their careers, and a few women who had left the field in mid-career. For three days, they spoke and listened to each other, frankly, openly, and from the heart. At times, they were surprised by their own revelations.

Said Louiselle Lévesque:

> When I joined CJBR (Radio-Canada) at Rimouski, there were no women on permanent staff in the newsroom. I was told women had passed through but not stayed because they weren't competent or didn't fit into the newsroom team, which they also told me was one great big happy family. When I arrived there, I was the only woman. Another was subsequently hired, also on temporary. Two years later I am still on temporary staff. People say that there is no discrimination in unionized shops. I don't agree; there is. I do not think women have the same access to permanent employment. In our newsroom, all the men are permanent staff members, and they tell me that is just happenstance.

Said Hélène Lévesque:

> I began working at the [Quebec] press gallery for the *Globe and Mail* as a researcher. When I arrived, there were two women journalists and about sixty men; when I left there were four women and now it's back down to three. The promise is always held out to women researchers: someday they might become journalists. They are told they have to study the basics first. In my experience, no man was ever told he had to apprentice as a researcher, clipping newspapers, in order to become a journalist.

Said Armande Saint-Jean:

> Why is it that I made the aberrant decision to abandon a career which was both enviable and envied, which certainly was leading me to glory and fortune in that most prestigious of all fields of journalism — national politics? Why did I leave it all to work with women and become a farmer? Well, I have to go back a bit. I began working in journalism eighteen years ago, when I was

eighteen. The first ten years of my professional life were golden years. I was young, pretty enough without being too pretty (as they say), intelligent, and available. I had no family or children; I was ambitious and worked extremely hard. I mastered the rules of the masculine game, I learned to win and to like competition. I even became "one of the boys." Then I decided to have a child. And I believe that's why things collapsed and why I made huge changes in my life.

First of all I had to resign. I was sick and there was a risk of losing the baby at five months, so I had to have time off. I was told I would violate my contract and I had no choice but to resign. I objected and finally got a verbal commitment that I would be reinstated when I returned. So I spent seven months without income, because as a freelancer I had no unemployment insurance, and when I returned I was given a much inferior position with lower pay. I was returning to work with a small baby and all the difficulties that entails. At work there was the usual pressure, schedules, and long hours — it was like having two twenty-four hour jobs at once. I protested about the situation and discovered quickly that it was better to say that I was sick than to mention the baby. That was more acceptable and lowered my credibility less. I think, however, what hurt the most was the contrast: the difference between the treatment I had known before and the treatment I got after the baby was born. I realized that in my early years I had represented the living proof that discrimination doesn't exist in current affairs because I was there. I had been a *femme-alibi* in the strictest sense of the term and I had absolutely believed the motto of all good token women, "If there is the will, there's a way."

The conference was a powerful and moving experience for many of the women attending. "A wall of silence is broken," announced *La Presse* in its report, accurately pinpointing the significance of the event. As the women talked, the isolation of their daily professional experiences evaporated; the feelings of frustration and anger which poured forth lifted into a kind of euphoria, which comes from discovering that your experience isn't unique. The meeting turned into a celebration of the resilience, imagination, and drive of the "hidden face" of journalism — their own. Moreover, the meeting had been called into being as a tribute to the memory of Quebec's greatest pioneer television journalist, the late Judith Jasmin. Just remembering Jasmin, seeing her legacy in that room, was a grand reaffirmation.

Who was Judith Jasmin? Why have we heard of René Lévesque's prodigious efforts in the establishment and definition of television journalism, but not hers? Why is her name unknown in English Canada, when she has inspired the entire current generation of women journalists in Quebec?

Judith Jasmin worked most of her life for Radio-Canada. At the very beginning, she was an actress in radio drama. She never really liked the work, however, and soon left to join Radio-Canada International. There she worked in information, doing radio reporting. She later wrote about those years: "When I began, realism was rather frightening to people. However, as we were supposed to be sending an accurate reflection of Canada abroad, we were finally given permission to *descendre dans la rue*, to go into the streets to speak to Canadians. They [the programme directors] realized that reality has its usefulness and can also convey something."

Eventually it occurred to someone that Jasmin was presenting programmes to foreign audiences that ought to be made available to Canadians as well. So, the news service of the French network was conceived and brought into the world by Jasmin and the department's other employee, René Lévesque. That was 1953, and two years later, Jasmin made a decision which altered the course of her career. She asked for an extended leave without pay and, at her own expense, went off to India and Indochina. Drawn by the philosophy and rhythms of eastern culture she went on an intellectual and spiritual pilgrimage (long before the Beatles made gurus fashionable). She went to Vietnam, where she interviewed the generals and diplomats, and with an interpreter talked to

the Vietnamese people. When she returned, she had enough
material for five programmes.

The trip was the first of many journeys — or perhaps it
was one stage in a lifelong journey. In 1957, Jasmin made a
second, more astonishing decision; she quit her staff position,
moved to France, and worked freelance for two years. Her
friends say that it was during those years in Paris that Jasmin
found herself, completed the journey of liberation she began
in India. "You learn many things alone, with no money, in a
room in Paris," she once remarked. In Paris she came to
terms with herself and her talents. An old friend and
colleague, Marie-N. Choquet wrote, "Judith always thought
of herself as the equal of the men she worked with. But the
other side of this deep conviction about her intellectual
capacities was a total lack of confidence in herself as a
woman." At the same time, Jasmin was coming around to a
new view of her homeland. She no longer saw Quebec as a
"poor, provincial cousin," and she realized that she wanted to
re-establish herself there. She also decided to take the plunge
into the great new medium of the age, television.

The next ten years of Jasmin's life were the most scintillat-
ing and passionate of her career. She was at the height of her
creative powers, and she became immensely popular, admired,
and respected. She introduced Quebeckers to Algeria, Peru,
Spain, Le Corbusier, racial segregation in the American
South, and hunger in the Third World. She became a
familiar figure, elegant and eloquent, on television programmes like *Champs Libre* and *Premier Plan*.

For four years, she was posted abroad as foreign correspondent to the United Nations and then to Washington,
where she reported on those turbulent American times —
civil rights, riots, assassinations. What made her reports
remarkable was her ability to get to the heart of complex
subjects and to find, invariably, the right people to explain
what was happening and explain it well. As much as anyone,
she invented television interviewing. And there is something
else that people who knew Jasmin say: that she seemed
somehow to have avoided letting her job become an addiction,
as so many foreign correspondents do. They can become
burnt out and empty, with just one reflex, the one which

sends them hurtling to an airport at the first sound of conflict anywhere on the international map. Something that should be there is missing: the sense that somewhere is a place where they belong.

Speaking to the assembled crowd of women in 1981, Gisèle Tremblay had this to say about Jasmin:

> Several months ago, when we were reflecting on the lot of women journalists, I suddenly thought of Judith Jasmin. With that memory I felt my admiration for her, vividly. But it's now almost nine years since I used to see her every day and I found that I was forgetting what inspired my admiration. One day I happened to see one of her reports again, and it all came back to me: that rigour, the clarity of exposition which she had mastered to perfection, and to which she added something which is rare today, a quality of emotion. She knew how to restore the emotive dimension to the facts she was presenting, and it is my conviction as a journalist that the emotions are part of the facts and are part of the journalist who is reporting them. She understood that.

Maison Radio-Canada on Dorchester Boulevard in east downtown Montreal is a monument to the federal presence in Quebec, twenty-three floors of chrome and glass rising over two levels of studios and workshops buried underground. Erected in the seventies, the Maison is a hive of activity both loved and hated by its inhabitants. It is the headquarters of the French network, and every bit as stylish and self-assured as the city surrounding it. Here the cafeteria serves wine and has a *table d'hôte* section. Men and women dress up for work: the women are eye-catching whether in couturier ensembles or the studied inelegance of haute punk; the men, wearing their hair a shade longer than is fashionable in Toronto or Vancouver, are just as fetching in leather and silk. The scent of Gitanes and French perfume hangs in the air.

Tucked away on two floors halfway up the tower huddle the offices of CBC English radio. The local current affairs people have cornered off a section of the fifteenth floor and superimposed their own informality on the hard-edged highrise environment. The place looks comfortable and lived-in with a busy drop-in centre look; you expect to find lumpy Sally Ann sofas and old newspapers lying about. The people are dressed to match in well-worn denim, running shoes, and Mexican cotton shirts.

Sheila Moore sits cross-legged in an office piled high with tapes and file folders. CBM radio is playing discreetly in the background, but loudly enough so the boss can keep an ear on today's *Radio Noon* show. Moore, as executive producer of radio current affairs, is captain of a team that produces three shows and seven hours a day of radio for the Montreal area, plus *Cross-Country Checkup* on the weekend for the network. She looks out at the world through sturdy red-framed glasses, surveys the office and counts off six producers — four women and two men — and a corps of researchers, editors, and reporters. The world she sees is a perpetual-motion machine of events and people and ideas. The necessity of preparing seven hours a day of programming hardly leaves anyone time to think, let alone plan beyond Friday — anyone, that is, except Moore, whose job is to do that. "My ambition in life right now is to have a job where I don't have to wake up workng," she jokes, and hurriedly admits she can't bear listening to other stations. She doesn't even listen much to CBC's stereo service. Moore says of her work:

> What I do is damage control. There is a lot of organizing and training to be taken care of. Because, for one thing, the turnover of people in the regions is high. I never have the luxury of having a unit with everybody operating at the same level. There is always someone who is not yet as strong as you'd like.

Controlling damage includes dealing with the odd disaster, such as the morning Dr. Henry Morgantaler, the doctor who helped set up free-standing abortion clinics in Winnipeg and Toronto and has run one for several years in Montreal, appeared on the show with host Dennis Trudeau.

Trudeau didn't want to do the show and was very rude to Morgantaler and also to callers who were supportive of Morgantaler's position. I was at home listening to it with three friends and the man I live with, and they all kept asking me why I didn't call up the studio and tell the producer to make him stop. I told them there was no point in doing that. The producer was probably doing everything she could and didn't need me phoning up to tell her to do what she herself wished she could! If an on-air person chooses to ignore his producer, there is a point when, short of cutting the show and going to music, there is nothing you can do. My argument, after the fact, was that I do not think we can allow hosts in current affairs to provide us with lists of no-no topics. Either you are a professional current affairs broadcaster or you're not.

Thirteen years ago, when Moore first joined the CBC in Regina, it was to produce the same sort of morning radio show. She was then the entire production team. She worked with a host "who shall remain nameless" who would show up only for the bare three hours he was needed on air and who, she finally concluded, was incapable of doing an intelligent interview, *ever*. That left Moore holding a very large bag, with all the research, writing, organizing, and lining up of guests, plus the production to do, all by herself. "Here, the morning show has a producer, a full-time host, two researchers, and a writer — and they still think they are understaffed." But, she notes, those Regina days were back in the stone age of information radio.

In the early seventies, CBC radio, having been in eclipse for several years, had just undergone a thorough examination that led to modernizing current affairs. Immodestly, but perhaps correctly, radio people called it the radio revolution, and Moore came to town just as it was starting to roll.

They were frantically hiring anyone who could name more than a dozen politicians. I had been doing some freelance work for the Manitoba government and wanted out of that. I heard that the CBC was looking for someone to produce the show in Regina and I applied. I was too dumb to realize how ignorant I was about the work I would have to do. I got the job — I think I was the only one who applied — and I was lucky to find some good people to work with.

For instance, there was a newsman who was able to help Moore with the interviews and who was knowledgeable enough about Saskatchewan not to require detailed briefings. In time, with persistence and pleading, she also got a researcher. When Moore moved on, the researcher, Pamela Wallin, took over as producer.

Network radio in Toronto occupies a ramshackle red-brick warren on Jarvis Street that once was a girls' private school. Kate Aitken, Claire Wallace, Claire Drainie (Bronwyn's mother), Kate Reid, and Maggie Muggins all worked there, as have Barbara Frum, Helen Hutchinson, Jan Tennant, and Judy LaMarsh. The radio building itself is forever being rearranged. Yesterday's hallway might become today's closet or editing room. These days, *As It Happens* and *Sunday Morning* are produced out of an ungainly sprawl of meeting rooms, staircases, corridors, and open offices occupying most of the south end of the third floor. You pretty well have to know where you're going before you start out, or you're not likely to get there. Not only is there no obvious floor plan, but this may be the only building in the world with its first floor in the basement. The stairs creak, the cafeteria serves umbrella juice for coffee, and it's hard to get yogurt. However, the windows can be opened and you never have to wait for elevators.

Entering *Morningside*'s crowded territory, the visitor is treated to an unusual sight: a waiting room. Well, it's not quite a room: it's a corner with a brightly coloured rug, two comfy sofas, and a coat rack. To the right, past the receptionist's desk, a clutter of people, desks, copy machines, paper, and plants claims every inch of space. In this unit, the two top jobs are occupied by women.

Cora Hind in her prime. The world renowned agriculture expert and journalist began her career with the *Winnipeg Free Press* in her forties and pursued it with vigour through her seventies. (HARRY STEELE, MANITOBA ARCHIVES)

Lise Bissonnette, the editor-in-chief of Montreal's *Le Devoir* and the only woman editing a major city daily newspaper in Canada. (*LE DEVOIR*)

June Callwood addressing demonstrators in front of Toronto's Central Reference Library, September, 1983. A former Chair of the Writers' Union, Callwood has campaigned for the payment of a lending right to authors of books in public libraries. (RANDY HAUNFELDER)

Columnist Barbara Amiel relaxing at her computer terminal. Amiel was editor of the *Toronto Sun* between 1979 and 1984. (FRED THORNHILL. TORONTO SUN)

Claire Wallace at the microphone in 1936, with one of the many pet cats she introduced to her radio audience. A year later Wallace switched to the CBC, where her programme *They Tell Me* was a daytime favourite. (KEN BELL)

Cooking and etiquette expert, author, world traveller and housewife extraordinaire, Kate Aitken was a Canadian radio institution from 1934 to 1957. (GILBERT A. MILNE/CFRB)

Christina McCall, an astute political analyst whose study of the Liberal Party in power, *Grits*, became a bestseller in 1982. (STEPHEN CLARKSON)

Singer, comedienne and CBC staff announcer Margaret Pacsu. The familiar voice on the stereo network and *Listen To The Music*. (CBC)

Betty Kennedy interviewing Prime Minister Pierre Trudeau in 1982 for her afternoon show on CFRB. (CANAPRESS)

Jane Hawtin, the ''grande dame of rock radio,'' newscaster, interviewer and host of *Barometer* over Toronto's Q–107. (BRUCE MCCAULEY)

Katie Malloch and co-host Wayne Grigsby clowning around the set of their entertainment magazine show, *Stepping Out*. (CBC)

Helen James, the assistant
supervisor of CBC radio's Talks
and Public Affairs department,
who was responsible for
Women's Interest programming
from 1952 to 1965, during the
creation of *Trans-Canada
Matinee* and *Take 30* where
Helen Hutchinson, Barbara
Frum, Adrienne Clarkson and
Elizabeth Gray got their start.
(HERB NOTT/CBC)

Elizabeth Gray in her *As It
Happens* gear. A twenty-year
veteran of CBC radio, Gray nearly
refused the offer of the top job in
information radio in 1981. (CBC)

Jan Tennant arm-wrestling with co-anchor Peter Trueman during a publicity photo session for Global News. The candid shot was later used in a 1984 network ad campaign.
(GLOBAL NEWS)

Helen Hutchinson preparing to interview Mila Mulroney, wife of the newly elected prime minister, in 1984 for *W5*. (CTV)

Adrienne Clarkson in her *Fifth Estate* office, 1981. (CBC)

Nicole Belanger is *Morningside*'s executive producer, just finishing off her last few weeks in the job before moving upstairs into management as the Deputy Head of Radio Current Affairs. She is widely regarded as one of radio's most talented producers. Her first love, however, was not radio but television; that was where she began as a freelancer in the late sixties in Ottawa.

Belanger had just arrived back in Canada from Geneva, leaving behind a marriage and a diplomat-economist husband. She had married very young, at twenty, partly to escape from deciding what to do with her life:

> I always assumed that I'd marry, and that then I would decide whether or not to work. I realized a few years afterwards what a dumb thing it was to do but there I was in Switzerland, playing chatelaine to a much older man, circulating in a society where everyone was years older than I was.

Belanger occupied herself with the life and the people in Geneva, and read her husband's papers at night for amusement, but she gradually realized that she couldn't be a traditionally passive wife for the rest of her life. Her husband, however, didn't understand her desire to work. So she left, arriving in Ottawa to live on her own, a divorcée not yet thirty with two young children.

At least Belanger knew where she wanted to be — in the thick of things. After checking around a bit she headed straight for the producer "with the best reputation in town" and besieged him for a job. That was current affairs producer Cameron Graham, who has collaborated with Patrick Watson on numerous programmes and television series. Graham buckled under Belanger's determined onslaught and gave her a job clipping newspapers for two hours a day. "I was fortunate that Cam recognized that a person who clipped newspapers might be capable of research." After research, she went on to story editing and producing, and finally decided that she wanted to produce her own films, which she did on the local news show *Something Else*.

After a time, Nicole Belanger began freelancing for radio, and in 1971 took the jump into a full-time position on *As It Happens*.

> The kids were going to live with their father for a year, so I came to Toronto looking for work. I was actually coming to see Alex Frame, who was executive producer of *This Country in the Morning*, to find out from him about work, when I bumped into Mark Starowicz in the hall. He asked me what I was doing and then said I had better come talk to him. I discovered he'd been asked to take over *As It Happens* and change it, though the appointment hadn't yet been announced and he would not be signing on until the following January. When he asked me if I would be interested, I had to say I didn't know the programme or anything about it! Next thing I knew I was sitting in front of a little Japanese lady [Margaret Lyons, the executive producer] and being told to show up in October.

Although Belanger had no idea what Lyons and her protégé Starowicz had in mind, she knew it wasn't going to be a rose garden. She also knew it would appeal to her more than television.

> I loved film, and I still do. Initially I had thought that you could have a kind of independence in television; certainly working with Cam I did. Subsequently, though, I found out that television is extremely bureaucratic and over-supervised. By the time you got an item done, you had spent an awful lot of time for what now seemed like something you didn't want to say in the first place. I got very frustrated. Radio is wonderful because it's hands-on and very little intervenes between you and the material. It is very direct. I also like the idea of appealing to people through the imagination. It's a wonderful medium that way — creates very strong impressions for people, and I think people listen to radio more actively.
>
> My main interest in television was journalistic, and I'd gone there so I could make my own films and have

control over what I was making. To be a story editor on the show, however, meant that you had to do interviews on-air. I so hated that, I'd deliberately keep myself looking unkempt so that when they cast around the room for someone to go on camera that evening they'd pass me over. Finally the executive producer tumbled to it and told me I couldn't get away with it anymore. "Comb your hair. You're going on to do the interview tonight," he announced.

As It Happens was a very important step for CBC radio. It brought a younger group of listeners (in the twenty-five to forty age group) to current affairs radio and especially to Canadian current affairs. "There were a lot of people working there then for whom that really mattered and who were not content with ripping off items from the *New York Times*."

Belanger wasn't to be at *As It Happens* for very long, though. Her children returned to Canada and didn't want to live in Toronto, so she moved back to Ottawa, where she went through a tough period trying to string a living together. She spent a year on a government project, "the most terrible job," and then, when Starowicz was getting *Sunday Morning* started, he asked her to come back as a senior producer.

This time she refused. With the kids in school, it didn't make a lot of sense to sign away all her weekends. So she produced segments for shows called *The Senator's Diary* and *The Watson/Lapierre Report*, from Ottawa, as well as a weekly programme, *Canada Watch*, one of the "mandate" programmes that fell like manna from the CBC head office following the election of the Parti Québécois. Belanger also sensed that, though she had gotten along exceedingly well with Starowicz before, they were moving in different directions journalistically.

In 1980, Belanger was named executive producer of *Morningside*, bridging Don Harron's last year and Peter Gzowski's first comeback year. She was not the first woman in the top producer's chair; Krista Maeots had been in charge for a couple of years until her tragic death in 1978. The unit had changed somewhat from the early days when the programme was called *This Country in the Morning* and

Gzowski and executive producer Alex Frame ruled the roost over a large pool of mostly female underlings. "It was a very sexist arrangement. I used to watch it from *As It Happens* and get mad," says Belanger — and now she was going to be Gzowski's first woman boss.

> I had no idea how that was going to work and I was extremely nervous about it. But it's never come up as an issue. More importantly, he has sensibilities as a journalist that I used to think were peculiar to women, although I think that sort of categorizing is becoming more complicated. Women as journalists used to be much more subtle and thoughtful than men. On the whole, I think, my opinion has always been that women are predisposed to being better journalists. They tend to see things in a surround, in a context (historical and otherwise) which may come from trying to understand their own evolution. And in an emotional surround women tend to have a better eye. I think, though, that men are changing and we're getting more of that kind of journalism from them.

Belanger is not alone in sensing a difference in the atmosphere of radio. "It astonishes me when I run into people from television or from the business world. Radio is by comparison a remarkably unchauvinist place; you almost forget it's an issue." She and Sheila Moore find themselves working in the company of men and women in roughly equal numbers, taking an equal share of the power and the responsibility. They point to women at the senior producer levels and among management: the chief of network radio is the first-ever woman vice-president of the CBC, Margaret Lyons.

Belanger muses:

> There are a lot more women working in radio, both on-air and in production. There is no question about that; just look. The technical areas always seem to be the last where women are allowed, but there are now a fair number of women in technical jobs too. Women feel accepted in radio, and I think that radio management is

more enlightened. I believe it is reflected in the programming we do, which I think is socially and politically more progressive than television.

Radio has a real history to it; it has a memory — the faculty television, for all its magic, hasn't yet developed. Belanger has a personal theory about this, one that she is rather cautious about, not being able to vouch for its veracity:

> Television is a glamour profession, so it sometimes attracts people for the wrong reasons. It is seen as a place where you hold power and it has all the Hollywood showbiz pizzazz. There is nothing like that in radio; there is nothing glamorous about current affairs radio, so it tends to attract people who are journalists in a truer sense. Moreover, technically it is simpler and less cumbersome than television. You can do things more quickly.
>
> For another thing, radio is much older than television; it has had the time to cultivate a tradition. The people who are currently in management have been around for a long time and have a keen sense of tradition. For reasons I've never been able to exactly determine, there were a lot of women around in the forties and fifties, so the men in the upper echelons of management today are used to working with women. To them, there is nothing odd about having female colleagues working in absolute equality with them. When I arrived in 1972 I saw that in the older generation. Yes, there were injustices; all kinds of them. I have heard amazing stories about women who had working husbands not being eligible for pensions. But at the same time, bright capable women in radio were not unusual.

Elizabeth Gray calls them "the CBC Ladies." They were a stalwart band of exceptionally clever, worldly, and strong-hearted pros who came into CBC radio during the war or just after, to the department then known as Talks and Public Affairs. They came from a variety of backgrounds and beginnings — teaching, social work, the army — and they shared an intense interest in the country and in public broadcasting. Few of them were married. Asked why, one of them replied, "Because I never had time." They were pioneers, rather than radicals, and what they achieved had long-lasting effects on radio as much for the influence they had on younger people as for the programming they created.

One of the first people Elizabeth Gray worked for at CBC in Montreal was Margaret Howes. It was 1965, and Gray had just returned from five years in England, where she had been doing some freelance items for various radio programmes — none of which she ever actually heard. These included interviews with London teenagers for a kids' show called *Countdown*, feature pieces for *Trans-Canada Matinee*, and commentaries for *Focus*. "CBC radio was more open in those days to freelance items from abroad, and it was open season for all the programmes in the schedule," she remembers. Working from such a distance, Gray had all the autonomy you could wish for; she chose her own stories and cut her own tapes, but she never heard how they were produced or integrated into a finished programme.

Howes had a desperate situation on her hands: a producer was going on sick leave, and there was no one around who could step into the job. Gray was at home with a tiny baby at the time and at first was reluctant to take on a full-time job. "When I said I couldn't come and take the job they told me I had to. So I hired a housekeeper and went." If she had been left to her own devices, claims Gray, "it might have taken me a long time to get going. I'm slow at deciding things like that."

She was not slow, however, at picking up the basics of production. Although Gray had never seen a producer functioning or a programme being put on air, Howse was there to help.

> What did she know about me, after all? Someone tells her, "Look, this kid can cut tape." So Margaret sits down with me for about an hour-and-a-half to tell me how to be a producer. I took notes and I could kick myself that I didn't keep the notepad, because it was very straightfor-ward stuff about who does what and what the pro-

grammes were. And beyond that, it was a short snappy lecture about the producer's essential role. "Basically," she said, "your job around here is to make the broadcaster sound good. That involves going through the script thoroughly: everybody makes grammatical errors, scripts can always be better. If they want water, get it. Make sure they're sitting up straight. And don't bug them! You — the producer — are not the most important person; the person on air is, and everything depends on that." No one had ever talked to me about broadcasting like that before. I'm sure it was as much background as you'd get in four years of journalism school. It was incredible.

Then she took me over to the studio in another building, where she was producing *Speaking Personally*. Those were nine-minute essays which followed the 10 P.M. news every night. (We don't have commentaries like that much any more; it's a lost art form except for the two-and-a-half minute commentary which follows the eight o'clock news in the morning.) Howes got people from all over the country doing those commentaries every damn night. In the studio that day there was a man in shirt sleeves, tie off, sitting at the mike talking about growing up in Victoriaville — the place where hockey sticks and Jean Belliveau come from. The man was Gérard Pelletier, then editor of *La Presse,* and Margaret Howes kept him there for half an hour making changes in his script. I just sat thinking, "Oh, that's what you do!"

Howes was the regional supervisor for English-language public affairs at the time. She had been hired in 1946 to fill in for someone who had gone off to the war and who never came back to claim his job. Howes was thirty-six when she joined the CBC. She had a degree from the University of Alberta and had worked for the Student Christian Movement and later the YWCA. She was also a volunteer and strong believer in the Canadian Association of Adult Education and helped organize the study groups for the programme *Of Things To Come*, which later became *Citizens' Forum*. Howes was very keen on the adult education approach to programming, as was her mentor at the CBC, a woman named

Elizabeth Long, who had started with the CBC in the 1930s. It was Long who was responsible for developing a sub-department of Talks and Public Affairs that she called Women's Interests.

After a very brief producing career, Elizabeth Gray went to work as a researcher and later host for a new show called *Cross-Country Checkup.* "I would never have had that job — because there wouldn't have been a *Checkup* — if it hadn't been for Margaret Howes," she told a radio audience in 1979. As Gray recalls:

> She [Howes] had acquired on her staff a young, very brash producer named Andrew Simon, who managed to scandalize the network brass by proposing a national open-line show. I say "scandalize," because the technology was such that a thing like that had never been contemplated let alone done before. At the time, too, open-line shows were regarded as a vulgar aberration of private radio.
>
> Simon fought hard, but he was losing the battle when suddenly he was sent out of town on assignment for a month. Time was running short for a fall launch of his show, but he had to leave his project in the hands of Margaret Howes, whom no doubt he regarded as a nice but pretty hide-bound school-marmish lady who probably hadn't the faintest understanding of what he wanted to do. When Andrew Simon returned, Howes called him into her office to tell him that she'd completed the arrangements with Bell telephone and the network management and that he'd now better get busy and set up his show.

So began one of CBC radio's long-running popular successes. Howes retired shortly after, and Simon, who has often credited her with that strategic bit of road clearing, moved up the ladder to his present job as head of Radio Current Affairs.

For the entire twenty years Howes worked at the CBC, she was classified as a temporary employee. In 1946, married women could not be hired on permanent staff, and even as temporary employees, married women were not tolerated gladly by corporate policy-makers. In 1947, there was a brief attempt to purge all of them to make way for presumably more deserving single workers, but when the production staff suddenly found themselves without secretaries and switchboard operators and planners they protested vehemently and the firings ceased. Howes and other married women were allowed to remain, but as temporary help they were still not eligible for pensions. It took a personal appeal to the Honourable Judy LaMarsh (then the minister responsible for the CBC), on the eve of Howes' retirement, to get her pension instated, over the heads of her CBC bosses.

The injustice was clearly attributable to the attitude of top policy makers and bureaucrats; the men who worked with women like Howes in Talks and Public Affairs appear to have been much more tolerant and willing to bend the rules behind management's back.

Take the case of Marjorie McEnaney. She was hired on a part time basis and ran into problems similar to those experienced by Howes. McEnaney's troubles began in 1943 when she informed her superiors that she intended to take three months' leave following the birth of the child she was expecting. "Impossible" was the verdict, and a man was hired forthwith to replace her. However, McEnaney simply turned up for work one morning — three months after the birth of her baby, as she had promised — and picked up where she left off. Her male boss was not about to press the case, and was no doubt happy to have her back. So she stayed; and though it took another three months, the personnel department eventually reinstated her — as a temporary, of course. McEnaney stayed with the Talks department until 1958, when she resigned to work freelance. She was then at the height of her career and responsible for some 500 broadcasts a year, including the controversial *In Search Of Ourselves* which was ahead of its time in dealing with touchy issues like rape and homosexuality.

Margaret Howes was succeeded in Montreal by another woman, somewhat younger, named Kay MacIver. MacIver became a mentor for Gray and is still fondly remembered by many women around the CBC for her radio work and the support she extended to other women in broadcasting. MacIver rose through the ranks of CBC radio from producer at *Trans-Canada Matinee*, to the first woman director of radio in Quebec, to head of the Features and Humanities section for the radio network. She was a superb organizer and deft at policy development, which won her a special assignment, helping the Malaysian government to set up its public broadcasting service. In 1974, she headed the CBC's internal task force on the status of women.

Elizabeth Gray regards MacIver as an outstanding example of the tradition of women in current affairs radio, and when she died of cancer in 1979, Gray spoke about MacIver to a *Morningside* audience with great emotion:

> MacIver's death brought me one happy realization, that all the best I've ever learned about braodcasting has been from women who came from that tradition. In the same way that Margaret Howes saw the potential in a programme that must have offended her training and instincts in many ways, so Kay MacIver was always concerned with reading the time rather than fighting against it.
>
> When she took on the CBC Task Force, the women's movement was at the height of its militancy — and verbosity — and I think she could have been forgiven had she regarded it all a little smugly. After all, she was fifty-four years old then; she had fought all those battles herself outside of a popular political context and she'd forged her own highly successful career. She could also have been forgiven had she resented those bright young women whom she led and spoke for on the Task Force, who were combining careers and marriage and family, but she didn't. She simply thought they were wonderful. I know she did, because ten years before, when I would despair of doing justice to three small children and a shaky career, my most sympathetic mentor was a woman who'd never had to change a diaper in her life.

Tracing the tradition back a couple of generations, MacIver's

great hero was Elizabeth Long. Long (also Margaret Howes'
mentor, as MacIver and Howes were Gray's) was neither a
producer nor a broadcaster. She was an influential figure all
the same, and she played a pivotal role in the evolution of
radio because of her commitment to broadcasting serious,
wide-ranging public affairs programmes for women, and
because she hired women to do political commentary, which
had never been done before. She established a tradition of
daytime current affairs broadcasting that reached down to
our own time with programmes like *Take 30*.

Elizabeth Long hired Helen James in 1946, just as James
was being discharged from the Army Medical Corps. Because
of something called "veterans' preference," Long, who needed
a Women's Interests producer quickly, could get the paper-
work done immediately. The day James was discharged, she
began work for the CBC, little guessing she would be there for
twenty years, the last thirteen of them in Long's position, as
head of Women's Interests and assistant supervisor of Public
Affairs. James was in her mid-thirties, with a university
degree and a variety of work experiences behind her already.
She'd started off at the St. Catharines *Standard,* had worked
in advertising at Lever Brothers, in the employment department at Eaton's, and as a secretary to the editor of the
Financial Post.

The CBC department James joined was made up primarily
of women. There were only two men: John Fisher and the
department head, Neil Morrison. "This was partly because
of the war, of course, because men were not available," says
James. Through the post-war period, the department grew
and the proportions evened out. However, until the late
fifties or so, when television current affairs took its Great
Leap Forward into the future and left women behind, public
affairs, which operated as a single department for radio and
television, was a good place for women to work.

Elizabeth Long, James remembers, was a journalist from
Winnipeg who was cousin to the CBC's controversial first
general manager, Gladstone Murray:

> She was an ardent feminist. Really militant. I don't mean
> that she went out and paraded; people didn't do that in

those days. But she used the word feminism all the time. Initially I didn't want to be associated with what I saw as the women's ghetto and so I resisted working only for Elizabeth. I made it my business to do other things. My first year, when I was anxious to learn as much as I could and was very enthusiastic, I put in seven-day weeks and did programmes for the school broadcasts, and the music, religious, and children's departments as well as my own. I particularly remember a programme I did called *Doorway To Fairyland,* which had a cast of children.

When I first arrived, I think women's interests had about twelve minutes per day of airtime. Shortly after, it increased to fifteen, in addition to a three- or five-minute commentary each evening. Then when television, God bless it, got going and the soap operas were pulled from radio, suddenly there was a clear forty-five minutes in the afternoon. I managed to persuade Mr. Dilworth, the director of Programme Production, that we should have a magazine format programme for women in the afternoon. As far as I know, it was the first of its kind anywhere and what I wanted to do with the concept was to have the room to broaden the content of women's broadcasting.

We were the first to read adaptations of books on the air and one summer we did something I was particularly pleased with — a thirteen-week daily drama series called *Neighbours*, about two families living next door to each other in Quebec, one English- and one French-Canadian. The series followed the relations between them: the romances, conflicts, and arguments, what the children learned in school, and so on and it was all written by *one* woman.

The programme was *Trans-Canada Matinee,* and Marjory Whitelaw was the woman who wrote the sixty-five episodes of *Neighbours* for a fee that James says was ridiculous.

Helen James, like Long, was not a broadcaster. Only on rare occasions did she go on air. One day, Max Ferguson, who had introduced *Citizens' Forum* as he was supposed to, forgot to return for the sign-off. James had to slip into the studio and breathlessly give the final announcement and wrap-up of the season. "Radio," says James, "attracted me very much. I have really always been a spectator rather than a performer by nature, and so I was very glad to be on the editorial side of broadcasting."

James and Long used a large number of freelancers for their expanding roster, and many of the experts they called on for information were women. There were special difficulties associated with getting some of them on-air:

> Elizabeth really did an extraordinary job of persuading people to come on the air and talk, because women weren't broadcasting very much in those days. Some of the women needed a lot of encouragement. We all know that women who've been at home while their children were growing up feel very tentative and almost apologetic about going out and looking for a job again. Well it was the same sort of thing getting them to come to the microphone. They were fearful; they didn't have the self-confidence.

Although James and most of her colleagues were single, they collaborated in several efforts to change discriminatory practices against married women. James recalls:

> I remember the shocking thing that the CBC would not employ married women, so that Marjorie McEnaney had no sick leave and no pension. One of the things I spent a lot of time on during my first two years there was circulating a petition that married women should be eligible for permanent employee status. Even though Andrew Allan (the renowned drama producer) told me it was the best worded petition he'd ever read, it didn't succeed! And there was no change until after I left.
>
> It's true most of us were single and I don't think any of us were under thirty-five, which is roughly the age we thought was a good one for a producer or programme planner; someone who'd lived that long and had that much experience.

Since radio and television Public Affairs departments were not separated until the late sixties, James and her colleagues were also responsible for television. *Open House,* the precursor of *Take 30,* was started under her. For quite a long time, it was the only place in Toronto where women were hired as television producers. Peggy Nairn was the first, then Helen Carscallen, who was executive producer of *Open House,* and Margaret Fielder.

In 1964, Public Affairs got a new supervisor: a British immigrant, ex-lawyer, and businessman named Reeves Haggan. Haggan's main interest was television and specifically the brave new experiment that was to be *This Hour Has Seven Days,* combining the talents of Douglas Leiterman, Patrick Watson, and Laurier LaPierre. (For the "female touch," Dinah Christie came on each week in slinky outfits to sing satirical lyrics to familiar songs.) Radio took a backseat, a *long* way back, and it was generally perceived by the women in radio that Haggan was unsympathetic to the work they had been doing.

James began reassessing her position and counting her options:

> I had been doing the same job for thirteen years and there was no possibility, at that time, of my ever doing anything else. I was tired of it. But that wasn't the only reason I decided to resign. I didn't get along with Reeves Haggan. I thought he really despised women in senior positions and didn't see any place for them. Moreover, though I admired the President, Alphonse Ouimet, tremendously as an engineer, it seemed to me that he was frightened of ideas. And I felt it was having a deadening effect on the CBC. So I quit.

Somewhat to her amazement, Ouimet travelled to Toronto especially to see her. "It was very funny. The president actually came to ask me to change my mind. He didn't suggest another position; he just kept repeating, 'I wish you'd change your mind.'"

She didn't. And following her out the door were Helen Carscallen, Margaret Howes, Margaret Fielder, and several others, most of them taking early retirement because, as Carscallen said much later, they realized "the lid was on the advancement of women." Even at the time, though, everyone involved knew it was an exodus. And it was going to be a long time before women would once again have as much power and creative influence so close to the CBC's heart.

Helen James had been pretty bored for the last years at CBC. Now she set out on a new career with rekindled enthusiasm. She returned to university to do an M.A., and for two years revelled in the freedom and irresponsibility of going to the library when she wanted and being answerable to no one. She went on to become a head social worker with North York's Children's Aid and served as a part-time commissioner on the CRTC (Canadian Radio Television and Telecommunications Commission) from 1968 to 1973. To a young Barbara Frum, who was just starting out in Helen James' last years at the CBC, James was an awesome figure: "She was formidable. I think everyone was scared to death of her, including (her boss) Bernie Trotter. Subsequently I liked her so much; you know, over a period of time people who seemed quite fierce become less so. I was probably very naive but she seemed very powerful to me."

The women left because they were victims of discrimination. Had they stayed, they might well have become victims of the changing times. Jean Bruce was a radio producer then and one of many talented women the CBC lost because they married other CBC employees and had to resign. "It embarrasses me now, but I never asked to see the regulation or objected to it — none of us did. And there was no question which of us, me or my husband, would leave." Bruce has written about the women in public affairs in the journal of the Canadian Oral History Association — the only published record of their accomplishment so far, though several histories have been written about broadcasting. Bruce points out:

> The frustration felt by these long-time CBC employees involved more than career disappointment. They deplored the trend towards looser and more flexible programme formats and more importantly, the weakening of CBC's traditional ties with citizens' organizations. These connections had been nurtured by James, Howes, and others, not only for their input into programming but also for the support they offered the CBC generally.

Nonetheless, there was a legacy. It was there, for example, for Elizabeth Gray:

> I always had the sense I belonged at the cbc because those women were already there and already doing things. They were real forces and I figure today most of the influences in radio are still coming from women. Nicole Belanger (whom I didn't work with until 1976), is an incredibly bright, wonderfully erratic producer and one of the most stimulating people I have ever worked with. Some of the best professional relationships I have had have been with women. The women on *As It Happens* now are similarly strong people. In terms of programming and the development of the radio service as a whole, the most important people I have encountered here have all been women.

Gray herself, and her predecessor at *As It Happens,* Barbara Frum, are part of the tradition of women in current affairs. They are leaders of their own generation of broadcast journalists, both male and female. Frum, at the *As It Happens* mike for ten years, questioning the movers and shakers of world politics, has changed the public perception of women's role in broadcasting. When she moved to television, she took that reputation with her. Time will tell if this will make a difference to television women, who lag behind their radio sisters in collective power and prominence within the medium.

When Frum left *As It Happens,* Gray was the obvious choice for the job. Everyone knew it and the columnists predicted it. It was a job she was cut out to do, but she almost didn't take it. Following the period in Montreal, she and her newspaper-correspondent husband, John Gray, moved to Ottawa. There she became the first host of the new local rolling home show, *Now Just Listen.* For two of her three years on the programme, Gray's producer was Evelyn Gigantes (later elected to the Ontario legislature); together they discovered and explored the intricacies and intrigues of Ottawa politics. This was also the period when she discovered her aptitude for political reporting.

Over the years, Gray made a few forays into television. In 1975, she did a series on women's issues for CBOT called *Lady's a Four Letter Word*. But, she says:

> To be honest, I don't like television and I don't watch it. I don't like it because I never feel I have accomplished what I wanted to. I don't like waiting around a lot or putting out such an enormous effort for so little. You spend an hour in make-up for a six minute interview. It doesn't make sense to me and I feel I might as well write or be on the radio.

The problem with the job at *As It Happens* was that it meant she would have to work in Toronto. Unwilling to leave her family, she turned the offer down.

> I'd done just about everything there was to do in Ottawa and had had a lot of fun hosting *As It Happens* when I'd gone down to Toronto to do replacement shows. So I was sunk in gloom because it was the job I'd always wanted to do. I'd had a long talk with the producer and it was clear that there could be no compromise. The show couldn't have functioned with me in Ottawa three days and the unit in Toronto.
>   Then at Thanksgiving John and the kids and I were driving to the cottage for the weekend. John said, "Look, I really think there are some barriers that have to be lifted here," and he went into a long spiel. And then the kids, who were in the back seat, chimed in, "Yeah. You'd better go." It was actually like that. John and the kids telling me to go. One of them was at university at that point and now two are, so they aren't babies. The more I think of it, the more absurd it was ever for me to wonder. But you do!

Like Barbara Frum's, Gray's career has spanned radio, television, and the written word (magazine articles, mostly). She's had the accolades, the attacks, and the awards, and says with some pride, "Ever since I began in radio, no guest has refused to come on my show because they were afraid of being intimidated."

Over the years, the press has been enthusiastic about her, if a bit repetitious: "one of Canada's best, toughest interviewers." "She has matched wits and challenged top politicians, tackled controversial subjects, voiced her opinion on issues and generally made a name for herself in broadcasting" said the *Ottawa Citizen*.

It is not just her radio manner or her questions that are distinctive. Her voice has also become a trademark, with a quality that leaves people casting about for adjectives (throaty, sexy, smoky are popular). It's clear, strong, expressive and, though hard, registers subtleties. She is able to be insistent and sound friendly at the same time — a rather useful feat for an *As It Happens* host who, by tradition, doesn't let any-one off the hook. And she has a terrific sense of humour which, when well-aimed, can be devastating.

In January 1981, the *Citizen* gave her the Best Line of the Week award for her comeback to the acting President of the Advisory Council on the Status of Women, Win Gardner, who was attempting to evict journalists from a council meeting. This was following the dramatic resignation of Doris Anderson and four council members, who had accused the Minister responsible for the status of women, Lloyd Axworthy, of applying political pressure to dissuade the council from holding its planned constitutional conference. The majority of the council, including Gardner, had voted to postpone the conference. (A bad move, as it turned out, for the women's groups of the country would rally and hold their own highly successful, "unofficial" meeting in February.) Gardner had promised Gray an opportunity to question her about that decision. Wrote the *Citizen*, "Gardner, who has signed an affidavit renouncing the minutes of an executive committee meeting that support the allegations of political influence, denied she'd made any such promise. 'In that case, Mrs. Gardner, I'm afraid you'll have to sign another affidavit,' shot back Gray. Momentarily stunned by the remark Gardner agreed to accept reporters' questions."

A very significant ingredient in Gray's success has been her marriage. She and her husband have been working in tandem as journalists and parents for twenty-five years, since they met on the student newspaper at university. Working in the same field has been a bonus for both of them. (He has always been a newspaper correspondent while she has mostly freelanced.) She feels that it is an unusually good marriage "which surprises everyone, including our kids" and obviously the shared interest in politics is part of it. Moreover, the family has risen to meet the challenge of her career more than once, while also making sure that neither parent's career pushed the family's interest aside. There was a time when the Montreal *Star* wanted to post John Gray to Washington.

> I'd been doing the morning show for just a year; we had young kids and I thought, Christ we'll have to get a dog and put a whole lot of locks on the door and I don't want to live there much and anyway what am I going to do? How could I possibly match the show I had here, in Washington? So he said okay, and we didn't go. Our friends thought we were mad; they have often reminded us about what we missed — Vietnam, Watergate, and all that. And again in 1975, there was an offer of a show in Toronto, but the kids were still very young and John couldn't move so we didn't go there either.

Great marriages like Gray's are unusual in the media world. So is her apparent success at raising children while managing a career. The secret may lie in having the children early on *and* having them with a good man who wants to share parenting.

If it is still impossibly difficult for women who try to combine journalism and motherhood, the distance travelled by women in the profession since Helen James' time is impressive nonetheless:

> When I think back to the days when it was unthinkable that there should *ever* be a woman announcer, unthinkable that there should *ever* be a news commentator except in that little women's ghetto, unthinkable that there should *ever* be a woman regional director, I still

find it all quite shaking. It hasn't happened all that quickly; yet somehow it *does* seem to have happened very quickly. And speaking as a viewer and a listener, how pleasant it is to see both men and women doing the same thing. But I never thought I'd live to see the day when a Margaret Lyons would head the cbc radio network.

FIVE

The Evening Stars

JAN TENNANT crosses the driveway in front of her apartment building to the white Audi 4000 and slides in behind the wheel. It is a brilliant afternoon in late fall. The sun falls purple and yellow on the trees lining the Don Valley as she makes her way to the Global television studio in Toronto's north end. It's 2:30 P.M. and the start of another working day for Canada's top female newscaster.

The Audi and Global arrived together in Tennant's life. For the twelve preceding years, her life had revolved around College and Jarvis Streets and the CBC's radio building, just a stone's throw away from home. Being a staff announcer meant running a schedule that looked like a patchwork quilt, with duties ranging all over the broadcasting map. Reading the news, narrating documentaries, introducing programmes: Jan did it all at one time or another. For years she was host of *Reach for the Top*, the popular quiz show; hers was the familiar voice introducing *Gilmour's Albums, Quirks and Quarks,* and *Opera Theatre*; and for three years she had her own programme, called *A Little Night Music*. It was her pride and delight, for she had proposed it herself, and was then assigned to choose the recordings and write the script for it. What made Jan Tennant famous, though — what put her on the front page of the newspapers — was reading the national news on TV. In 1974 she was the first woman in Canada to anchor the evening news on network television.

Tennant drives the way she walks, with a swift sure pace that has a touch of the athlete in it. She has her own style, something the fashion magazines used to call classical elegance, and which seems to have more to do with the way she wears her clothes (simple, neat, and stunning) than any identifiable look. She prefers the colours, the fabrics, and the cut of clothes in men's shops. She knits and sews for herself (and her friends) and always does her own make-up. These days her dark, curly hair is bobbed, à la David Bowie, and is left to grey at its own rate — but, she says, "I haven't gone punk and I haven't been made over by Global. The changes are my choices." And her choices have just as much to do with common sense as with fashion sense. More often than not, for instance, you can catch the flash of sparkling white running shoes below the well-tailored pants. They are concessions to a bothersome arthritis condition, but given the chance Tennant will earnestly hold forth on the crippling effects of high-heeled shoes.

Tennant exercises regularly and follows a disciplined regime that includes weight lifting and avoiding certain foods. With characteristic independent-mindedness, she wasn't content to accept traditional medical advice that all anyone can do about arthritis is to take aspirin and learn to live with it. Tennant did some reading and investigating, and then made up her own mind about what to do. She is no mid-life convert to physical activity, even so. She has been a sportswoman all her life and has dabbled in just about everything, including archery and jazz dancing. At university she won letters for women's basketball three years running and in her final year at the University of Toronto was one of six women to win the silver ashtray for athletics. (In the 1950s it didn't seem odd to hand out ashtrays as prizes for athletic excellence!)

After graduating with a degree in physical education, Tennant taught for two years in an experimental high school in Toronto that was starting a special programme for "problem" students who hadn't passed grade eight and probably wouldn't make it into technical school either. It turned out to be an unhappy experience:

Here I was trying to teach basketball to grade nine girls who couldn't care less. It's a very complicated game and you have to have some basics to build on — it doesn't work if you are just fooling around. I would go to meetings of the Phys. Ed. Teacher Association, where they would spend hours discussing the relative merits of a 7 inch bladder ball and I would be saying, "Listen, you don't understand, the kids I have are not interested in *anything*. They won't even go swimming because they don't want to get their hair wet." So I was caught. Either I had to re-do my whole training or get out.

Originally she decided to transfer to another school, but when that attempt ran afoul of Board of Education procedure she left teaching altogether.

Tennant had married while still in university, and had accompanied her husband to Switzerland, where he had a teaching post and she got a job modelling for a dress designer. "In the fifties, marriage was a way of leaving home for all of us. But it was only substituting husband control for parental control. The divorce was my idea and he was insulted; but I simply wanted to make my own mistakes and decisions for myself." Fortunately, a Swiss divorce was easily obtained. It went through without a hitch and Tennant returned to Toronto alone in the fall of 1963.

She slipped back into a single life, and resumed her old name. She did not, however, slip back into the approved single lifestyle of the time. To the extent that there was a bohemia in Toronto in those pre-hippie days, Tennant became part of it. She moved in with actor impresario Don Cullen, the owner of the famous Bohemian Embassy which, to everyone's glee, was listed under "Embassies and Consulates" in the telephone book. It was the coffee house where everyone who was going to become anyone in the folk scene came to hang out. They lived with another couple in a quasi-communal house downtown but "in those days living together wasn't done, so we pretended." For the benefit of parents and relatives, she claimed to be living with a girlfriend in a boarding house rather than living in sin with a boyfriend.

The times were carefree, the company amusing and

talented, and Tennant, now in her late twenties, enjoyed it all. It didn't faze her that when she had left teaching, she had walked out on a secure job; there were other jobs going and security wasn't a priority. For a couple of years she supported herself with odd jobs that led nowhere in particular but which paid the rent. She had modelling jobs; she was an exercise coach at a charm school; and one summer she and Cullen packed themselves and their dog Rasputin into a Volkswagen and headed east for the Charlottetown Festival, where she worked as wardrobe mistress while he performed in *Turvey*.

That was in 1966. Just before leaving Toronto, Tennant had, on the advice of friends, gone to see the CBC's television news chief, Bill Cunningham, who was looking for a female reporter. Lunch with Cunningham led to an audition, and then, to her surprise, a second one.

> The first audition was absolutely fabulous; there were no nerves or hesitations. Their problem was they couldn't believe it; they thought it was a fluke. At the end of the second audition they asked me to write up a story for them — just anything. So I sat down and wrote a piece about the closing of the Bohemian Embassy after five years and eleven months; who was there when it started and where they had gone and how it will always be fondly remembered as belonging to a particular time and place in Toronto. I read it to Cunningham afterwards and he exclaimed, "Is that true?" because it was big news, that day's news in fact, and they hadn't heard about it yet. It seemed to me they didn't really know what to do with me, whether to hire me or not. So I told them it was their problem and left for Charlottetown.

Cunningham, who took over CBC news in the mid-sixties, recalls that he was quite serious about hiring a woman:

> The first most glaring and obvious deficiency to me was that there were no women. I didn't have any particular sensitivity to the injustice of the situation at the time, but from a producer's point of view it was like a missing

tooth. Moreover, the guys were all starting to look alike. So my first attempt to do something was very traditional and superficial in its way. The sixties was happening; the lifestyle, the music, the dress, poetry, and the arts (a) weren't being covered and (b) were, I thought, a natural journalistic form for a woman. I had a reputation for taking journalists and teaching them television skills because it is a difficult thing to teach both at the same time. There weren't too many hard-hitting female journalists around at the time — there were, but we, or I, didn't know where to look — so my notion was to recruit someone with bright broadcasting qualities and then to develop them. I auditioned and interviewed many people but the most attractive and compelling natural talent with broadcasting character was Jan Tennant.

Through the summer Cunningham called Tennant periodically to talk about the job, somewhat to her mystification, but finally it seemed to her that he had made a firm offer. A starting date was discussed and when she arrived back in Toronto she went down to see him again, only to discover that the job was off. The newspaper guild wouldn't permit it. Cunningham would have to get along with his missing tooth.

Though it sounds like a short trip from the sublime to the insignificant, Tennant went over to CBLT and got herself a job as a secretary on the local supper-hour news programme. She was hired by the mercurial Ross McLean, whose own star was still rising in current affairs and who played star-maker with an intensity that was already legendary. For a pittance and the chance to learn about television production first-hand, Tennant signed on staff, swore allegiance to the Queen (as was required in those days), and became a clerk-steno Class 3B. Her duties included moving people's cars off Jarvis Street at 4 P.M., laying in sandwiches for McLean each morning, and serving as a short-order secretary. By the end of the season, when the unit was being expanded, she decided that she wanted to move into research and asked McLean for a promotion. He talked her into a job as script assistant instead. "No," she says, "I wasn't upset. It's funny

because he said so many things that you'd think would have
sent me off screaming. He used to tell me Don Cullen wasn't
good enough for me; he said he hired me because he thought
I was a failed person and felt sorry for me; he also thought I
had a Pollyanna complex because I was perpetually cheerful
and forever propping things up just before disaster struck."

The place was bursting with eager young talent, including
an impressive group of women (Barbara Amiel; Susan Dexter,
who went on to become a producer at *W5*; Louise Lore, who
is today the executive producer of *Man Alive*) who were
invariably smart, beautiful, and locked into junior positions.
Very quickly the unit acquired an aura. Louise Lore
remembers getting on an elevator one day with another
young, nubile, and mini-skirted colleague and being greeted
by a male CBC producer who looked up and down their long
legs and declared, "You must be some of Ross's girls."

It wasn't always easy being one of "Ross's girls." As Barbara
Amiel recalls:

> It was a can of worms. When you are in your twenties
> you're unaware of office politics which are, perhaps,
> more difficult to deal with among creative people and
> amid all the showbiz hype. Ross could spot a winner but
> he also had the most amazing ability to self-destruct —
> taking others with him. It is a quality I have found in all
> talent. These are people who command intense loyalty
> from their staff by charming them and telling them they
> are going to be superstars. But they have a dark side
> which destroys people who don't have the fibre, stamina,
> or experience. Most of us didn't have the experience
> and Ross would play us off against each other. He would
> turn on his affection like a spotlight; you would be in
> one day and out the next.

Somehow Tennant survived unscathed, perhaps because
she was out of range of McLean's spotlight and could see
what was going on better than the others, perhaps because
she didn't have stars in her eyes and couldn't be held hostage
to her own ambitions. After two years, though, she started
scouting around for greener pastures. With a little self-

promotion and patience, she got the script assistant's job she wanted on her favourite programme, *The Nature Of Things*. It was while working there that Tennant saw something truly remarkable, something that set her off on a voyage of discovery. She had occasion to look at some film footage that had been shot in East Africa and couldn't get over what she saw. "It was the most spectacular footage. There wasn't a dud roll or frame anywhere, and I thought to myself, it must be like that all the time in East Africa." For a year she saved her money — half her monthly take home pay of $400 — and in 1970 went off on her first safari. There have been many trips since, many continents explored and many wildlife preserves visited. She has been to India, the Antarctic (via the Falklands a few months before the war), and most recently Namibia, Botswana, and Cape Town. In all these places, her main interest has been observing and photographing nature.

On her return from Africa she had an unexpected call from the announcer's office to say a staff position was vacant and asking if she would like to audition. Tennant had already auditioned for summer relief announcing several times, with negative results. Since only a couple of women had ever worked as announcers before — and none permanently — she didn't expect anything to come of this audition either. What she hadn't reckoned on was the fallout from the Royal Commission on the Status of Women, which had made its report to Parliament that same year. The report documented women's inferior position in the workforce and identified the public service as one of the leading culprits. Crown corporations were criticized for their abysmal record and exhorted to "encourage women to move out of traditionally female occupations, emphasizing in recruitment programmes that all occupations are open equally to women and men." There could hardly be a more public "public enterprise" than broadcasting. All any citizen or MP had to do to check out its record was switch on the radio, and in 1970 the absence of women on the CBC's airwaves suddenly became an embarrassment.

Tennant blithely went ahead with the audition, having reassured her boss that she would never get the job.

At the end of the interview you have two minutes to talk

extemporaneously, which you are supposed to do to
time, and naturally I talked about Africa. It was such an
incredible experience. It was easy to wax eloquent — I
actually persuaded Monty Tilden, who was conducting
the audition, to go on safari himself. There were something like sixty applications from male announcers all
across the country hoping for the spot in Toronto. To
everybody's amazement I was hired.

Once the job was offered, Tennant couldn't possibly refuse.
So now she had to move from the comfortable shadows of a
traditionally female occupation to a high-profile position
among an all-male staff with the entire country listening. She
would have to learn fast and break the ice carefully. She was
put on probation for six months before she was accepted as
permanent staff, by which time she had won the men over:

Often, what I think happens with the first person [who
breaks a barrier] is that the novelty aspect takes over and
masks any resistance. As a script assistant I had worked
with many announcers so I knew them and had some
strong supporters among them — Harry Mannis and
Ken Haslam, for example. So I went to those I particularly
respected and I asked them to tell me if they ever heard
me say anything on the air which was wrong — pronuncia-
tion, choice of words, enunciation, anything. And they told
me, *all the time*. I would get wonderful notes in my mailbox.

Four years later, history repeated itself. In February, the
CBC was up before the Canadian Radio and Television
Commission for the renewal of its network licences, and at
the public hearings several women's groups intervened again.
They were highly critical of the corporation's portrayal of
women on television, and accused the network of sex role
stereotyping, both on the air and in the division of labour
behind the scenes. Within the CBC, moreover, several women's
caucuses had been formed and they too made representa-
tions, noting among other sins that the CBC had never
allowed a woman to read the national news.

Meanwhile, Tennant had spent two-and-a-half years doing

a little programme on Sunday mornings called *News Profile*.

I had been chosen by the producer Barry McLean to do it. It ran fifteen minutes, with four minutes of news and then a profile on something or someone. Hardly anyone knew it existed; I doubt that the news department knew it existed. So it was a wonderful way to begin. The profile was frequently voice-over and not pre-taped, so I was doing live narration.

Sure, doing that sort of thing live can rattle your nerves, but eventually there is no more reason for it. Something happens inside your head somewhere which tells you that being nervous isn't going to help; it won't make you better at what you're doing, so why bother? It took me several years of announcing to arrive at that point — to know that the mind has a control over the body that way.

Suddenly, like magic, the newsroom was calling.

My supervisor was getting calls asking for me to do the weekend news. I said no, that I didn't feel I was ready. Mike Daigneault was head of news then, and when I went in to see him he said he wanted me to do *The National* sometime. I felt it was nothing but a publicity gimmick and said so. He assured me it wasn't, and that he would never ask me unless he thought I was ready. Finally, around Easter that year, they called again. George Finstad wanted the weekend off. Reluctantly I agreed to do it, but told them I still thought it was a publicity stunt. Given the time of year, I asked, did they want me to wear a bunny costume or wear purple or would some fake ears do? No, I didn't leap at the chance. Not at all. And that Saturday morning there was a picture of me on the front page of the *Globe and Mail* and a report saying I would be reading the news. So I knew what they were doing; I knew *I* didn't give that story to the press.

I do remember *The National* that Saturday and Sunday, and it was nerve-wracking because of the build-up and because I knew I absolutely could not screw up. It was so important to the women of the country. But I was fine; my voice not so terribly relaxed, but the country recovered and the response, especially from women, was wonderful. About twenty-five percent was negative and the rest was terrific. I had all sorts of telegrams and letters, but I was most touched by the response from women, young girls, old women; and the housewife who wrote to say she never thought she would live to see the day. It all made me realize just what a tragic comment it was on our society. Because, in truth, reading the news wasn't that big a deal, and it shouldn't have been considered such an amazing event.

For eight years Jan Tennant was the CBC's popular female voice. If she couldn't be called the top news broadcaster in the country, it was only because Knowlton Nash held *The National* and she only sat in occasionally — "when the men were on holiday or playing golf" during the week. Her own regular spot was the *Saturday Evening News,* which she did for four-and-a-half years.

In retrospect, Jan Tennant's defection to Global seems inevitable, though when it happened it came as a major surprise. Staff announcing had exhausted its challenge for her and was no longer stretching her talents. Repeatedly she had applied for the job anchoring the CBLT evening news, and repeatedly she had been turned down — first in favour of a newcomer from the Maritimes named Sharon Dunn and then, in the summer of 1981, for Valerie Elia, whom the show's new producer Ivan Fecan was wooing back from retirement with a special contract. Only once was Tennant offered the supper-hour job — and that was at half Elia's old salary — so she can be forgiven for concluding that the producers either didn't want her or wanted her only at a bargain basement price. At *The National,* the dim prospects were getting dimmer. Knowlton Nash, who had been hired over union protests about the irregularity of his candidacy (he was at the time chief of News and Current Affairs and was therefore applying to himself for the job), was settling in with a new pair of glasses. George McLean and Jan Tennant were on the roster as substitutes on his nights off until 1981, when suddenly they were bumped to clear a path for Peter Mansbridge, who was being groomed as Nash's new understudy and heir apparent. Moreover, with the much-heralded move of the news back to 10 o'clock, it was no time for the CBC brass to be considering changing news anchors, and, in any case, it seemed fairly unlikely that after putting two women on *The Journal* they would hire a third for *The National.*

So, when Henry Kowalski at CBLT told Tennant yet again, "We've decided to take a pass on you this time," she began to think seriously about taking a pass on the CBC. Enter Ray Heard and Global News with an offer to co-anchor two daily newscasts with Peter Trueman. She would also have the opportunity to develop her journalistic skills by doing some commentary and possibly some reporting. Still, she wasn't eager to leave the CBC, and made a pact with herself not to go unless Global doubled her salary — which they did.

The CBC's response to her imminent departure was ungracious. She was immediately yanked from TV news and put on the graveyard shift for the last month. There were the obligatory farewell parties, which had the air of a requiem: they were losing Jan Tennant, the CBC's premier "token" woman. It seemed to be an admission of a failure on the corporation's part; an acknowledgement that it didn't really know how to develop female talent past a certain point.

Says Peter Herrndorf, who was then chief of CBC English services:

> Jan Tennant at Global is relaxed, easy, warm; her clothes, her manner, and body language all project that. Moreover, she has the vehicle which gives this very bright, *very* unusual woman a lot of latitude to show it. And she's fabulous. On *The National* she was highly tailored, neither loose nor warm. Perhaps it was a function of the CBC not being able to use her well — I suspect it was — because the Jan on Global is the Jan I've always known and the Jan on the CBC was some stranger.

The CBC's loss was Global's best gain in years. Tennant blossomed; her arrival was as much a tonic for Global's

sagging spirits as for her own. Under Bill Cunningham, Ray
Heard's predecessor, the network's news had suffered through
bad times and several unfortunate choices for anchors. Gord
Martineau was hired away from CITY-TV and lasted only a
few dismal weeks; Suzanne Perry was brought in from the
prime minister's office and bombed humiliatingly on air.
Peter Trueman had been carrying the load by himself for the
better part of two years and he was getting restless.

Tennant arrives at Global's studios, parks alongside the
president's Mercedes, and nips in the side door. It is three
hours to airtime and already the newsroom, which spreads
its clutter out in all directions around the anchor desk and
the set in the centre of the studio, is frantic. The coffee-
maker in the corner strains to keep up with the traffic and
Jan, on her way to get some hot water for tea, cracks a few
ritual jokes about too much cigarette smoke and bad coffee.
Despite the fact that she'd like to reform the place, Tennant is
much admired and appreciated around Global. Ray Heard is
not alone in thinking she's the best thing to happen to Global
since the invention of satellites. Senior reporter Christina
Pochmursky, who watched the anchors come and go at
Global, tries to pin down with words just what it is about
Tennant. "She projects a warm, intelligent personality and
can convey the sense of a *whole* personality in fifteen
seconds. She has a genuineness that overcomes the cold static
set and she has real, regal grace." For all the classy looks and
classic fashion, Tennant comes across as a vibrant and
approachable, likeable person.

For the real Jan Tennant, being liked by the audience is
both a blessing and a curse. First of all, there is the endless
torrent of commentary about her hair, her clothes, her jewelry,
and so forth, which sometimes makes her feel that the entire
viewing audience is made up of hair fetishists and frustrated
fashion coordinators. Few people ever get used to that kind
of intense personal interest from total strangers, especially
when at times it gets rather nasty. Barbara Frum remembers
the comments that telephone operators used to log about Jan
Tennant in the early days. "People would call in saying 'Why

doesn't she shave?' — horrendous, hateful comments from people who just couldn't accept her reading the news."

At times, too, someone does cross that invisible line into a twilight zone of unacceptable behaviour: men who call up for dates, or turn up at the studio door with flowers insisting they are friends, or who send in proposals of marriage. Some may be on the level and just insensitive to the effect of their direct approach; some are not totally sane, and it isn't always easy to tell which is which.

> There was a teacher at a local boys' school who kept calling me up and asking me out, and no matter how often I turned him down he kept calling. I mentioned him to a journalist who was doing a piece for *TV Guide* and a couple of nights after the article appeared, as I was leaving Studio 6, a man in a trenchcoat looking like the Detroit mafia came over. It was him and he was angry that I had mentioned him by name and called him a loonie. I simply went berserk. I yelled at him that he had no right to involve himself in my life, or take liberties in assuming that he had anything to do with me. It always happens, I am sorry to say, that when you are pushed into behaving like that they disappear.

Not quite, and not always. There *was* Ethel. Ethel from Woodstock wouldn't fade away.

> Originally she thought I was a man and started writing letters, which I never answered but didn't think of sending back unopened until some time later. Last summer Ethel decided to come and pay a visit. She had it all worked out: she would come on the bus and stay with me and we would get married and adopt a child. Global was notified and so were the police, who knew Ethel and paid her a polite visit. But she came anyway; turned up at Global and had to be escorted away by the OPP.

Tennant does make wonderful stories of these encroachments on her privacy, but beneath the mirth she is philosophic. She has not let the few unpleasant encounters put her off making contact with people, and she likes meeting the public. She is also generous with her time for students and young people who approach her for advice.

Long ago Jan Tennant came to terms with television and its all-seeing eye. She figured out a way to square the public preoccupation with her looks and her own sense of professionalism.

> Confidence (on-air) comes from being able to forget what you look like and what you're wearing. When I first started on the supper-hour news at the CBC, Don Cameron was constantly asking why I only wore turtlenecks. The truth was that I didn't have any extra clothes — only my own regulars, including three turtleneck sweaters which I rotated. People are concerned and do pick on how you look. If you are at all worried about it, it can destroy your ability to concentrate. You have to be able to forget all that, to focus on the story you are telling.

Self-confidence of that order takes a while to grow and is not easy to achieve in the best of circumstances. Being the token first woman on the job is rarely a good circumstance. Tokens are watched; their performances are minutely scrutinized, and worst of all, the haunting suspicion lingers that "she got the job because she's a woman." At the CBC, Tennant felt that prejudice in other people's perceptions of her. "I always felt that in the news department I was considered an efficient newsreader but that I wasn't a news-woman; having never been a foreign correspondent and lacking experience as a journalist worked against me in people's perceptions of me and there was no way I could overcome that — ever. I was not going to get the background; it simply wasn't going to happen. 'Once a copy clerk, always a copy clerk' seemed to be the mentality." As Tennant says, it is hard to imagine a man who began by lugging cables in a studio and went on to win international Emmys as a pro-ducer being labelled as a camera assistant who went too far, but she noticed that attitude towards her from many CBC current affairs producers. She was never invited on *Front*

Page Challenge, for example, or other such programmes when there were legitimate reasons for asking her.

Tennant is not a woman who waits around for people to change. She has her own ideas, her own life, and prefers to get on with it. That should make her the sort of woman — self-assured, clear thinking, and strong — who sends some men running scared for their own egos, but it doesn't seem to work that way. She is a good team player, a trooper and a pro. Her ironic sense of humour, her debating skills, and her steady hand with politics have gotten her onto more than one union negotiating team. Still, imagine the reaction when she turned up for one committee meeting with her crocheting! Scandalized, the men told her she would give the impression she was not taking the proceedings seriously. Tennant quickly announced to the stunned gathering of men that while she realized crocheting was a mindless occupation, so was smoking; and, if there were people present who were offended by her crocheting as she was by smoking, she would be glad to stop if the smokers did.

Wherever she works, she notices what's going on and will speak out if what she sees isn't right. She listens, especially to women in junior positions, and she encourages them to stand up for their rights, for the pay and respect they're due, and if need be, she'll stick up for them too. Around Global she exercises the power of her position as a kind of moral authority. She sees hers as a position of privilege: she is making excellent money, has a comfortable life which she shares (cooking, travel, music, and all) with CBC documentary producer George Robertson, and has few familial obligations, the main one being her two elderly parents. If worst came to worst she could walk. Her feminism and her sense of justice give her a perspective on a work-day atmosphere that is always chaotic and often cut-throat. She deplores the tendency of news executives to avoid direct criticism of people's work, abandoning them instead to the agonies of the rumour mill when things go wrong.

Global is not immune to such behaviour, but it does have a good record for advancing women and Ray Heard has reasons for claiming his laurels as an equal opportunity employer. Following the 1984 leaders' debate on women's issues, Global was the only network that could muster three top newswomen to discuss the event. Still, Tennant sees women floundering because they were promised a chance and it hasn't worked out or because they have been subjected to sexist behaviour. When she does interfere, it is with tact, caution, and unassailable integrity. There was the case of a director, an old boozer from the fifties with a ribald tongue who harassed women with his seedy wit. To a recently married and still impressionable young woman from a straight-laced background, he heaved remarks like, "If your husband's not sticking it to you enough, you know where you can come." Everybody who heard was transfixed, and the woman was mortified. Jan had a quiet chat with Heard and before long was looking across her desk at the old boozer, who thought she should know his side of the story. She wasn't interested in sides. She told him, not too gently, "That's for a judge and jury. But I do know that you have been left behind. The rest of us have grown up and behaviour like yours doesn't wash anymore."

After about a year at Global doing daily news, Tennant finally took on her own audience. The hair comments hadn't subsided; they even seemed to be getting worse. So one evening in June she took the concluding commentary and editorialized thus:

> From the female point of view there is one issue, however unimportant in the greater scheme of things, that engenders more telephone calls and letters than any other single topic here at Global Television News. That is the issue of women's hair on television. When I cut my hair last September it was seen as the symbolic final break with CBC. The switchboard was swamped with several hundred calls over the next few days. Even the security guards were taking calls. I am not the only target of this obsession. I share with Deborah Burgess the puzzlement about why the Women's Bridge Club in Cambridge would call to say "Deborah's hair is disgusting because it's straight." Or why Mrs. Cooper of Ancaster called to say Deborah's looks as if Jan cut it. Some callers

are more direct: "Shoot the hairdresser." But my favourite letter goes this way: "Your hair is a mess, the earrings are ridiculous. Let's have a bit more style on-air. You're not a spring chicken." Now, I have never claimed to be a spring chicken. I don't even want to be a spring chicken. I want to be what I am — a 46-year-old woman with naturally greying hair who works in news.

No one has yet been able to define what it is that makes a person magic on television, much less what personalities will mix well together on-air. Heard's search for a suitable partner for Trueman ended on a weekend when he caught Jan on the CBC and realized his answer was sitting right in front of him. "It just clicked," he says — "it" having had to do with credibility, professionalism, her tremendous popularity, and the CBC cachet. Global, English Canada's third TV network, had been licensed in 1974 amid showers of promises for the new dawning of Canadian television production. Within months it was in financial trouble and reneging on its promises to produce original Canadian programmes. Today its main contribution to Canadian content, and thus the most important part of its schedule, is the three hours a day of news that Heard and executive producer Wendy Dey produce on a relative shoestring of $11 million a year.

Heard, in the quasi-military jargon beloved by newsmen, refers to his news outfit as the Vietcong. Poor in reporter-power and resources, it has had to pick targets carefully, stretch its coverage thin, and carry many imported news reports — mainly from the US networks. When Heard took over in 1981 he set out to change Global's image as an also-ran operation. Trueman and Tennant were part of the bid for journalistic respectability, but he also had something else in mind: female rating points. "The bottom line in news ratings are female rating points. I don't think it should matter who watches but the advertisers want women because they make most of the buying decisions. Some might find it condescending or demeaning to say that women are treated as bait for advertisers, but that is how all television is sold, until the evening." Heard was chasing a larger and more female audience, and he made a conscious attempt to highlight and accentuate the contribution of women to the news programme and to appeal to women viewers. Jan was part of the scheme. But, he notes, this defies the conventional wisdom which says women don't like female anchors. Though Tennant still draws the usual catty comments from viewers about her appearance, the statistics show the pairing has worked. Warm, witty Jan alongside of somber, craggy-faced, pipe-smoking Peter: it's a match made in heaven. Jan is "skewing" a female audience and Ray Heard is a happy man.

As Helen Hutchinson tells it, she fluked into a career in broadcasting. You could say she was tricked into it. As a child growing up, she never thought about becoming a journalist. True, she had always loved the radio and as a small child had been so addicted to the family radio set that her parents had worried about her health: a four-year-old who'd rather listen to *Our Gal Sunday* or *Ma Perkins* than go outside to play! She had also been a keen sports fan from childhood. The only child of a Newfoundland Irish father and a Russian mother who fully expected her to be a boy, but who weren't deterred when a daughter arrived, she was encouraged to play every sport imaginable — which she did with the style and enthusiasm of a natural athlete. In fact, several members of the family were athletes: an uncle was a professional golfer and when Hutchinson first married, it was to a pro football player.

Jack Hutchinson later became a CBC radio producer and it was he, in 1962, who first lured Helen into a studio. He pressed her into service to read a script he had written after the early peace marches called "Don't Ban the Bomb."

> He was working for *Trans-Canada Matinee* at the time and had been told that because he was a staff producer he could not go on the air. His reply was that he'd get his wife to do it, and they laughed. But that night he took me down to the studio, carefully pointed everything out — this is a studio, this is a green baize table, this is a microphone, and that's the control room, and I'll be in there. Then he told me to read the script through to get comfortable with it, which I did, only they had flipped the

machine on and were recording it. It was an eight-minute script and it was a clean take — first time.

An auspicious beginning, maybe, but Hutchinson didn't take the bait. She does remember that after her reluctant debut, people at the CBC like Helen James began to urge her to do freelance items, but she wasn't really interested. Her attention was somewhere else, for she had completed graduate work in Canadian literature and had her sights set on university teaching.

Hutchinson was well ahead of the times with her passion for Canadian writing. CanLit hadn't really been discovered yet and few Canadian universities acknowledged its existence, let alone taught it. Hutchinson and her husband had just returned from a two-year stint in Winnipeg where, at Jack's insistence and because of CBC rules about spouses not working for the corporation at the same time, she had not done any radio at all. When a friend suggested she do a programme about books to fill a fifteen-minute slot in the network schedule, she was happy to:

> So I started with a programme called *Paperback Reader*, because I had looked around me and seen that all we owned were paperbacks which we had carted around the world with us and I realized that's what most people read. At that time the newspapers and magazines only reviewed hardcover books. I also began interviewing people about the books they read, trying to cross-match people and themes — say, Lister Sinclair and thrillers. Within two weeks the *Toronto Star* called up and offered me a column, which I also did for three years. I was also getting calls from people wanting to come on *Paperback Reader*, so I put together a thirty-part series on Canadian writing for *Matinee* and...just never looked back.

Before she really realized it, Hutchinson's radio career was in full flight. The ideas kept coming, people kept offering her work, and Helen James kept up the gentle pressure. "She used to take me out to lunch and tell me I was a natural, that I had the right background and the voice — that I ought to do it." For some while yet though, Hutchinson held back. She kept thinking about going back to university to do a doctorate and had reservations, anyway, about "this crazy business" she was becoming involved with. Later on she would credit James for dragging her into radio, and a second woman, Dodi Robb (James' successor), for deciding to put her on television.

The year 1969 was a momentous one for Helen Hutchinson, in more ways than she expected. Her television and radio commitments had ballooned into a seven-day schedule, which included five days a week on *Matinee,* two hours of television with a show called *Women Now,* and another TV series called simply *Helen Hutchinson,* which featured interviews with Torontonians. On Sundays she was dong *The Morning After* with Bruno Gerussi and Dannie Finkleman. "At that point I dropped the book column as I couldn't get all those books read and the column written too."

It was during this period that it finally dawned on Hutchinson that she was never going to be an academic and that her life had taken a detour which had opened into a main thoroughfare. Then the day came when she definitively — if painfully — proved to herself that she had turned into a thorough-going professional:

> It was the day after my husband left me to go and live with his girlfriend and I collapsed into a fit of hysterics. Collapsed because I had no idea it was coming. Good ol' me. The *very* last to know. I cried all night and the next morning Jack arrived at about 7 A.M. He knew I had the Gerussi show to do and I think he wanted to make sure I got myself together and didn't start developing a reputation for missing deadlines. I think that may have been the best thing he ever did for me. He actually drove me down to the CBC. I had a book review to do and I still remember the title, *The New People,* and it was about the Age of Beige. I took off my dark glasses, put on my reading glasses, and, having no notes prepared, I just flipped through the book and talked spontaneously for twenty minutes. Bruno, I remember, thought it was terrific. We went to commercial and the producer came

on the talk-back and said, "Fantastic, can you do another ten?" So I did and then put back my dark glasses and went snivelling out of the building.

In the middle of that personal crisis Hutchinson remembers saying to herself, "You're a broadcaster; you can do this under any kind of pressure."

Helen Hutchinson is a diminutive person and when you first meet her, her size is surprising. Television tends to make people seem slightly larger than they are in real life, but with Hutchinson it is her voice that's deceiving. She has a rich, alto-toned voice with hints of raspiness around its edges, which she modulates with consummate authority, and she sounds bigger than 5'1''. Many Canadians got to know her first by her voice, and got to like the person it revealed: neither stuffy nor fawning with guests, she was always genial and knowledgeable, and fascinated by the topic or person at hand.

Today, after a decade in current affairs, Hutchinson still thinks of herself as an interviewer rather than a news reporter. She has made her reputation through interviewing, by her ability to take charge of a conversation without seeming to, pushing an issue or a question at the right moment, being tough with those who deserve it and drawing out the hesitant ones. She is tremendously versatile and was lucky enough to establish herself as a generalist from the beginning. Although she came into broadcasting through book reviewing and daytime programming, it never seemed to hold her back. She was not tagged as a "soft item" interviewer.

I was never really slotted anywhere. One of the things we were trying to do, for instance, on *Matinee,* was to make it into a public affairs show that dealt with more than how to get puke out of the baby's bib. We did serious interviewing on the programme. And the same thing is true with just about every show I've done. I don't recall being relegated to "women's stuff," perhaps because of the book reviewing and the fact that from the outset, I ranged all over the map — politics, poetry, fiction, cookbooks, and back to military history. I think I avoided being branded, as so many women are, with that attitude, "Oh, the little thing has an idea, how cute."

Being a woman, she concedes, wasn't a great disadvantage for her. There was help at the start from some men as well as women. "I know when I first went into radio I was fortunate to be adopted almost immediately by de B. Holly and Allan McFee, who I used to call my curmudgeonly fairy god-uncles. They taught me a lot of little tricks that would take a lifetime in broadcasting to learn and were always protective and good to me." Actually, she has found being one of a very small number of women has distinct advantages at times:

I think women have an advantage; I know I do. Doing all those live interviews for *Canada* AM you could really see it at play. As soon as two men sit down together there is a contest. The guest says something and the male interviewer says, "Of course," and passes on. Whereas I, as a woman, can stop and say, "I wouldn't know a Keynesian theory if I were sitting on it. Please explain in layman's language." At that point I'm being a good interviewer because I'm being a surrogate viewer. If I don't understand or suspect that some viewers might not, I'd better get the guy to make himself clear. I learned that the hard way, talking to writers and poets who'd throw out an allusion or metaphor that I'd understand and I'd let on by using the same phraseology myself. Then a couple of smart producers hauled me in and told me to simplify my language.

The break-up of her marriage meant that Hutchinson abruptly found herself alone with two kids to raise. Max and Megan were nine and thirteen then, and just heading into the time-consuming and most costly phase of their growing-up years. Because it was a bitter separation, she really was on her own; and with no child support coming in she plunged back to work, accepting everything that came her way. She was doing *The Morning After* and hosted *This Country In The Morning* for a time; TV Ontario was just beginning, so there was work to be had there. Freelancing continued to offer flexible hours so that she could fit herself around the children's schedule and be there when they returned from school. It must have been gruelling, but Hutchinson says with characteristic understatement, "Listen, for a lot of years it was not easy. Think back; it was 1969 and not only was there still a social stigma about divorce, I had to work my butt off juggling six to eight jobs at the same time, all of them overlapping so that just when you think you can take a breather at the end of a thirteen-week contract you find yourself ensconced in another project."

The sobering experience of having to make a living and a home on her own to support two children was also a liberating one. Deep down she had known something was awry with the marriage, as she trailed Jack Hutchinson back and forth across the country and over to England, in pursuit of his ambitions. "This still small voice started saying, *Me Me*. When I think of it now, it sounds like a women's manifesto. But even as a child I never wanted a nurse's kit, I wanted a doctor's kit. And Jack's idea was that I would be the forever faithful Penelope while he would, well, come and go as he pleased." The end of the marriage was a beginning. She poured her energies into work — and her income rose obediently, enough to send the children to private schools. She proved to herself she had the mettle and the wherewithal to be a good single parent. Without help at home all three Hutchinsons managed together. "And I did it all by myself. I reared those kids by myself and that's the proudest accomplishment of my whole life. It made me work harder and it made me realize I was strong."

Still, she remarried quite quickly, and though she soon realized it too was a mistake she stuck it out for five years, primarily, she states matter-of-factly, because of "materialism": for a little badly needed moral and financial support. "I needed help. I had five jobs at that point. David [Harrison] was good to me and the marriage was a Good Thing. Remember, I was Catholic and didn't go to bed with people I hadn't married."

Still, the freelancing pace was crazy. In 1973, with a sigh of relief, Hutchinson moved to CTV and joined *Canada AM* as co-host with Norm Perry. She took the job mainly to bring some stability into her life, to be able to say she would be somewhere on a certain day and have some confidence that she would be. To most of us, the prospect of getting up every morning at 4 A.M., heading out to CTV's studios in the nether reaches of Agincourt before the sun is up, and putting in a long day that ends (or should) when most people are just sitting down to dinner hardly sounds like a solution to anything. Indeed, it required a total realignment of Hutchinson's metabolism: rearranging sleeping patterns and eating habits. It took her a whole year to adjust to it. CTV is still the only Canadian network producing a live public affairs show for early morning audiences. When the show was introduced, critics, cynics, and soothsayers all said it couldn't be done: Canadian audiences could never be pried loose from the American programmes. By 1975, however, the ratings had inched their way up until they topped the US competitors. Norm Perry and Helen Hutchinson became household faces.

Anyone can be briefed by researchers, but out there in front of the camera, curiosity and native intelligence are your only protection — and Hutchinson has them both in quantity. On *Canada AM* she had the added challenge of working live — no retakes if something goes awry. David Cobb once described Hutchinson's grace in the midst of total confusion for readers of *Canadian Magazine*:

> To watch her first-hand as she and Perry thread items together in the pressure cooker of live production... instills a further respect for the cool professionalism involved. To interview strictly to time in a crowded studio with a score of people shuffling about in the background getting ready for the next item, and nobody except the immediate guest and (with luck) the cameramen paying attention to you, is harder than one ever sees on screen. Hutchinson, rapt with interest, intelligence, and timing, makes it look particularly easy.

While on *Canada AM,* Hutchinson caught the eye of the executive producer of *Hockey Night In Canada,* Ralph Mellanby, who was impressed with her interviews on sports. He signed her up to do the between-period interviews for the 1976–77 season (which turned out to be the last season CTV was involved in with the programme). Hutchinson is still the only Canadian woman who ever has been admitted to the holy ground of hockey. It was the sports equivalent of Jan Tennant reading the national news. Hutchinson carried it off with customary aplomb and professionalism, stepping adroitly around the traps lying in wait. Sports editors were dying for headlines like "Tiny timid interviewer tackles the hockey hulks — and melts the ice." But Helen knows her sports (which is why she had been covering that beat for *Canada AM* in the first place — ask Wayne Gretsky) and her work could not be trivialized. Those who remember her interviews probably remember the probing questions about motivation and intellect: What makes an athlete push beyond physical endurance? What is the mechanism, the philosophy, or psychology that gives the mind such control over muscle? Hutchinson's approach guaranteed fascinating revelations.

Canada AM gave Hutchinson a chance to concentrate her efforts for the first time, while also allowing her to range over a variety of topics. It is not, however, a programme to do forever. There is a price to pay for working odd hours. At dinner with friends on weekends Hutchinson would find herself nodding off during the soup course no matter how stimulating the conversation. After five years of hard work and no social life, she was thankful for the chance to move to CTV's weekly prime-time current affairs program, *W5.* With *W5,* her role as host changed, along with the schedule: she is now on the road with a producer and a film crew about 200 days of the year, doing interviews that will eventually be edited into a mini-documentary item. It means putting some distance between herself and the audience, sacrificing some of the control she had doing live interviews. With co-hosts Jim Reed, Bill Cunningham, and Dennis McIntosh, she introduces items in the studio, but always from a carefully worded script. It is a long way from the days when she virtually produced herself, doing everything right down to booking the guests, and sometimes she wonders if she hasn't become a little detached from it:

> It took me a long time to get used to the fact that here we go out, shoot film, come back in, and then I get handed another pack of research to start on the next story while the producers go into the cutting rooms and bring me down the final product. The script is more or less written while the editing is being done, so all I'm left to do is really fine-tuning.

Although she is close to the story and part of the production team — a group of people she gets along well with — she no longer has overall control of what she says on the programme and, on occasion, that can be treacherous. When *W5* did an item about foreign students in Canadian universities which brought charges of racism, she was the one who presented it on-air and so she was the one who caught most of the public blame — and it hurt. The host of a programme which is produced by a team (there are eleven producers at *W5*) can never know all the dossiers in depth, but the person on the screen is often assumed by the viewers to be the expert.

Leafing through press clippings that follow Hutchinson through her career, you get the picture of a highly disciplined and determined person. She was once even called the Iron Lady of CTV and described as tough, competitive, and single-minded. David Cobb, the journalist who wrote the *Canadian Magazine* profile, also accompanied Hutchinson to one of the exercise classes she was taking. This apparently impressed him more than anything else in Hutchinson's life. Exercise wasn't glamorous in those days: Jane Fonda hadn't turned leotards into high fashion, and the idea of women pumping iron in a mixed gym would have raised cat-calls.

Astonished by the spectacle of a group of women seriously working out, Cobb seemed to take it for some kind of cult. Furthermore, he interpreted it as an indication of Hutchinson's near-obsessive drive for control — over her work, her life, and her body. The 1976 article is a wonderful period piece, a benchmark to chart the distance travelled in eight years by the media males.

If Helen Hutchinson was among the first Canadian media stars to champion the cause of fitness, it was mainly for self-preservation. It was the shortest route to developing the physical stamina she needed to meet the stress of the *Canada AM* grind. A hardy, hard-working, and efficient Hutchinson seems a long way from any fanaticism about order and control. Her schedule has gone back to predictable irregularity; she's at the top of her profession having the best years of her career, and she's married for the third time, happily.

Most of Hutchinson's encounters with journalists, profile writers, and personality hounds have been friendly, just like her relations with the Canadian public. She is happy to be recognized by them and is pleased when people call her by her first name. Sometimes they recognize the voice before they see the face, and crews accompanying Hutchinson often amuse themselves by walking behind her down a street in small-town Canada watching the effect she creates. She's rarely been plagued by crazies who, she says, you learn to spot. "They're the ones who send letters in three colours of ink written up one side and down over the other side of the page."

Hutchinson is open to the experiences and emotions of the people she reports on. On occasion, as when covering the Italian earthquake, this can be harrowing:

> I was lying in my bed with a dreadful head cold when Bill Cunningham phoned to tell me I was on a 4 o'clock plane to Naples. When I got to the disaster area it was horrible, just horrendous. There was unbelievable confusion and mess and filth, and those poor frightened people were sleeping twenty-five or thirty to a tent. There were no toilet facilities whatsover. Everything was mired in mud and human excrement was flowing all around. You had to pull to get your feet up. Mountains of medical supplies, clothing, and food sat rotting in the excrement and the rain; I can't understand why there wasn't an outbreak of typhus. I was there three days and it was tragic and awful. After we returned, one of the

cameramen who had been there too berated me when he saw the rushes of my stand-ups. "You were on the verge of tears, weren't you? Well, you should have let yourself cry," he told me. "It would have been much more effective."

Helen Hutchinson belongs to the first generation of women who made careers for themselves in television journalism, and she has been there longer and more consistently than most of them — a dozen years in front of the cameras. That makes her a pioneer and a role model to a second generation of women journalists who are now just appearing. Jane Hawtin, who at thirty has her own hour-long daily show on FM radio, considers herself to be one of Hutchinson's protégés, though the two have never actually met.

> I watched Helen Hutchinson on *Canada AM* and decided that if I was ever going to do that sort of work, I wanted to do it like she does. She can be tough, but is also nice; and she wants to know things and she *cares*. Even before I went into radio I enjoyed listening to her interviews more than anyone else's. If she was excited by something, she'd get excited. So do I when I come out of an interview. I'm high as a kite, but if someone is conning me I go for the throat like Helen does.

Looking back over her career, Hutchinson admits there was luck and a lot of hard work behind it, but she confesses, rather sheepishly, that she never had to go on the rounds, beating on doors to get opportunities. "I hate to say this because it sounds awful, but I probably dragged my heels a bit. I wasn't as ambitious as I might have been and I've never in my life had to ask for a job." For that reason she doesn't feel herself to be any sort of spokesperson for women in the media; her situation has been too easy. Men have not given her a hard time; she's not had to hustle or endure being harassed about her looks by over-zealous producers. She has seen mighty changes in the attitudes, nevertheless. Originally, when she began freelancing, people assumed that she was there because of her husband. They would ask if he was writing her scripts. She remembers the days when producers were forever "discovering women." "I had one male producer, who'd known me for donkey's years, say to me at a cocktail party one night after I had begun doing a lot of television, 'You know, I could kick myself up and down the street for not having discovered you years ago when you were right down the hall.'" She has also seen changes in the attitude of women. "I certainly think that the women's movement has affected us. It's made women more conscious of each other, and of trying to help each other out. I think we stick up for each other more." It's true still, she adds, that women work twice as hard as men. "It's a work habit we have developed and yes, it does mean that employers are getting a damn good deal for the money, and it does mean we set higher standards for each other and for ourselves."

Hutchinson learned to succeed in a man's world by capitalizing on her natural talents. "I was born with a deep voice. I can write. I was trained academically. I have an insatiable curiosity and am a compulsive talker and I've always taken the job that would extend me, let me learn new sides of the business." She has made it pretty well on her own terms and has not shied away from risks. And long ago she learned to horse-trade. She has always made sure that her position is equal with the male co-hosts. "In fact, my contract is possibly better. Norm (Perry) wept when I left *Canada* AM because he used to go in a month after I did and he would usually ask for 'whatever Helen got'!" Standing up to CTV executives is not hard for her — she's been standing up to large powerful men all her life. And though she doesn't divulge what she is making, she is thinking of the women following. Each good deal she negotiates, she hopes, will make it that much easier for the next woman.

Women, she believes, have achieved a great deal in the media over the last decade and some power, "by dint of sheer numbers." "The CBC's task force [on the Status of Women in 1974] was very important. The figures in it were absolutely shocking; I think the powers that be began to move and hire more women because they were pressed."

Helen Hutchinson's children are grown now; she's a grandmother, and her age now puts her out there on yet another frontier. Having won the battle to get women on the air, the next stage is to see if they remain on the air into their fifties and sixties as the men do. Hutchinson jokes, "Maybe when the men tell me I'm too old and ugly I'll go back to radio, which I still love and miss. I won't, of course. I should stay in television. And I've told them all that's exactly what I intend to do.

Adrienne Clarkson's break into television was another case of an academic career nipped in the bud. It was 1965 and she was back in Toronto after several years studying in Europe (England and France), hard at work on a Ph.D. in English literature. For the women of her generation university had a special purpose. Academe offered one profession — the only one really — where bright, young women could gain entrance on a roughly equal footing with men. One degree led to another, and with so few opportunities beckoning from beyond the ivied walls, many stayed. What other profession would accept women as apprentices in such a number, or allow them to pursue their own goals with such freedom?

Not that university and academic institutions were any the less hidebound, socially speaking. Clarkson went to Trinity College, the University of Toronto's training ground for the Establishment, which suffered the presence of women with little pretense of equality and actually kept them segregated in their own sub-college (and still does). There were professors at Trinity with reputations for being anti-woman, like the Greek and Roman History professor who told the same lewd jokes at the same places in his lectures every year and always posted his list of essay topics with certain ones designated "for men only."

Clarkson knew she wasn't suited to the academic life, and when an opportunity happened along in the guise of a suggestion from a friend at CBC's *Take 30* to try for a job doing book reviews, she did. "She told me they'd had nothing but boring old professors apply, so I prepared a little eight-minute piece and had it all memorized. When I walked into that studio, I loved it instantly...it was wonderful.

I knew this was what I wanted to do. I never really liked classrooms — in fact, I don't like live audiences that much — but I always loved the studio and talking to that camera."

Consciously or not, Clarkson had been scouting the horizon for openings. It wasn't simply work or a career she was searching for; it was something more adventurous and intense. She had always wanted to be a writer, and thought of becoming a journalist, "but I didn't like newspapers much, so I didn't see much point in writing there. I think television writing is interesting because it's such a mysterious medium, because there is the image and the voice. So many elements come into play. In television, once you've got somebody watching you, you can hold them." It was the medium that seduced Clarkson: television with its power over the audience and its emotional resonance. Yet there was something else. At *Take 30*, doing public affairs television on the CBC, she became a part of the world of ideas even more actively and prominently than she ever would have as a university professor. By being there, at the centre, an eye-witness to the people and events of the day, she herself became a woman of the world. It wasn't only a case of having the right background and telegenic good looks. Clarkson had imagination and flair, and wrote with a sharp-edged wit that appealed to the producer who hired her, Helen Carscallen.

Clarkson enjoyed *Take 30* and jumped right into the spirit of things. Though academically trained, she wasn't above jazzing up her topics: "anything to get the audience interested in reading." She probably horrified a few viewers with the item she did on summer reading, wearing a bikini and reclining on a fake studio beach, but most people were utterly entranced.

The following year, *Take 30*'s host, Anna Cameron, left the show and a cattle call went out for hopefuls to apply. Clarkson auditioned with the rest and was hired. Dodi Robb, who was just returning to the CBC after fifteen years to take up Helen James' position as head of daytime information programming, started work the same day as Adrienne and has always thought it was highly symbolic. She acknowledges it was a bold decision to hire Clarkson. Bold, because Clarkson is Chinese and there was some concern about negative reactions from the audience (what there was, was squelched immediately by Robb, who had the letters acknowledged and then destroyed) but mostly because Clarkson had so little television experience. Robb, though, was sure it would work. "Adrienne was so lovely to look at; she had such élan and class and a mind like a razor. She could absorb anything; you never had to go over things twice."

Thus CBC acquired its most favoured and popular host and Adrienne Clarkson acquired a career. With a distance of twenty years it may be hard to imagine how unusual Adrienne Clarkson was when she burst on the scene. Virtually the only woman in English television hosting a public affairs show, albeit an afternoon programme (and thus lacking somewhat in the aura and audience), she was also what we'd call today a "visible minority."

Clarkson was born in Hong Kong to well-to-do Chinese parents who fled to the British protectorate in 1942 following the Japanese invasion. Her father had worked for the Canadian Trade Commission and was one of the few Chinese who joined the Hong Kong volunteers and fought with the British army. The Poy family lost everything but not the taste for the gracious life and beautiful possessions they once had. "We were Chinese refugees who had a lot of this world's goods before we came to Canada and we were quite intent on getting it back." Although the Poys arrived with one suitcase apiece, Clarkson recalled, "my brother and I were brought up with a great deal of hope for the future, not with a sense of loss. And that's a difference I've noticed between myself and other children from Europe, for example, who think of nothing else but what life was like 'then'; they are often brought up with a crippling sense of nostalgia."

The early years in Canada in a tiny Ottawa apartment are still fondly remembered: watching her mother struggling with unaccustomed household chores. "We'd had servants in Hong Kong and she had never really been in a kitchen before," and for a while there were hopes of returning. "My father had been going back and forth getting his import-export business established, but in 1944 when the Communists took over China my parents decided they would not go back; that Hong Kong wasn't going to last. We became Canadian citizens that year." Adrienne and her brother were to grow up very Canadian.

"There is a part of me so hideously and ineradicably rooted in the Ottawa Valley that I'm more Canadian than I would ever want to think I am. On the other hand I feel totally alien everywhere; and I have always felt that way." A curious mixture of belonging to a place, fitting into the landscape, and yet feeling like an outsider; it's common to newcomers, minorities, and especially to women. It is also where Clarkson gets her drive. "I don't think I have thirsted for recognition; it's the idea of being able to be a part of things that are really happening. I just didn't want to be shunted aside. I didn't want to be a part of a minority group as a woman, as Chinese, or anything. I wanted to be right in the centre of it; right out there on the firing lines."

Adrienne Clarkson may not have looked like mainstream Canada to some people in the sixties, but her voice, her education, and her demeanour betrayed someone who was supremely at ease with the lifestyle and those values. Part of it, paradoxically, came from her Chinese parents:

> There was a great emphasis placed on public presentation in my family. My parents insisted I take dancing lessons but it was only to ensure I walked properly and didn't slouch. My father would tell us, "Always present yourself well in public." It was a matter of great importance to him, perhaps because he envisaged me in business someday. We were constantly corrected on the way we ate and spoke, and it was done as something we ought to do for ourselves, not because of an idea that it "wasn't done" to drop your g's or whatever. There were no moral values attached to it, they were aesthetic values.

The positive Poy approach apparently served Adrienne and her brother well. He became a prominent plastic surgeon; she, a nationally known broadcaster before she was thirty. She also married into an Old Toronto family, taking up residence in Rosedale with husband Stephen (a political scientist who ran for mayor of Toronto on a Liberal ticket in 1969), and joining the world of the Beautiful People. She became, as they say, more establishment than the Establishment.

No one knows better than Adrienne Clarkson, however, that looks and posture and grammar guarantee nothing in television. The most beautiful person in the world, so goes the adage, can fade into nothingness under the gaze of the TV camera. No one quite knows why, but some, Clarkson included, claim they can recognize the royal jelly when they see it: "I can tell when I see someone on-camera if they're going to be good. It *is* mysterious. You can't just learn to be on television; you just can't. That's why it's an avenue of broken dreams and why I seem to speak with an arrogance I don't intend. I am speaking as somebody who was in it for eighteen years and knew she was successful at it." The magic, she adds, can't be conjured up by producers or glitzy production values. "I know I was at my best when I was working with the best producers and directors. They gave me the chance to be wonderful. But I also know that on bad days I was still competent and at all times I connected with the audience."

Partly the success has to do with being natural and understanding what you are on the air to do. "It isn't acting: you are *informing*, not performing." There are techniques, she admits, which can be learned, but training doesn't necessarily help:

> I was thrown in to sink or swim on my own, which is typical. The only advice I got was on the level of having my hair cut or getting new glasses, which is no help. What would have been useful is what a director does for an actor — telling her when she is putting too much emotion in the voice, or moving the eyes too much; asking her what she really meant when she said such and such. Of course, there were lots of men around plying me with advice. But I always had a rather individual style and, in part, my defence against men telling me how to look was to become the best dressed person around. That was my best defence as it turned out. I wasn't really conscious of it, but I realized after that I had been carefully creating an armour which could not be

penetrated by men and their criticisms. And once it was
in place I could forget about it and not worry.

Clarkson clicked with the medium and the viewers immediately. She knew instinctively that she was connecting with the
audience, but it was confirmed by the powerful and personal
response from the audience who would pour out their hearts
in letters. "The audience always liked me. I made no bones
about it. The CBC doesn't give you the secret surveys that they
do on performers. I do know, however, that after I had been
on camera for a year or so I developed a large constituency,
and that's what the CBC also knew; whatever it was, it was
there and still is and that means whatever you do, people will
watch it because it is you." That is called a following, and in a
medium that has an attention span of 56 minutes and
where nothing is reliable, this is bankable gold.

In 1967, a new executive producer arrived in the person of
Glen Sarty, with whom Clarkson was to work right through
her *Fifth Estate* years. An improbable match, it nevertheless
seems to have been made in that department in heaven
which specializes in happy endings. Sarty, whom no one
would ever accuse of being a feminist and who is quite candid
about his prejudice, nevertheless became Adrienne's sup-
porter and defender. Colleagues noticed the way he ran
interference for her, particularly at times when other
journalists were taking pot shots at her professional qualifications. Since she came from the "soft side of journalism,"
there was a good deal of resistance to her within *The Fifth
Estate* unit. According to Peter Herrndorf, it was a good
three years before she established herself and won the total
respect of her colleagues there. For her part, she is
philosophical:

> Everybody has their problems. Some men drink, some
> womanize. So [Glen's sexist attitude] was just one of
> those things. I'd point out the stuff to him because we
> had one of those special relationships which permitted
> that. I'd just tell him he was being a chauvinist. Of
> course, he never did a thing to me; he didn't dare. I
> vividly recall one day when he was complaining about a

woman who'd come into his office and cried and how he couldn't stand women crying all the time. I suggested that maybe she was upset and that I cry sometimes myself. He looked at me and said, "Oh, you're not a woman." I had basically become an honorary man to Glen. To him it was a tribute!

The old black-and-white kinescope rattles and shakes its way through the projector, making the image jump. Something happens to the space in the picture when it's filmed off the TV screen the way they did it in the days before videotape, flattens it and turns it dark. Somehow it's a surprise to realize that in the 1960s colour had not yet come to Canadian television. There she sits in the middle of the ancient *Take 30* set, young, with-it, and elegant: her hair in a puffy back-combed creation, clad in an impossibly short and narrow skirt. But even then Adrienne Clarkson looked as if she were in charge of her image, author of the style and not the wearer of someone else's idea. You feel her presence even when the camera is turned away; her voice, a major element in the effect, is rich and damask-toned, drawing attention and holding it, as irresistible as sugar syrup to a humming-bird. Time has refined Clarkson's features, accentuating her eyes and sharpening the outlines of her face and figure. She's more attractive now — her style is more splendid. She wears silks, fine wools, exquisite and unusual jewellery and you don't have to know fashion or even like it to be fascinated. She is an *objet d'art*.

The Clarkson look has, of course, been an integral part of her success, but it also stuck in the craw of some colleagues. People who haven't been able to get past the chic also find her too cool and aloof. She was once asked whether the shift to *The Fifth Estate* was part of a concerted effort to get away from the sophisticated career-woman image of *Take 30*, and the inquirer was treated to a lecture on the solid current-affairs record of *Take 30*. What Clarkson didn't comment on, though, was the implication in the question that someone who appears to be a "sophisticated career woman" cannot be a working journalist. The resistance, which seems to have been more pronounced among male journalists, came out in full force at the time Clarkson made the move to *The Fifth Estate*. It had to do with a general contempt for *Take 30* as "serious" current affairs programming, but was aggravated by her image as a fashion plate.

Fortunately for her, Adrienne Clarkson had two strong and loyal mentors. Glen Sarty was one and Peter Herrndorf was the other. Herrndorf was the Head of TV Current Affairs and the driving force behind the creation of *The Fifth Estate*. He was responsible for her first break into prime-time television during her last season on *Take 30*. It was a series called *Adrienne At Large*, for which she travelled the globe to interview all sorts of international movers and shakers and thinkers, then weaving them into quite personal essays on various themes, such as modern Sweden. It wasn't a huge success but it was excellent preparation for what followed.

Herrndorf didn't hesitate to hire Adrienne as the host for *The Fifth Estate*; he hired her even before he appointed an executive producer. "I hired Adrienne because I thought she could instantly give the programme a kind of identity and visibility, a look and feel; I thought she was very able and particularly attuned to the kinds of reporter-based stories that we wanted *The Fifth Estate* to do. Remember, that had not been the style for some time; we recreated that style where the reporter is incredibly obtrusive in those pieces. And I thought Adrienne was a natural for it."

The launching of *The Fifth Estate* was accompanied by great fanfare. It was a big gamble, and a dramatic new departure on which several careers were riding. And it also took to the airwaves with a woman highlighting the event and anchoring the show.

For Clarkson, the switch to *The Fifth Estate* was the right move at the right time. All the money and attention of the Current Affairs division were going into the programme. The transition required adapting to a new format and working conditions: half the year on the road and a new editorial role. "Because of the volume [three items a week] and the sensitive nature of the material, I didn't have the same personal control that I'd exercised on *Take 30*. At *The Fifth* there was an overall thrust to the programme and an editor in charge of it [Ron Haggart]. I did my interviews as part of the overall effort and of course controlled them, which is considerable control." But Adrienne had something else to add. Cachet.

She was a drawing card, for viewers and for guests. One producer who worked with her remarks, "In addition to journalistic skills, Adrienne brought a star quality which helped enormously. People responded to her, were flattered to be interviewed by her, and so she was a lure to get interviews."

The Fifth Estate came out punching. In its first year, it had the audience and the headlines and plenty of controversy. One of its first pieces, on the Panarctic plane crash, ended up in court. Clarkson was a smash — though not everyone loved her. Some were outraged by her manner, found her superior and rude, especially to the Shah of Iran (when he was still the Shah and no one had yet heard of the Ayatollah Khomeini).

One incident was especially nasty, involving racism in the highest of places, the Senate. It followed one of *The Fifth Estate*'s early items, on the McCain Foods Ltd. conglomerate of New Brunswick. The report had traced the growth of the family business from a small potato-processing plant to the world's second-largest producer of processed foods, and reported that it had received about $20 million in federal and provincial grants and loan equities to get there. The item, which Clarkson still considers a classic *Fifth Estate* piece, was very outspoken and caused an uproar in the country among people who weren't used to such incursions into the private affairs of private enterprise. Two maritime Senators, Josie Quart and Rosamond Norrie (an in-law of the McCains), were apopletic, and wasted no time before denouncing the CBC and all its works in the Upper House. In an intemperate moment of anger, Quart accused Clarkson of repeatedly "downgrading successful Canadians on *Take 30* when she was not herself a naturalized Canadian." (The Senator later attempted to have the comments expunged from Hansard.) Thinking back on it, Clarkson says she would pursue such a thing today, but back then "We were hurtling about so much, I didn't do anything about it."

This was not the first time Clarkson was hurt in an encounter with one of the other estates. In the early years, the TV reviewers sometimes became uncritically infatuated.

Profiles and newspaper accounts gushed, "Adrienne, Love, You're Terrific." Everything about her was charming and perfect. Then, around 1972, a new generation began writing magazine articles; women who were part of the Women's Movement, who had dropped out of the middle class, shed its values, and were re-evaluating everything (including Adrienne Clarkson) with radical eyes. Clarkson, in that perspective, was not so much a success as a sell-out. Melinda McCracken wrote an infamous piece on the Clarkson image for *Maclean's* in 1972. It was Crunchy Granola meeting Vichyssoise-on-ice, as one reporter later quipped, and in a way he was right. The article records the clash between two cultures, two feminists headed in opposite directions:

> Mrs. Clarkson is wearing a short green-and-blue cotton sun-dress that ties around the neck. She sits with her ankles together, feet in white leather clogs. Her black hair is loose, brushed back; it is professionally trimmed. I can only assume she wears a bra. Diamonds and emeralds sparkle on the third finger of her left hand.
>
> What she sees from her end is a tall, slightly tanned person about her age, with longish brown hair, a straight Irish face, wearing faded jeans, a top that looks like jungle fatiques and a red bandana around the neck; your original freelance revolutionary, Miss Natural. Nothing sparkles on the third finger of my left hand; I've not let anybody near my hair with scissors for years. She, the first-generation daughter of a Chinese family, went up. I, the fourth-generation daughter of Irish-French-Scottish prairie people, went down. We stare at each other across that gulf.

Had Clarkson ever questioned the status quo, McCracken wanted to know. Had she ever been distracted by rock music or experienced the drug culture? Had she ever experienced the injustice of the society she was so eager to join? How did she square her oh-so-upper-class Anglo-Saxon image with her Chinese heritage? Wasn't she part of the problem, living a totally contrived and fabricated life by a set of other people's standards, now accepted as her own? McCracken was not generous or kind, and seems to have been genuinely appalled by Clarkson's privilege and hob-nobbing with sinfully powerful people. The question she was asking, though, was very much on people's minds at the time, and wasn't glib. Can one be a wife/mother, a middle-class professional, *and* a feminist? The women's jury is still out on these issues.

Clarkson remembers the article as being anti-woman and vaguely racist. "It was basically asking what right this person had to live in a house in Rosedale, to work while she has children because she can afford a housekeeper and there are those who cannot afford daycare." If it was racist, *Maclean's* was complicitous, for Clarkson was featured on the cover in a ravishing photograph over the headline "Scrutinizing the Inscrutable."

"All that stuff about being mysterious!" Clarkson sighs. "I remember Dodi Robb used to joke about it, saying I was about as mysterious as yesterday's stew. I never thought about it much until I was out of the scene, but I guess I was misunderstood because I was so new and one of the factors must have been that I'm Chinese and people didn't know how to deal with that, or didn't initially."

If Clarkson was freaked out by the *Maclean's* article, it was as much because of the confrontation politics as the invasion of privacy. For several years she refused all interviews, and when *The Canadian* commissioned Doug Fetherling to do a piece on her she only agreed to be interviewed if it was published as an interview. Adrienne Clarkson in those years felt ill-prepared for success. Furthermore, things weren't going too well at home; McCracken had touched a nerve, spotted a few cracks. Clarkson spoke of having long periods of deep melancholy which left her empty and able only to go through the motions of life. The "ideal marriage" was coming unstuck; separation and divorce followed, and some basic rethinking about husband/wife relationships:

> I recall coming back from a *Fifth Estate* trip, having been out six or seven days instead of the two or three we had packed for. One male producer made the remark that when he got home, he was just going to open his suitcase at the top of the cellar stairs and dump the dirty clothes

down. "What's going to happen then?" I asked. "My wife's going to wash it," came the reply. Myself, I would have loved to have a wife; my life would have been a lot easier with that kind of help. But it would also have been degrading for the other person because the whole idea of a wife is...it's why I don't really believe in marriage and why I don't want to be anybody's wife myself. Articles are written about a new kind of wifehood and it simply puts the other kind down. I don't want any part of it.

Clarkson has since found a way to live with herself while in the public eye. She has settled on a private lifestyle which suits her; having made the radical decision to leave her two daughters with their father, she has devoted herself to her career and independence.

I am still a very private person, but I made a deal. I let certain things become public. I don't mind people writing about what I wear or do publicly. But nobody knows where I spend holidays or what I do with my spare time. The price you pay for being known is having to explain certain things, but I don't think you have to go into detail. When I say that my divorce was a very painful, excruciating event, that is what it was for me and I don't think it betrays anyone else's confidence. The standard question you get is, how did my career affect the marriage? How do I know? I certainly wasn't divorced because I worked. I have no idea if the pressures of the profession had anything to do with it. I would think my divorce had to do with my age at the time I married, my generation and so forth. It had nothing to do with my being a journalist.

Despite the rough ride Clarkson has had in spots, she says now that she is prepared for success:

People like me, who had Total Approval, have a fundamental psychological advantage. "The beloved of the mother are never failures," as Freud says, and I've had that from my father. He identifies with my life and everything I've achieved. He came to a speech I gave recently and said afterwards that I was fifty percent better than the others and only made two grammatical errors. He thinks I'm terrific. He would never deny my stumbles and falls but he was there, and I've always known that.

Clarkson has thought about this:

I've met a lot of women in journalism whose motivations are different and who had different father relationships, and it seems to me, if the world out there is basically male, the way we approach it and the relationship with the father is terribly important. Perhaps a critical one. My mother was very motherly, cooked wonderful meals and made beautiful clothes and gave her life for us, as she is fond of reminding us. She is a classic "Jewish mother." But the preparation for success is the preparation for the father-world out there.

In 1982 Adrienne Clarkson made a surprising move; she bowed out of television to take a high-profile job with the Ontario government. She lives in Paris now with her companion, author John Ralston Saul, where she leads an even more glamorous life than before, as the first Agent-General for the Province of Ontario. That makes her a member of the diplomatic set, a life which she finds actually eats deeper into her private life than television did. "I am constantly having to have people to dinner who I don't really know," she laments. But the drawbacks are more than compensated for, by the opportunity to build something new from the ground up. And Clarkson's had experience with that role:

I was a pioneer [in television] and accepted it; I was eternally conscious that I must never make a mistake. That pressure was always there. I was also aware that if a woman fucked up it would not only affect her personally but would somehow be letting other women down. So I always asked for the top dollar; I asked around and had an agent, and although I was realistic about not setting out to bankrupt the show, I made sure I was properly paid and from about 1968 on, I was.

Part of the pressure, of course, is being out in front, knowing you are being watched and judged. Part of it is knowing that, for women, the margin for error is slim indeed. "Men are always given second chances; somebody is there to pick them up and there are lots of old-boy networks to rely on. Women don't have that. Not yet."

In her experience, the work relationships with women are vastly different from those with men and, given a choice, she prefers working with women.

> I like them better. I understand what makes them go. Even if a woman is an absolute horror, I still know what she's like from the inside out. I understand how her body works, how she works; and while I may not like her I can understand all that about her. We still don't understand men, which is probably what makes love possible. But I really feel the easiest and most warming relationships are with women.

Then what does that say about men, who occupy most positions of power and are responsible for hiring women in the media? "They hardly understand us, and hiring women is, most of the time, very difficult for them. Women often put on a show for men, pretending to be efficient, organized, and unemotional in order to get the job. And whether or not that's what they really are, it is a mask. It is still a male world; we haven't changed that. To say so would be self-delusion, which is the greatest sin of all." Women, she avows, will kill themselves working because they want to prove that they can do it — in journalism or anywhere. "They also don't waste time like men do, drinking, for instance. I don't know one female who drinks like men do, and it, is an activity that consumes several hours a day."

Adrienne Clarkson, like all women who have "made it" in prime time television, got there because a man hired her. Success came because he (or they) recognized the talent and

wanted to see it grow. On *Take 30*, however, most of the
people Clarkson worked with were women, and she retains
close friendships from that unit. "The women," she says
ruefully, "made most of the decisions and did most of the
work while the men took the credit." On *The Fifth Estate*,
arrangements were a bit different. "The tendency [there]
was to hire all men as producers and all the researchers
seemed to be women. I was older and more experienced
than most of the other women, so I felt I could help out in
that sense by putting forward women when producers' jobs
came up."

Clarkson doesn't mind admitting that she is successful or
that she is ambitious. It's like her attitude to sports: all her life
she has detested competitive games, but loved doing things
like cycling and swimming and, lately, aerobics. Ambition, she
finally realized, doesn't have to be competitive either. It can be
positive, life-enhancing, and creative. "I have this little engine
inside me and there have been times when everything was
going wrong and I would be lying down, exhausted, wondering if I could go on, and gradually I'd become aware of a
little hum inside. Call it life force; it keeps me going."

It is a warm, cloudless afternoon in late May and, for once, it
looks as if summer will arrive in Toronto on schedule.
Barbara Frum walks out of the CBC office building into the
sunshine and opens up a large, clear plastic umbrella for the
short walk down Mutual Street to Studio One. "It's to protect
the hair-do," she grimaces. It is one of many little ignominies
exacted by her job at *The Journal*. Whatever else preoccupies
her, she must still make sure that her hairstyle is intact and
her makeup stays fresh through an entire day of interviewing
and taping sessions. "In this neighbourhood," Frum jokes,
motioning towards the nearby red-light district, "you get a lot
of comments."

Barbara Frum didn't have to go to *The Journal*; she
certainly didn't need the aggravation of doing daily TV,
which she knew would magnify the pressures and complexities
of radio a thousandfold. She had mastered the medium of

radio and, though her experience in television goes back almost as far, she never really adjusted to it. In 1967, she was co-anchor of CBLT's local news programme and stayed on as host/interviewer of *Weekday*, the show's current-affairs section. During the 1970s, she hosted and anchored several series, including TVOntario's *True North* and CBC's *Quarterly Report*.

Television is a very tough medium to master. The addition of the visual element is the least of the difficulties, but it is responsible for forcing people to be selfconscious about their looks right when they are taxing their brains over an interview or a late-breaking news item. It is a trivialization, and one that is harder on women than men. Television is an extremely awkward and heavy-handed medium, a "ten-ton pencil," as it's aptly been called. All the satellites and portapacks and squeeze-zooms in the world can't change the fact that it is a laborious and time-consuming enterprise. Space-age technology can make everything look simple, spontaneous, and swift on the screen, but it is like seeing the head of a brontosaurus weaving gracefully through the jungle, with no hint of the lumbering hulk thrashing around below.

When pressed about why she decided to take the job, Frum replies:

> *The Journal* was the logical extension of what *As It Happens* had come to mean to the country. I guess I thought if I wasn't willing to take the risk, I'd be denying the thrust of everything I had done. I had mastered the format and all I could do there was to maintain the quality of what I had already done, as opposed to risking the free-fall into disaster of daily television reporting. Now, after two-and-a-half years, I have reached the same stage [in television]. I am not afraid of it anymore. I don't worry if I am intellectually up to it, or wonder if I can take the interview technique and adapt it to television. All that is known. Now the question is whether I have the physical stamina to keep on going.

Frum's sense of obligation also stemmed from the knowledge that few other people in the country — perhaps no one else

— had her expertise. Mark Starowicz, *The Journal*'s executive producer, had no illusions and frankly admits it would have been very difficult to start the programme without Frum:

> Who's done a thousand interviews a year for ten years and encountered all that before? A lot of *The Journal*'s senior staff came from radio and knew how rough daily interviewing is and how wrong-headed the idea is that you can just brief someone. We know you need a pro who is *au courant* with events, someone who can do four minutes with Duarte on El Salvador *now*, if need be, and we have a colossal respect for the interview form. Any idiot off the street admits he can't do a documentary but thinks he can do an interview. We know that interviewing with countdowns in your ears and all that is harder.

For Starowicz, Barbara Frum was simply the best professional interviewer for topical daily news; no one else had her range and experience. It was a conservative decision, Starowicz maintains. "Everyone thought it would be easier to overcome Frum's discomfort with television than to grow her skills in someone already at ease with it."

So it came about that Barbara Frum, premier political interviewer and the best-known journalist in the country, suddenly had to worry about her looks. Friends like June Callwood took to calling her up after the programme to tell her she looked great. "To me," says Callwood, "that would be no compliment and wouldn't help me at all. But telling Barbara her interview went well is meaningless; she knows that. What she needed to know was that she looked all right."

However, her concern about making the grade, visually, in TV was real enough. Television was not kind to Peter Gzowski when he tried to make the transition from *This Country in the Morning* to *Ninety Minutes Live*. Moreover, Frum's impact on television audiences has never been overwhelming. "She's superb on radio, merely good on TV," one critic carped. To what did she owe this lackluster performance? Was it as simple as her appearance and manner? Can qualities that work well in the fluid, informal atmosphere of radio ever be translated successfully to television?

As an interviewer, Barbara Frum grew up on *As It Happens*. She joined the programme in 1971, a few months before Starowicz came on as executive producer. At that time, the programme was sleeping in a corner of the schedule virtually unnoticed by the CBC brass or, for that matter, by the public. The tone of the show in those days was radical and irreverent, and when it wasn't busy muck-raking, it was exploring the exotica of far-out cultures; it was not a place you would expect to find a wealthy dentist's wife from York Mills. For Frum, it meant forever explaining to people that she wasn't a Marxist in favour of destroying private property. Contrary to the image of the show, she's a middle-of-the road liberal with little patience for armchair radicals.

> *As It Happens* was constantly evolving from the time I joined it until I left. In the first years, it was about fifty percent music and the items were eight to twelve minutes long. It was altogether a softer and looser format, although the subject was hard news. The arguments presented were more controversial when it was more of an underground programme. As it became mainstream, that political radicalism disappeared, both because of the people hired and because of the realization that if we were addressing a general audience we couldn't be a think-tank for intellectuals. So instead of saying "Let's construct utopia and nationalize the gas industry," we had to be more topical and popular and speak to people's real lives.

What Barbara Frum was doing on *As It Happens* was poking her nose into other people's business — something which is right in character. "I was a nosy kid and asked questions relentlessly. It drove my father crazy. So journalism is probably a logical place for an inquisitive person who likes to tell people what she has found out."

It was also the perfect spot to develop her on-air skills as a professionally nosy person for another reason. The public was not yet used to the sound — much less the sight — of a woman taking on politicians, VIPs, and authority figures. Frum had driven some viewers to the telephone to complain about her blunt questions and tenacious manner. They found her rude and aggressive and said so, often rudely and aggressively.

Ross McLean, who had been her boss on *Weekday,* said later, "Most interviewers dress up a personal question or politely back into it. Barbara just blurts it out for two cents plain. It is the quickness of her mind, her reluctance to fudge over anything. She asks the best bloody questions and gets the most dramatic answers."

She was perfect for gonzo radio. She would ask the impertinent questions no one else would. She could be gutsy and direct, and if that infuriated and offended some people, it was all part of the show. As *As It Happens* matured, so did Barbara Frum and so did the audience. Canadians gradually got used to the sound of an "uppity woman" on the radio and accepted her for the same reasons the interviewees themselves did: because if she was brash and impertinent at times, she was never flip, and she always knew what she was asking about.

They also accepted her because of her voice — that most remarkable, mellifluous, sensual voice that manages to be worldly and homey at the same time. "She talks Canajan, a slangy, vivid, colloquial jargon that instantly puts people at their ease and gains their confidence," wrote Heather Robertson in a 1975 profile. Moreover, contrary to her reputation, Frum is in fact the soul of politeness. But she concedes on aggressive:

> I think I am very aggressive, and those listeners who said so were right. I just happen to think that aggressive got a bad name unjustly. The most lively, wonderful people in the world are aggressive. You've got to be, to get up in the morning and if you want to get anything out of life. If you're not passive — and that's the opposite of aggressive, not "ladylike," — well, who wants to be passive?

Besides being industrious and scrupulous about preparing herself for interviews, Frum has never been an ego-tripper or an air-hog interviewer. She lets people talk and she listens. Ten years on *As It Happens*, experiencing the world through earphones, sharpened her aural faculty, and Frum reads voices the way some people read body language. She has a finely developed ear for lies and hypocrisy, and her own natural intolerance for manipulation and evasiveness, as well as her love of a good mystery, egg her on. Like Mother Nature, La Frum doesn't like being fooled. She wants to know what people's real motivations were, why they did what they did, and she's uncompromising when she sniffs a con. As for her own motivation, Frum is not interested in editorializing on the news or expressing her own opinions, which she claims are quite ordinary. "I have tons of opinions but presenting them on air doesn't appeal to me and never has. I'm just curious."

Barbara Frum grew up in upper-middle-class comfort, the eldest of three children. Her father owned Niagara Falls' largest department store. Her mother had been to university, which was very unusual in her circle, and although she herself only worked after her youngest child reached high school, there were other women in the strong matriarchal family who had always worked. It was a warm, supportive Jewish family.

Barbara was brought up with a sense of social responsibility and expected, if not necessarily to work, at least to do "good works." She married when she was nineteen and still in university, had her children, and then decided to try her hand at freelancing, partly because she could manage it from home base. Her educational background was in general arts, and she had no particular ambitions: she had had the typical succession of fantasies as a girl growing up — becoming a ballerina, a champion equestrian — but she had never thought of journalism. "I suppose, if anything, I might have been expected to go into politics — Judy LaMarsh was a family friend and lived down the street." She first began writing magazine articles and flogging ideas around CBC radio. Helen James remembers her as a very stimulating person, and determined. "Day after day she turned up with ideas. She was bound to get on the air!"

She was also bound to get into print. Her first foray, sending in an article to *Chatelaine*, brought immediate results. Doris Anderson recalls:

> We read all the slush that came in over the transom because we never knew when we were going to hit a good story or a good writer. A story came one day on daycare which didn't have any particular new angle, but the writing was good. So I called up the writer and said to come on in and see me; I don't want this story, but let's discuss what else you can do for us. For a while Barbara did quite a lot of writing for us. She just had a flair.

Frum's first published article in *Chatelaine* was a lovely, ironic piece about why lawyers don't want women on juries. Women are prejudiced, they told her. But when trying to explain how it worked against their clients, the lawyers were contradictory, cancelling each other's arguments.

Eventually, Frum got a weekly spot on a radio programme called *Audio* with Lorraine Thomson and Jim Chorley. "The first year, I came on and did my chats based on my experiences as a young mother. You know, how to amuse your child and what to do in Christmas week. But after several months of that, I ran dry and had to convince them to let me broaden my scope." She bought herself a state-of-the-art portable Euer tape-recorder — standard equipment for experienced freelancers — and began selling items on all sorts of things, at $35 a piece. These were her little "pocket documentaries"; she would go on location, do some interviews, and put them together with an intro. "I went to the very first Vic Tanney's and interviewed some women on the machines and did something that would still make you laugh. And I did a nine-minute piece on the visit of the king of Bulgaria and his meeting with all the old monarchists in the Bulgarian community." Like all freelancers of the period, she made her way by bringing in ideas that the producers hadn't thought of.

> You have to appreciate how good freelancing was at the time, for both men and women. There were lots of men

out there with Euers, too. And there was an enormous
market for freelance tape. Moreover, you could come
into the CBC, use its facilities, edit your own tape, narrate
your documentary, and sell your stories. It was quite a
scandal in the late sixties when the CBC stopped using
freelancers and gradually chopped people off. The
whole morning market disappeared with the Gerussi
show. Even *As It Happens* used to be freelance territory.

But before she got that far, Frum had pulled off a scoop
which probably, more than any other single thing, set her
irrevocably on the road to journalism. It was the kind of story
old newshounds dream of and lie in wait for: an exposé of
the misuse of funds in the TB seals campaign.

"My first blissful beginning memories are about calling the
Toronto *Star* and asking to see the already legendary Ralph
Allen. This was absurd, bloody absurd. What was more
absurd was that he saw me." She went in and told him about
the story she had stumbled on. "I must have been shaking. A
person who is putting out a daily newspaper has got a lot of
things to do besides talking to someone off the street who
claims to have a story. I had it all typed, though, and left it
with him. He said he'd get back to me, which he did, and
asked me to come in again, which I could hardly believe."
Allen wanted her to substantiate her allegations and, when
that was done, to do a rewrite. The *Star* ran the story and it
was a sensation. Frum was thrilled. "I thought it was
wonderful. I was quite excited with myself and became
infatuated with this notion you could know something other
people didn't and get it printed in the newspaper."

In the course of that first foray into the newsroom, Frum
met Robert Fulford, Peter Gzowski and the legendary theatre critic Nathan Cohen, and sold another story, on her way
through, to the education editor. More than anything else,
Frum loved finding a story, researching it, and then telling
others about it. She has never been attracted to the editorial
side: "I wouldn't have traded places with Doris Anderson for
all the tea in China," nor with the producers on *As It Happens*
or *The Journal*.

What Frum did sacrifice by going to *As It Happens*, however, was the travel and the life out in the field, moving around the community. It is something which perplexes other journalists, who regard the life she led in the dingy bowels of the radio building as a sentence to solitary. For ten years Frum ran her life from "that horrible pit," as Starowicz affectionately calls it. Virtually everyone she met, she met by telephone: she hired help, talked to the plumber, communicated with *As It Happens* staff editors and researchers in offices upstairs by phone.

The beauty of the way Frum worked is that it mirrored exactly the way her listeners listened. She heard what they heard and didn't have any visuals to go with it either. She too had to use her imagination and intuition, and her capacity for sensing what people were feeling. "I empathize with others as a way of experiencing things instead of having to do everything myself. It is not so much vicarious living as putting myself emotionally alongside them." She calls it mind-travelling. It is a very intense, concentrated working method but it has its own special, hidden pleasures. "You know you are doing something potent when the people you meet are feeling that you are making what's going on somehow vital to their lives. That is a thrilling thing to do in this world. How many people are doing something they know matters in other people's lives? It is what makes broadcasting so interesting. It matters."

Frum not only enjoys what she does, she is involved with it the way a hacker is involved with computers:

> It's like getting hooked on an intellectual game. Interviewing is an intellectual puzzle. That's why I had to keep you waiting today; I had something to do for tomorrow that wasn't adequately thought through. As I express it to the producers here, it's as though you hand me a pumpkin, a pineapple, and a poached egg every day and say "Go juggle." And I have to make it work. I have to find the intersections between the arguments so that I can create a coherent piece. The intellectual demands of that are intoxicating.

Frum continues:

> I would like to be able to play chess but I don't think that
> far ahead. I am concentrating on how long I can keep
> the thing going. If I ask the question this way how will
> they respond? Can I channel the answer by the way I ask
> the question? I reword it, write the questions out long-
> hand, and I jig the nuances of the question. I can nail it
> down more precisely if I write it out, but my notes are a
> hysterical jumble which no one can read, and sometimes
> I can't. I listen to myself silently ask questions and then I
> can hear the problems and change or adjust. If I ask this
> first, and then get that answer, where will it lead? I am
> the architect of a building, doing a kind of construction
> with the goal of really wanting to understand. I figure, if
> I can get it, the audience will also understand.

It may be a game, but not one with winners and losers:

> I am not playing against the people I'm interviewing
> or trying to defeat them. What I am trying to do is
> illuminate the ground. When there is a second guest, it
> gets more complex. With three or four, it becomes a
> nightmare of complexity, because they all have their own
> personal agendas (and that seems to be truer in televi-
> sion than radio). On TV, everybody has an agenda and
> everyone takes a question, no matter how plain and
> simple, and gives back their little rant. When there are
> three guests, there are three agendas you have to dodge
> and that's marvellously taxing.

When Frum says she has "no respect whatsoever for
authority" and states that, so far as she's concerned, prime
ministers and popes are "just the same quivering pieces of
meat" inside as she is, she is explaining an attitude that is the
essence of what people find so compelling about her character.
"If there is anything that makes me nuts," she says defiantly,
"it is hierarchies. I viscerally can't bear any work or human
situation where people have rank over other people. I believe

people work most happily without hierarchy and I, for one, couldn't care less what someone's title or so-called 'power' is."

There are few people so close to the nexus of power in this country who are so genuinely liked and admired. Frum's popularity seems to be of this superior genre. The consensus is surprising, in that it exists at all in a business famous for its jealousies and rivalries, and because it includes people who are dubious about Frum's work on other grounds. Even her critics are captivated by her professionalism. But at the same time, people sense her own considerable power. Along with recognizing her consummate prowess as an interviewer and journalist, the consensus also holds that Barbara Frum is the most powerful woman in broadcasting: powerful because of her position, her sway with the public and the politicians, and her personal charisma.

Marjorie Nichols gives a fairly typical assessment.

> Barbara Frum's done more for women because she is so good. You don't hear sniveling, snipping things about her. Everyone knows she's one of the best in the country — no, I'll go farther — one of the best in the world. She works hard to keep herself better informed than anyone else, to stay on top. At the Liberal leadership convention, there was Barbara Frum down on the floor milling about two days before it started, notebook in hand. I didn't see any of the other TV stars wandering around talking to people like that.

Of course, there are hierarchies at *The Journal* and there were hierarchies on *As It Happens*. Which is not to say that the working atmosphere isn't "generous and collegial," as Frum describes it, but the usual rug-ranking, status-tending, and rule by chain-of-command exist and Mark Starowicz, Frum's "boss," is no stranger to any of it. This alone invites specula-tion about the Frum/Starowicz relationship. No one would suggest with a straight face that Starowicz is Frum's Svengali, or that either is the creation of the other, but some people do wonder how she could possibly be comfortable in the *Journal* straitjacket. All such formats are designed to limit and shape the presentation of information yet one wonders how much is Frum and how much is Starowicz's tailoring of her talents. Barbara Frum is not complaining. As she describes their modus operandi as a team, going back to the early days on *As It Happens*, "I have this memory of us leaving each other alone, as in an 'I trust you; you trust me: you do what you do and I do what I do' understanding. I have a history of working with producers that way."

Starowicz, being the succesful, canny producer that he is, knows Frum, knows what conditions she needs to work well and knows which side of the toast his pâté is on. He does not believe in stars, is only interested in "people who work for a living" and frankly says he thinks that Barbara Frum is, comparatively speaking, underpaid. For at least a decade, she has been pulling in one of the top salaries in Canadian broadcasting and, in her third year at *The Journal*, is reputed to be making in the $150,000 to $200,000 range. Says Starowicz, "Barbara's and Mary Lou's salaries are, indeed, the highest on the programme, but they are not that high compared to the salary of the president of CBC or the heads of other crown corporations, which I've seen as high as $260,000. This society will still pay the goalie of the Winnipeg Jets more than it will pay Barbara Frum."

Through her career Barbara Frum has been blessed with good opportunities and good people to work with. Even the stories about how she was fired from *Weekday* for being too abrasive and rude are exaggerated. She was "let go," she says, for reasons that were political — in effect, she was being disciplined by CBC management for committing the indiscretion of signing a private petition that was sent to the Prime Minister protesting the War Measures Act. She credits no mentor or protector except good fortune; no one slotted her or watched over her career. But still, once on her way, she never stumbled or had to hustle for work. "I have always had too much to do," she laments. And when she left *Weekday*'s shop, she merely marched across the parking lot into the radio building and history. Nor did she have to deal with the overactive imagination of producers "on the make" as some women have, thanks to her face. "That happens to women who are beautiful. I'm not the type — just look in the mirror; I've been protected by God."

Success and public recognition, when they came, stole up on her quietly.

> Things happened gradually. Perhaps people are shoved forward suddenly in the entertainment world but not in journalism. There was a delicious moment in 1974 when there was a strike at the CBC and we were closed out but still being paid. So they sent us off across the country as a way both to show the flag of the network radio service and also because they thought we would be helped by meeting some of the people in the field and talking to them about local stories. *As It Happens* was very underground then and through that experience, for the first time I realized people were listening. We'd had no sense of it at all. Then my book *As It Happened* was published three years later and I did a national tour for McClelland and Stewart, the publishers, and I got incredible line-ups in Vancouver — people with babies strapped on their backs wanting me to autograph the book. Same thing in Ottawa and Halifax. I was shocked; I continue to be shocked.

Rarely has she been offended or bothered by public attention. She accepts it as the icing on a cake which is plenty grand and gooey as it is. Like everything else, it's absorbed into her life, mulled over and marvelled at.

Barbara is something of an anti-star: she is the last person to believe her own press clippings and she doesn't seem to be preoccupied by the trappings of success. Part of the reason is that she is already rich. Her own family had money and her husband Murray made more of it in real estate. Financial security made it possible for her to take the high road of freelancing, to weather the lean years of apprenticeship and to resist the temptations of security. She remains on contract, not on staff, at the CBC — technically in business for herself. It is a position of privilege she readily acknowledges. "I think if you have got the freedom to say no and don't use it you're a fool. I've always felt that I was privileged and I was going to enjoy it by saying no or yes to work. I appreciate that people like Helen James didn't have that choice. But in a way they did say no when they left the CBC. And they did succeed."

Frum's economic independence purchased political and creative independence. It may also contribute to a quality of detachment you can sometimes detect in her attitude: not detachment from the work at hand, or from the people she is working with, but from the human fray. Like a Taoist monk who contemplates infinity in a grain of sand, she too guards a quiet centre that seems unaffected by time present.

In the middle of whatever frenzied activity is going on Frum is always still, calm, and unruffled. She husbands her time carefully; she has some assistance to help stick-handle her schedule and *The Journal* has a PR person who, among other things, keeps well-wishers, publicity hounds, and charity hustlers at bay. She never seems harried and probably made a conscious decision a long time ago to organize her life in a way that reduces the fuss and maximizes the efficient working hours. For reasons that are neither phony nor undeserved, people put themselves out for her. She's the kind of woman who attracts deference, a Jewish Princess not because she's spoiled or petulant but because she radiates "special."

When you talk with her, you have the sense of a reflective individual, someone who has thought deeply and carefully about many things, not simply about politics and current affairs. She has a time-tested philosophy along with a well-rounded, well-anchored personal life that has never led her to assume that it's "supposed to be easy." She has been married to Murray Frum for twenty-five years, and the relationship has served her well.

The Frums have lived in the same house for years and she spends most of her social time with family and friends. The big social scene doesn't interest her much. "It doesn't amuse me to buy a dress to see the crowd in on one occasion, buy another dress to see the same people again on another, and so on." Her friends tell stories of her loyalty and thoughtfulness. On one occasion, she rushed to the hospital when the child of close friends had been in a road accident and was in intensive care, thinking to take a sea shell with her, something beautiful that would be permitted in the patient's room.

Perhaps it is her conservatism or her individualism — it's

hard to tell which — but Barbara Frum is uncomfortable talking about the differences between men and women working in the media. "I prefer not to see the world like that. Or to have to say things like: I am not a sexist. Or I am not a racist. You just work with people." Then she proceeds:

> There are things that are harder for women (especially women who are also mothers) and it is still pretty much a "closed shop" at the top of management's ladder. At *The Journal*, the women work extraordinarily hard at proving they are not distracted [by children, family, husbands] and I don't notice the men have that problem. It's the men who talk about their babies and are always saying they have to go home to tend a sick child. It's unbelievably funny. I rarely make quips like this, but one holiday Monday recently I came in the office and exclaimed, "How come it's women's night on *The Journal?*" All the men had disappeared for the long weekend and the women were putting out the programme. Even Starowicz had checked himself off because he had to do the gardening and look after his family. I think women are penalized by that and still feel constrained. Men are not ashamed to say they have a sick child or have to go home because their wives will be angry if they are late another night. It has almost become chic for men to use their children as an excuse to get out of here.

When it comes to the question of men assessing the potential of women they might be hiring or promoting, again Frum is cautious and chooses her words. "I think they have difficulty not being irritated when a woman asserts herself and have a difficult time feeling she's entitled to be as assertive as they are. I find men are more irritable than women, crankier, more easily rattled. That whole stereotype about how women behave is absolutely the reverse in practice. Men get exasperated, expecting to give a word and have it enacted." She pauses. "I suppose they're spoiled."

Frum has been extremely important for Canadian women in broadcasting and helped change the face of radio and television current affairs while she was at it. There is no one like her in American television (the closest approximation would be Barbara Walters, who had one season anchoring the ABC Evening News and then went out to pasture as a celebrity interviewer).

Barbara Frum came of age in the fifties and so was present and conscious throughout the sixties:

> Women's liberation — I encountered it in 1968 and was furiously angry for six months. It was a period of seeing patterns I had never thought about before. I remember it very distinctly. I interviewed Ti-Grace Atkinson, Kate Millett, Betty Friedan, and Germaine Greer. I read it, all the stuff, wrote about it, and did a lot of public speaking.
>
> I accepted every invitation I got from women's groups because I felt a lot of women needed to be told it was okay to be ambitious, aggressive, to want things, and to be angry. They needed confirmation. I was never interested in radical feminism because I thought they were talking only to each other. I wanted to talk to women who were really frightened — afraid of losing their husbands, their status — who couldn't see the trade-offs and were immobilized. I did that for about a year and a half.
>
> I was asked because I was visible and because they thought I'd beaten the system.

Frum wanted to assure them that she didn't manage everything all that well either. "It's a raggedly-edged life we all lead. I wasn't going to lie to anyone. You can't be a professional about all the details. You can let some things go and the world doesn't come to an end."

Barbara sighs good naturedly at the question: does she think of herself as a feminist? "I don't think of myself as anything anymore. It's like saying I'm a Catholic, and then having Catholics bring up articles of faith I don't follow. That's not to say I disparage feminism or feminists. But it is just a word to me now." She looks up and smiles a bit quizzically. "I don't know what I am. I'm just...myself."

SIX

The Moon Goddess of Bay Street...and Other Television Journalists

GAIL SCOTT was in the right place at the right time. More important, she lost the crucial game of shuffleboard. It was the summer of 1966 and Scott, a graduate student of journalism from Carleton University, was working at the CBC station in Ottawa. The internship had been arranged by the university as part of its course requirements, for CBC television news didn't hire women as on-camera reporters then. Scott, who had gone into journalism because "it opened doors rather than closed them," wanted to explore the field to see what she might be good at. If journalism was going to be her chosen profession, though, it was a foregone conclusion that it would have to be in newspapers.

Towards the end of her stint with CBOT, Scott went on assignment with veteran newsman John Drewery, and they ended up at the Press Club, chatting and playing shuffleboard. Drewery told Scott about a summer relief job coming up and suggested that she try for it. He felt that it was high time for women reporters on television. But Scott didn't think there was any point. That particular door, as everyone knew, was firmly shut and locked. Drewery, however, was adamant. Finally, he challenged her to a game of shuffleboard; if he won, she would have to apply for the job. Scott lost the game and won the job.

Unknown to her, someone had quietly lifted the latch. Changes had been going on and a few news executives who were slightly ahead of their time had already realized they needed women on the news team. They were not always or immediately successful (as Bill Cunningham wasn't in his bid to hire Jan Tennant that same year) but theirs was an idea whose time had come. So it was by happenstance that Gail Scott was the first woman on CBC local news.

"When I first went to work, they made a great big deal out of it. There was a splash in the CBC in-house newsletter, with my picture, announcing that CBOT had hired a woman. It had an air of 'Aren't we wonderful? We've hired the first lady.' The newsroom in Newfoundland replied with an editorial declaring that they'd never let a woman into their newsroom: 'Next thing you know, we'll be getting pink curtains.' It was that level of banter — guys exclaiming that they'd have to clean up their language." The photo shows Scott sitting on a desk with her legs crossed, notebook in hand, looking (one might suppose) as if she were taking notes at a news conference. Scott is the last person you'd expect to see in a cheesecake photo. "It was all done in great jest," she laughs.

Despite the jokes and the titters, the boys did not give Scott a hard time professionally. She lacked television experience, but:

> At that stage everyone was learning. People were coming in, mostly from print, and anybody who was taking a first crack at TV was learning on-the-job. Film editors showed you how to select shots and string them together in a logical, coherent story; cameramen taught you how to position things, and each new reporter was taken under the wing of a senior reporter and taught how to script three-second lines to match the pictures. There was no school of instruction; you picked it up as you went along.

Rookies like Scott would start off doing early morning radio newscasts, "the only one they could afford to have you goof up," and she remembers a lot of those early shifts. But she also got her share of decent opportunities, and the highlight of that summer was having one of her reports make *The National*. There she was, being introduced by Lloyd Robertson to the entire nation on the 11 P.M. news. "I thought I had died and gone to heaven." In fact, she had passed the initiation. CBOT hired her full time in the fall, the same year CBLT in Toronto brought on its first woman reporter, Trina McQueen. So the gates were open, even though it was a decade before the flood came.

Television in the 1960s was still a new medium and very expensive. It had only been in Canada for a dozen years, though it was becoming widespread much faster than people expected. Rooftop antennae sprouted like mushrooms on a shaded lawn. Everyone wanted to watch; even the poor were buying sets. By mid-decade, TV had become *the* mass medium of consequence. Marshall McLuhan had already published *The Gutenberg Galaxy* and *Understanding Media*, and people were becoming dimly aware that what the motor car had been to the first part of the twentieth century, television would be to the latter part. The funeral of John Kennedy and the live television murder of Lee Harvey Oswald clinched it; television had become the pre-eminent newsmedium of the age.

But if television was the wave of the future, the men who set it up and pioneered its development in the sixties were, in some sense, a wave from the past. Early television news and current affairs programmes had to raid other media for journalists and, though there were women to draw from elsewhere, none were in fact recruited either as producers or reporters. Women had to start at the bottom again as if radio had never happened; as if their achievements as producers, supervisors, and organizers had been forgotten; or (if one were to be cynical) as if men took television as a golden opportunity to start up a whole new game where they could once again make all the rules and keep women where they wanted them. With exceedingly rare exceptions, men designed the shows, produced them, and invited women on air only as entertainment. Even so, there is one thing that can be said for television in its adolescent heyday: it gave a generation of bright, energetic, intelligent women a foot in the door and a chance to learn.

Kelly Crichton, until recently the labour reporter on CBC's national news, started out at CTV in 1966 when the network's first great adventure in current affairs television was getting underway. Hers is a classic tale, the kind young people build dreams on. She actually walked in off the street looking for a job and landed one in the promotion department as a writer.

> The title impressed me, but I soon discovered that all it entailed was taking the blurbs about American television shows sent up from the States and rewriting them for *TV Guide*. Although I hadn't finished college, I still had enough education and ambition to think that I could do a little better than that.
>
> I was sitting in the hairdressers' on Cumberland Avenue reading the *Star* want-ads one day when I saw an ad for a unit assistant on a new current affairs television programme. I recognized the name of the contact and the CTV telephone number. I literally jumped and hit my head on the top of the hairdryer — remember those old iron contraptions? — and straight away went after the job. If you can believe it, they were reluctant to let me leave the PR department. They thought I had promise! I persisted, letting them know if I didn't get the job, I intended to leave anyway. I have never had such chutzpah since.
>
> Sure enough, I was hired as unit assistant on *W5* and it really was a dogsbody of a job; you worked for the producers but you were everybody's slave. When I joined, Peter Reilly was the host and the executive producer, but within days he had a huge battle with John Bassett and quit in a rage. It was a revelation to me. I had been used to semi-professional theatre and I had

seen temperament, but never had I seen anything like that. The theatre was sedate by comparison with current affairs television in those days.

I came to people's attention on the *W5* unit for the simple reason that I was the person who figured out how to get Chinese food delivered to the studios up in Agincourt. We were often there on weekends when the cafeteria was closed and the closest thing to us was the Christian Reform Church so, on the weekends, people starved. Before I knew it, I was made a researcher — as I remember it, all the researchers were women — and over the next two years graduated to chief researcher, story editor, and finally producer. Current affairs was fairly loose then. At a certain point, when you had built up enough credentials by going out on shoots or helping producers edit, if you came up with a little story that wasn't too expensive, they would give you a chance on it. The job just developed; there almost wasn't a day when I switched from being a researcher to being a producer. At the end of one season it was simply clear that I was functioning as a producer, so the next year I was officially called that and stayed on producing for *W5* for the next three or four years.

The one thing that always stuck in my craw was the salary. I was paid less than the men. I think the feeling was that I should feel lucky to be earning what I was, because only a few years before I was just a little gofer. I wasn't their top reporter but I was doing a lot of serious political stories — elections and so forth. Yet they were paying me less than some of the men who were only doing light-weight stuff.

I would like to be able to say that I left over that issue. But the overriding reason was that I didn't really want to go on leading that crazy life travelling all the time. Certainly the dispute over money didn't dispose me to making any compromises. The last straw, however, was CTV's coverage of the October Crisis, which upset me quite a bit. CTV was not alone in this, but the refusal of senior management to allow any discussion of the issues on air at the height of the trouble led to a huge fight

about journalistic responsibility. Essentially, management decided to close ranks around the government.
They bought the whole argument that the world was
crumbling and they would not even permit someone as
tame as Claude Lemelin (who was writing then for *Le
Devoir*) to come on air to talk about what was happening
in Montreal. A number of us who'd actually been there
and talked to people were very perturbed by it. That was
why I left.

At the time I was not a feminist. In fact, I was an
anti-feminist and did not relate to the women's movement at all. I had all the standard arguments: there were
much greater problems in the world and how could you
talk about organizing women when there was terrible
poverty, and so on. I saw it strictly as a middle class
argument for more privilege, much as Betty Friedan's
Feminine Mystique had been. I had gone to hear Friedan
speak in Ottawa once, and I remember having fierce
arguments with my friends. You see, I took what she was
saying for granted; I assumed I was going to work and it
never occurred to me to get married and head for the
suburbs.

When I look back on it now, I realize I had a
completely naive idea of what work was and of my own
chances as a journalist. But I held onto my liberal
reasons for rejecting feminism for some time. The
conversion happened at a labour conference when I
heard a panel of working class women talking about
how important feminism was in their lives, about the
fights they had at home and on the job. For the first
time, I believed someone on the issue and I began
making connections in my own mind about my own life.

After leaving CTV, Crichton went almost immediately to
CBC Radio, working first as a senior producer on *Trans-
Canada Matinee* and then, after a year of freelancing, as a
producer for *As It Happens*. She was with the programme
during some of its best years, when it was making headlines
with the public and waves within the CBC. CBC's in-house
revolution was making radical changes to the sound and style

of public radio. Programmes like *As It Happens* and *This Country In The Morning* are often singled out as examples of the revolution's greatest hits. They gave CBC Radio a new personality: keen, bright, curious and in touch with the grass roots, or, as the buzz word of the day had it, *relevant.*

Crichton joined in 1971, during Mark Starowicz's tenure as executive producer. For Crichton, it was the best experience of her journalistic career.

Starowicz was a human dynamo. His energy level was incredible, his sense of story amazing, and his sophistication and sparkle, well, just so impressive. Everyone had to keep up with what was going on in current affairs; you had to do the reading and *Maclean's* and the *Toronto Star* weren't enough. It meant reading technical magazines, foreign affairs journals, and the like; it meant becoming a mature journalist. The atmosphere there was very exciting. Everybody was pouring it on and no one ever took lunch. Taking lunch would be disloyal. Besides, you might miss something while you were gone. I imagine it was like being on an Olympic ski team. So what if you don't get lunch. You're out there preparing to win a gold medal. There really was a sense of being involved in something great together and it was wonderful.

The best times were when something huge happened and the entire unit would buckle down to work on it. I guess the biggest event, the one I will never forget, was the fall of Allende in Chile in 1973. We put on an incredible effort, pulled out all the stops, got people from everywhere. It was a very emotional show and I think we were the first to have people on air saying that the CIA had been involved, which nobody else was saying and which is now, of course, well known.

As I recall, the editorial conflicts were the same ones they undoubtedly have today, for the show is still divided between people who consider themselves nationalists and those who are primarily interested in loony-bin stuff. There were always fights at story meetings about why we had to do the man who grew a thirty-foot bean in his garden in California and why didn't we do something on native land claims.

Crichton left *As It Happens* to return to television, first to *90 Minutes Live* and then *The Fifth Estate,* with a short stint on *The National* in between. Most of those years she worked as a producer, though she briefly hosted a radio programme when she went to Yellowknife for a year with her husband. Every so often, she flirted with the idea of moving in front of the camera. *The National* was not her first time out.

"Back on *W5,* producers routinely presented their own items on air. The studio segment was a very important part of the show, much more so than it is today; reporters would have to walk across the set keeping their lines to time as they moved, carrying microphones, and dragging cords. Sounds easy, but in fact it was a difficult feat to pull off with no training whatsoever." What she did get, in superabundance, was gratuitous commentary about how she looked.

"I'd be sitting in the make-up chair, having typically been up all night editing, after a straight run of forty-eight hours, and the producer would drop by and he'd look at me and ask the make-up artist, in anguished tones, 'Can't you do something about her eyes? Her eyes don't look right.'" Without any professional advice, Crichton was simply discouraged. Still, in 1972 she tried on-air work again, this time on a show called *Movie Buffs*, which included film aficionados Robert Fulford and Urjo Kareda. The producer, Dannie Finkleman, didn't want a film expert or trivia fanatic but someone who liked movies and went to see a lot of them. None of it worked. Crichton was eventually fired, she says, on merit. But again it was a case of the producer hanging around after taping sessions, full of unhelpful tips, critiques, and complaints about her performance, her looks, her hair, and so on. Yet he was never able to put his finger on what was wrong or why she made the audience feel uncomfortable.

"Finkleman was right in his heart. I didn't come across, but he couldn't define it in any professional way. It was like trying to cook without a recipe and without knowing what happens when you mix flour and butter together." It was an ego-destroying experience but it still didn't cure the itch. Later, when she was on *The Fifth Estate*, she decided to try one more time to settle in her own mind which side of the camera she wanted to be on. Crichton auditioned twice when openings came up for *Fifth Estate* hosts, and finally, for the first time, she got some useful help:

> The person who was most helpful to me was Adrienne Clarkson. I find this idea that women don't help each other out is just nonsense and it certainly hasn't been my experience. When I was trying for the *Fifth* job vacated by Ian Parker, Adrienne went out of her way to help me, and it wasn't just words of encouragement. It was solid professional advice: go and see this person who's the best make-up artist and can show you how to put on make-up for television; do this with your hair; try that style of clothes. And then, knowing that I had no experience reading lines from the autocue, she arranged for me to spend an hour with the autocue person to learn the ropes. She even spent time with me in her kitchen listening to tapes of me reading and giving me voice lessons — all of which no one had ever done before.
>
> It was a revelation: all those guys who tell women their hair and make-up isn't right don't know a bloody thing about either. It isn't advice really, it's worry. The trouble is that it reinforces the impression that she is not really there because she has brains or knows how to ask questions. Yet I am sure if you were to accuse the men of doing that, they would deny it and insist that there really was something wrong with her hair, eyes, or whatever. No doubt that is true, but the fact is, they don't know how to correct it.

Eight years after Scott and Crichton set out on their television careers, Christina Pochmursky took a two-week job that would eventually lead to the senior correspondent's position on Global News, where she remained until 1984.

I had previously been a production manager for one of Maclean-Hunter's trade magazines and had no inclination towards, let alone experience in, journalism. I did have an MA in English literature and a degree from the Ontario College of Education, when suddenly there was a glut of teachers on the market. I can't say that I was terribly disappointed when a teaching job failed to materialize; I had decided on it really because I couldn't think of anything I wanted to do better. It was a second choice and I didn't know what my first choice was.

About that time, Pochmursky, who was twenty-six, had what she calls a premature mid-life crisis. She left her husband, quit her job, and moved into a rooming house. With $300 to her name, she had to find some part-time work. A friend told her about a research job going begging at Global. It was 1974, and the new network had just been licensed. "I thought it would be exciting. Global was just getting off the ground and they were hiring bodies. They were launching a new station and a new idea and I thought I would stick around and watch the spectacle." She completed the research project and was immediately offered another job as an assistant to Raoul Engel, the business editor. For two years all she did was get the coffee, make photocopies, and take phone calls.

When a break came it was two men, Engel and Bill Cunningham (then head of news), who pushed her ahead. "They decided that I was too smart for the job I'd been doing; that I was being wasted — or so they said. Raoul needed another reporter to spell him off and there wasn't enough money to have someone doing my job as well. I was very good at my job, the ultimate in efficient secretarial back-up, and I'm sure Raoul didn't want to lose me. So, what did they tell me? I was told that I would lose my job if I didn't become a reporter!" Pochmursky insisted that she wasn't right for reporting. Although she is quite happy speaking to a live audience, she finds herself ill-at-ease in front of a camera. Perhaps, she says, it is the absence of human feedback. In any case, the men were determined.

It was part sexism and part pragmatism on their part. They certainly wanted me to stay, but Cunningham could see other possibilities: a tall, good-looking blond reporting on Bay Street. What a gimmick! He talks a bit like Humphrey Bogart and he would tell me that I had to cultivate a cool image, a kind of serene authority so that I could carry off this fairly unusual idea of doing the business beat. "Christina," he'd say, "You've got to be the Moon Goddess of Bay Street." All the same, business reporting is a very dry beat; there are few emotions attached to the twists and turns of the Toronto Stock Exchange. I remember at one point a media consultant was brought in who told me that, as he saw it, my problem was trying to be too cool on air. "You're projecting the wrong personality," he said. "You have a naturally sunny and open personality and you should exploit it." Which goes to show that everybody's got some advice for you as you go along!

I did the business beat and *Money Talks* for two years. I used to work sixteen-hour days for the grand sum of $10,000 a year. I did everything, including my old secretarial work, research, interviewing, some hosting, lining up interviews, digging out film, even putting make-up on the guests — at least three jobs. Finally I asked for a raise and they told me peremptorily that there were at least 100 Ryerson students who would happily take my job. I was being given experience and they weren't obliged to pay me into the bargain. I felt insulted and then angry. I was there four years before I got a decent pay hike and a salary that approached industry standards. But at the time, Raoul was making five times what I was and I was doing most of the work.

When I think of it, I know it may sound as if I pole vaulted ahead because of the designs others had for my career. To some extent that's true. But I also got ahead because I was a workhorse and never complained. I often got my way without confrontation by simply going out and doing what I thought was right despite criticism. I have found that people rarely challenge you after the fact. This way I achieved a freedom: by taking things and not making demands.

The freedom Pochmursky so prizes comes from having won the respect and confidence of her colleagues. She has won awards, two of them for an eighteen-minute documentary called "No Regrets," about a Brampton family who have thirteen handicapped children. She spent an intense three days with them, watching them going about their daily routine. "I wanted to know how those people connected with each other; to figure out how they functioned together as a family. It was the first time I had been given such a huge chunk of time (normally my items were five to seven minutes). And I only had a couple of weeks to figure the whole thing out and produce it."

After a while, Pochmursky felt that she was getting bored with Bay Street; she was too familiar with the beat and asked to move into general news. She was assigned to Queen's Park, but provincial politics didn't capture her imagination, even with an election in progress. Fortunately, Global gave her the latitude to find her own direction. One story she followed for several months concerned the plight of a young woman from Thunder Bay, Stephanie K., who was afflicted with a rare and virulent form of cancer that is horribly deforming. The woman had gone off to Texas in search of a miracle treatment. More staid networks accused Global of rank sensationalism, but Pochmursky's own journalistic sense tells her stories dealing with human resilience are not only appropriate current affairs material, they can be handled with dignity. But not without bruising her own emotions; she confesses there have been very difficult moments. Like the time she went back to see Stephanie and walked into the room to a sight that shocked her profoundly. The disease had progressed so terribly in six months that half of Stephanie's face was obscured by a huge trunk-like growth where her nose had been. Pochmursky's objective was not to shock the audience, so the camera angles were taken from behind Stephanie's head and the audience was told why.

Pochmursky has made her reputation treating "soft" news items — personal tragedies and social issues like poverty — with style and delicacy. Many of her stories deal with the particular plight of women, though she has never taken up "women's issues" as a cause. What she has tried to do is develop a female way of telling certain kinds of stories that men traditionally have shied away from.

I think there is a way of letting feelings penetrate along with the facts . I don't mean cheap, sentimental emotions. But I believe it is possible to show understanding, joy, and celebration. There are aspects of life which women have traditionally known about but which have never been allowed on television. Men are good at facts, politics, disasters, and the occasional foray into comic-relief. I find when I hit my stride I tap into a whole range of emotions which have never seen the light of day on television.

Pochmursky is able to deal with broken, hurting people by making them and their situation understandable to an audience that has never been there. She might, for example, tell the story of the beaten wife who returns to her abusive husband in a way that is comprehensible to women who have only been able to see such behaviour as self-destructive. Pochmursky is an open and very engaging person, and people talk easily to her. Because her manner invites confidences, she also has to be very careful not to exploit people: "I find some people are so emotionally tied to television that for them talking to a TV audience is cathartic. I can look at someone and tell if they want it or not. If they don't, I leave."

Her boss at Global, Ray Heard, admiringly called Christina's work her "sob sister tales": "It's probably a sexist thing to say, but Christina has this incredible way of handling people. It's something I've never seen in a male reporter. She gets to the humanity of it without seeming banal."

Although Heard appreciated Pochmursky's talents, he couldn't keep her at Global once he remodelled the news in 1984. Feature items were cut down to two minutes to fit the new format, and Pochmursky, whose work had been tending to longer documentary-style reports, could see it was time to look for another job. Before she did, CBLT called her. A deal was swiftly made and she moved downtown to host CBLT's local current affairs show, *Monitor.*

It is interesting to realize that, while Pochmursky was studiously avoiding making demands on her employers, she was also studiously ignoring much of the advice handed out to her by her male colleagues:

> Cunningham used to tell me that my biggest fault was that I was not ambitious enough; that I didn't have an instinct for the jugular. "Moon Goddess," he'd say to me, "go for it." He would tell me that I could become the most powerful woman in Canadian television. I never knew if he was drunk or if he really meant it, but my sense of the absurd is just too acute for that fantasy to carry conviction.

She remembers that another colleague, Andy Barry, who was with Global when she was desperately trying to make "No Regrets" under a nearly impossible deadline, helpfully added, "Your problem, Christina, is that you don't know when to say no. You don't make enough demands for yourself." With a wry smile, Pochmursky wonders aloud, "The secret of my success seems to be that most female of qualities — getting my own way without an argument. I manipulate my environment in exactly the same way that women do in traditional marriages and sometimes I think I am managing my own exploitation."

One stand she did take was over her name. Cunningham and Engel wanted her to change it to something more pronounceable. Pochmursky thought about it, and then told them no. The name would stay Ukrainian as it had been given to her, and she was quite sure a lot of people would respect that decision. The men gave in.

Both Crichton and Pochmursky have done well. After slaving in the trenches and paying their dues, they managed to get ahead with a little help from their male mentors. Both women admit that they did not have clear-cut ambitions and that, for a long time, they had a murky sense of their own talents and what they might be able to do with them. Pochmursky acknowledges that her opportunity was handed to her — on a pink slip — by men who also offered advice and encouragement. They had confidence in her when she had none in herself. But she sensed that their respect was tinged with a quality that they would not have felt for a man.

> I think they respected me because I was smart but they
> also liked me because I was helpless. So my insecurities
> may well have helped me. Had I gone in there brimming
> with confidence, I doubt if I would have succeeded. In
> other words, I allowed the men to feel they were needed
> and were helping me out. I was the perfect little project
> and it was a Pygmalion script.

Herein lurks a major difference in the way men and
women behave on the job — one which Kelly Crichton has
detected most clearly in the editing room:

> The editing process at *The Fifth Estate* has got to be one
> of the most intense I have encountered anywhere. You
> come back from the field with seven miles of film and
> you have to craft an item out of it! Well, the typical male
> comes in declaring that he has terrific stuff, fabulous
> footage, and it is all going to be just perfect. The typical
> female returns with a worried look on her face com-
> plaining that she didn't get this shot, and that interview
> didn't work out too well, and well it's all a mess. In fact,
> half the time when you look at the material objectively
> the men's is a lot worse than they let on and the women's
> is much better. Of course, the editors think everybody's
> material is a mess.

This difference in style can reinforce old stereotypes:
through gender-tinted glasses, optimistic, enthusiastic male-
talk is equated with confidence and competence; reserved
and pessimistic female-talk is taken as a sign of indecision
and ineptitude. As Crichton explains,

> The perception develops that women are weak and
> disorganized and don't really know what they are doing.
> The men, on the other hand, really have their act
> together. They have the right stuff and know exactly
> what they are doing.
> I think that women articulate their anxieties and

insecurities and men don't, and we all know where that comes from. Women were never expected to do a "man's work" and so weren't taught to hide all those feelings. We were taught that if we appeared helpless we'd get help. Men, on the contrary, have been schooled to see that as being an admission of weakness. So you can see why men naturally get slated for promotion. They hype themselves; they rarely admit they are wrong and it often isn't noticed when they are.

Pochmursky and Crichton are a rare breed: they belong to the first generation of women who have scaled television journalism's hierarchy to network news. They reached the inner sanctum of male ambition — and then each consciously chose her own path. Pochmursky left the news for current affairs, and Crichton ducked behind the camera again to become one of *The National*'s three assignment editors.

Since the beginning of journalism, the most sought-after assignments have been those associated with power — politics, business, economics, foreign affairs, and armed conflict. Crime reporting may be lurid and sensational; entertainment may bring you into contact with the rich and famous (and possibly the talented and interesting); but the real action is where the power is — with prime ministers and presidents, at summit conferences, and in war zones. Within TV news, there is a hierarchy: City Hall has less prestige than Parliament Hill, which in turn has less allure than Washington, Moscow, London, or (at the moment) Ethiopia.

It isn't simply a fascination with power or with the game of history being played between parties or nations that attracts journalists to news; they are also keenly aware that what they do affects the way the game is played, and possibly even the outcome. There is a symbiosis between those who make the news and those who cover it.

The CBC recognizes the social importance of the news and the fact that Canadians make important decisions based on the information they receive from it. CBC presidents have long been fond of stressing the importance of *The National* in

tones usually reserved for national institutions like the
Supreme Court or the Musical Ride. It is the one experience,
they tell us, Canadians share on a daily basis.

It seems, then, that the news has something to do with real
events but also with people's professional aspirations and the
cultural luggage carted around by television executives.
Every cub reporter knows that local news is small-time; every
ambitious striver wants to make it to network news. (In the
view of some Canadians, the ladder doesn't stop there but
leads on to the American networks.) It is predictable, then,
that eighteen years ago, when women first stepped in front
of news cameras, local news reporting was the easiest to
penetrate, while the networks were an exclusive men's club.
True enough, both CTV's and the CBC's national news programmes were very slow to accept women.

According to the statistics, a substantial increase in women's
participation occurred only in the last three or four years.
But it still frequently happens than an entire newscast will go
by without a single woman's voice reporting, while the
reverse has yet to occur. It took over a decade of persistent
pressure from women inside and outside the profession to
convince network executives that the world would not shud-
der to a halt if a woman were assigned to Parliament Hill.
Television still trails other news media on that point. CBC
and Radio-Canada combined have one woman in Ottawa:
Marguerite MacDonald (who doubles as a Social Affairs
reporter for *The National*), which means that the French
services have none. Global has had a woman reporting from
Ottawa for a couple of years (Nancy Wilson, who has recently
been replaced by Christine Gaynor). In a dramatic breakthrough, CTV appointed Pamela Wallin as its Ottawa bureau
chief in January, 1985.

The foreign correspondent represents the pinnacle of
prestige in news reporting — a prestige that has its own
particular patina, tinted with danger and the exotic colora-
tion of far-away places. So far, Ann Medina is the closest
thing to a female foreign correspondent in Canadian television. She has covered stories in the Middle East, the
Philippines, and Central America, as well as the United
States. Initially she prepared her reports for *Newsmagazine*

and more recently for *The Journal*, where she is a reporter-producer. Her work has taken her repeatedly into active war zones, and for two-and-a-half months she operated a temporary bureau in Beirut. Medina herself, however, points out that it is not quite correct to call her a foreign correspondent: "It's true I have done a lot of travelling for *The Journal* in the last two years and at one point I did ask for the title in lieu of pay but [her boss, Mark] Starowicz said no." While he doesn't bestow the title, he does most definitely prize the skills, for he knows how rare a gem Medina is in Canada: a journalist with a solid background in both foreign affairs and documentary production.

Ann Medina arrived in Canada from the United States in 1975 with her new husband, CTV producer Jack McGaw. She also arrived with an impressive set of American credentials that pretty well guaranteed her a job in Canada. She had first thought of going into television journalism when she was twenty-six, a drop-out from a Ph.D. programme in philosophy. It was the end of the sixties and, as she looked around and contemplated where she might go, she realized that issues such as student politics and urban housing interested her. Confident that she could improve on the reporting the local TV stations were doing, she selected a number of their reports, wrote an analysis of each with a paragraph about the treatment she would have given the same item, and proceeded to dazzle Chicago's news directors.

Medina comes from a fine old American family, studded with distinguished jurists, good connections, well-educated wealth — and a "family compound" on Long Island. Medina credits her confident outlook to the fact she was raised with brothers and went to private girls' schools, inculcating the "I can do anything" attitude early. She makes no apologies. "What I am is loud-mouthed, pushy, and not shy, which are good attributes in this business."

By 1975, Medina was a full-fledged TV journalist with experience in reporting and documentary production. She had worked for NBC in Cleveland and ABC in New York, and when she walked in the door of *Newsmagazine*, she was welcomed and hired on the spot. "It's a sad thing about the Canadian inferiority complex. You come up from the American networks and they think you're God. Little do they know, lots of us are lousy."

Her first shock was the realization that she was the only woman working for the National News. In the U.S., she had been one of a number of women drafted by the networks in the early seventies. Canadian television news seemed to be light-years behind. Trina McQueen was on the desk then, but there were no other women about and apparently none waiting in the wings. Medina also found the atmosphere different: "old boy, British-pub kind of clubby, and very macho." Once actually on the news team, however, she quickly discovered the treatment was much more egalitarian than anything she had experienced in the U.S., where they kept trying to saddle women with "fluff stuff."

Medina's first encounter with what she calls "the Side Door Syndrome" had been in Cleveland:

> I arrived in the newsroom, bright, not very attractive, and green. The news director came to me soon after, saying that he had a special project for me. I felt very important all of a sudden. He wanted me to do a regular segment of the sports news — it was going to be all mine — and I was to do the family angle, you know, interviewing the wives and so on. He was going to make me a big star.

Medina recognized the trap and immediately understood that, while such an assignment might appeal to one's weakness for glamour and showbiz, it would put her on a track that would bypass journalism. "What happens to the grind of writing, producing, editing, and making those phone calls when you're spending your time in a studio doing interviews? What happens is that you never learn the craft." Medina had just the right response ready for her boss. "'Yeah,' I told him, 'that would be great. Now, isn't the divorce rate higher than average among players — and what about a story on the neglected kids?'" She turned down the job, and her boss was undoubtedly relieved.

It was in Canada that Ann Medina blossomed. She was

given the opportunity to develop a track record and expand her considerable talents. As she herself acknowledges, the fact that she came with "made it in the Big Apple" stamped on her resume was a plus, sparing her the burden of having to prove herself. Moreover, there were other Americans around, including Vince Carlin, the man who advanced her for the job of executive producer of *Newsmagazine*, which she took over in 1981.

Medina is a compact, good-looking woman. In dress shops they would probably call her petite, but petite is not her effect. Her manner and her style are strong and boldly stated. The deep, throaty voice which drives conversation along at a brisk clip, her expansive gestures, and her physical demeanour indicate strength and stamina. And truly, work on the road demands great stamina: the ability to take long hours under pressure in highly abnormal conditions and to help the two-man crew lug its equipment from pillar to post. On a recent trip, she lost seven pounds hauling sixty to eighty pounds of gear around "like a mule."

Medina adores her work, but she recognizes how and why it burns out so many. It isn't simply the professional strain, the pace, or the unhealthy lifestyle (little sleep; bad food and water; endless uncomfortable waits for interviews, visas, airplanes, and meals). Covering stories in strife-ridden countries of the Third World, where danger has you running on adrenalin, and where you are also daily confronted with human misery, is emotionally draining.

> And it means dealing with the internal contradiction, that what is an upper for you as a journalist [the story] is a downer for everyone who is living it. What is harrowing isn't so much the danger as the fact that you are touching raw nerves. It's like the opposite extreme of the exuberance of Mardi Gras, and you can only take that whammo for so long.

Lately, this has driven a normally gregarious Medina into a more introspective state. She understands why some of her peers see a therapist on returning from such trips; in the field, there is no chance to talk things out. "You are by yourself, thinking about whether you were wrong on this point, wishing things had turned out differently for the poor people of Beirut." And she finds the residue of those experiences troubling. She is left with an intense desire to be alone, to have some "White Time" to herself. She explains, "Although one always talks about splitting the time between family and work, there is another kind of time. I remember a book which talked about White Time and the fact that the cost of a marriage and kids is not so much that a woman may not have the time to do this or that, but that she hasn't the time to be by herself to sort things out in her head."

Being a foreign correspondent and a woman is no longer the pioneering phenomenon it once was. Out there in the field, there are a growing number of women working for the international press. Viewers and news executives are also getting over their apprehensions and biases, as are Medina's own colleagues. When the Iranian crisis broke, she was slated to go but couldn't, because the cameraman assigned refused to travel with a woman. "He was very forthright and apologized, saying he knew he was wrong, but he would worry about me and wouldn't be able to do his job as well. That would never happen today. If a cameraman refused on those grounds, another would be found." In the field, especially the battlefield, being female is sometimes a protection. "Say you are at a checkpoint and all the guys there are masked with their guns out and you get out of the car, hands loose, and greet them, and you're a woman. You can see the tension go down."

An experience like Beirut, Medina says, leaves one with an acute sense of powerlessness. But she admits that there is a fascination in the mere fact that "I have touched history." For her, that is the kicker and the motivation. She does not fancy herself a political expert of any sort, nor does she aspire to being one. "I never know who's going to win [an election] and I don't want to go to experts, who are usually wrong anyway. I'm dealing with people. I think my strength as a journalist is in telling a very clear story without talking down to people, and telling that story with pictures because I think visually. I am not brilliant, but I do sometimes have instincts and hunches."

Like Medina, Gail Scott got her professional grounding on the "hard" side of journalism. She started out in news, worked for a decade at CBOT in Ottawa, and then switched to CTV and political reporting. After moving to Toronto in 1966, she joined *W5* as host/reporter and then went to *Canada* AM after Helen Hutchinson left. When Scott finally left television in 1982, she was looking for a change and a challenge. Her first step was into teaching (journalism at Ryerson Polytechnical Institute), which has given her some administrative responsibilities she enjoys. As with Medina's, her career has unfolded with very few hitches: the opportunities and encouragement came along when they were needed, and she had her share of firsts for women. Still, she regrets not having "a more glorious track record as a battling feminist." She accepts the label feminist with a twinge of irritation, because "none of the alternatives fit. I consider myself very pro-women and if that's what a feminist is, I'll accept the derogatory things that come with it. I think women are capable of doing whatever they damn well please, providing enough pressure is applied to open up the spaces. I have a lot of faith in women — and a vested interest in women achieving."

The younger generation of achieving women following Scott includes Pamela Wallin, who succeeded her on *Canada* AM. Wallin, still only thirty-one, has forged a spectacular career in a very few years. She is a journalist first and foremost, who happens to be working in television at the moment. She came up through current affairs radio, starting as a researcher for Sheila Moore, who was producing the CBC morning show in Regina. Her first job, however, was community work on a project for native prisoners and their families. Her introduction to radio came when she was being interviewed as a spokeswoman for a campus women's group, but it never crossed her mind to go into journalism. Then a friend entreated her to fill in as host on CBC's morning radio show, in mid-season. She went and, by the second day, "I was bitten," she quips. "A lot of things were happening then in Saskatchewan. I got people into the studio, where I could put all the questions I wanted to them: say, questions about health and safety legislation to the minister of labour. I thought I was in heaven by the dashboard light."

Wallin admits there was a large dose of idealism involved, but reality quickly set in. "It was an eighteen-hour-a-day job which left little time for meetings. You think you can use your career to help [people] and in a way you can. But not directly. Broadcasting is not a vehicle for you to preach your own philosophy, but it is worth the compromise. At least at story meetings I can make the case for doing an item on the Crow Rate, even though it's not very sexy: that makes it worth the trade-off."

Wallin feels only the slightest hint of nostalgia for the bygone activist days. Today she is riding high on an exciting wave. In quick succession, she moved from production and editorial work in radio (including three years on *As It Happens,* part of it as the show's national editor in Ottawa), to the *Toronto Star*'s Ottawa bureau, and then to CTV. She has established herself as a clever and hard-working journalist, earning the admiration of her peers. Although she occupies a glamorous role on daytime television, she treats it as Scott did, strictly as a journalist's job. Both women have a perfunctory attitude to the presentation of their personal appearance, putting up with the grooming but spending the least possible time and energy on it. On air, both project the image of reporters; their involvement is with the information and the substance of what is going on, and their own personalities are deliberately turned down. To underline that point, Wallin has steadfastly refused to join the actor's union because, she asserts, "I am not a performer. I am a journalist." CTV recognizes those abilities, and regularly used her in its coverage of important political events, until offering her the senior post in Ottawa. When the Falklands War broke out she was sent off to Argentina for the network. "I packed four dresses for a three-day assignment and stayed five weeks."

That kind of unpredictable change in plans is what makes the life of the international news reporter so difficult for women. There is something to the notion, Wallin agrees, that you get ahead faster as a woman in that sphere if you are not married. "You are more useful if you are free, able, and willing to travel. When suddenly you have to take off like that, it is one thing for all your plants to die while you're gone — but a family?" She lives with a man who is also in the business and therefore understands the commitment necessary. Yet she is cautious about the relationship, knowing the odds. "I am not optimistic about relationships surviving long-term. There is a lot of wreckage. When you get off an election campaign plane after eight weeks, you know in the next four months several marriages are going to fall apart."

The personal stakes for women in these high-mobility, erratic jobs are heavy. Medina's marriage didn't survive. Perhaps nobody's can. Still, the line-ups for a chance at a foreign posting are long and some younger women are queuing up. There are relatively few who are in a position to consider applying and anyone with children is almost certainly not among them. So, for the time being, the local news is still an attractive alternative for newswomen in television.

Women have gotten into television news by various side doors, back doors, and other circuitous routes, but there is only one who arrived by helicopter. Anyone over the age of twenty-five who lived in Toronto during the late sixties will probably remember Dini Petty. Even those who never listened to CKEY when she was their traffic reporter heard about her — the "traffic girl" who dressed in pink, flew in a pink helicopter over the Don Valley Parkway each morning, and drove around the city in a pink jeep with a licence plate that announced: DINI. Less well known is the fact that Petty flew her own helicopter. When she took the job she had no flying experience, and for a while had a male pilot as all the other helicopter announcers did. Not long after she began, however, she asked her pilot, a huge ex-OPP officer named Jim, how he felt about the fact that she was about to put him out of a job.

"He told me the idea didn't bother him at all because, he said, 'we know you'll never do it.' I guess from their viewpoint here was a twenty-year-old kid who certainly didn't look like a candidate for a job that takes two men. But that was it." A year later, she had her commercial licence and from then on, for the next five years, did all her flying and broadcasting herself, logging 5,000 hours in the whirlybird. She quit only when she was eight months and thirty days pregnant. That pregnancy caused a huge ruckus:

> One day I got a call at work from some official telling me that my licence had been suspended. My God, I thought, what did they catch me at that I don't know about? "Why?" I asked. "Well," he said, "you're pregnant and that's illegal." The rules apparently said you can't hold a commercial licence and fly when pregnant. I had about 4,000 hours by then and I was a professional pilot and I told him that. He insisted my licence was suspended and finally I just barked at him, "Listen, I've got to go fly; I haven't got time for this nonsense" and hung up. I remember one comment he made during the conversation as he was trying to explain. "What would you do," he asked, "if you were flying down the parkway one day and *it* moved?" I remember telling him that I'd do exactly the same thing I'd do if I were *driving* down the parkway and "it" moved. I also told him that if he wanted to go to war, we'd go to war, and to my surprise they backed off.

How Petty got the job in the first place is another amusing story:

> I'd gone out to lunch with a girlfriend for the express purpose of figuring out what to do with the rest of my life. (I had been working for a production company that had just folded.) We were sitting in the Café George above George's Spaghetti House and three people at the next table, who were from CKEY, were hashing over their problem, which was how to find a girl to do the helicopter reporting. I knew one of them socially and he knew that I had done some sky-diving. At one point, he apparently looked over at our table and told his colleagues, "That's Dini Petty sitting over there. Now maybe if she's crazy enough to jump out of airplanes, she'd be crazy enough to fly a helicopter." The timing

was amazing. I had just finished saying to my friend, "I don't know what it'll be, but it's got to be something challenging, something that uses my head, and I really don't want to work in an office again," when he came over, tapped me on the shoulder, and asked if I'd be interested in being CKEY's traffic girl.

The job was a great opportunity and for Dini flying was a lark, at least for the first two thousand hours or so. But eventually it became boring. "How long can you fly up and down the parkway looking at cars?" As a job, it was a great publicity stunt and an even greater career starter. Petty became a local celebrity. American television shows like *To Tell The Truth* and *What's My Line* invited her to appear. But by the time her daughter Samantha arrived, she'd had enough.

Petty had grown up on the periphery of show business. Her mother Molly ran the largest talent agency in the country for eighteen years, yet it had never occurred to Dini that she might make a career and a living herself in "the business." As a twelve-year-old kid, she landed the lead part in an NFB film, merely by turning up at her mother's office just when the producer happened by. One look at Dini and he announced that his search for a child star was over. In the same way, the CKEY job just happened. Now, however, she had a child and a second marriage ending; she needed plans and a job. She thought this might be the time to switch to television. CITY-TV was just starting up and its chief producer and man-about-town, Moses Znaimer, was in the process of putting Queen Street and CITY on the map (with some help from the so-called Baby Blue movies). Young, talented kids bristling with energy and ideas, the first generation weaned on television, were flocking to the station. And Znaimer was willing to give them a chance — male or female, he didn't seem biased. A good many of the women who went on to make names for themselves in television (Joan Schafer, Valerie Elia, Judy Jackson, Jane Fairley) started at CITY, and Znaimer's appreciation of female company seems to have helped. Says one, "Moses certainly enjoys working with women, but he's not afraid of their talent." CITY in 1974 was

just the place for someone like Dini. She called Znaimer and
told him he ought to hire her "because I'd be terrific." She
had never met him but he knew who she was, liked her gall,
"laughed and hired me."

For two-and-a-half years, Petty hosted *Sweet City Woman*,
an afternoon show that featured interviews and women's
features. When it was cancelled, Znaimer dropped her,
telling her that he only had openings in the news department
and couldn't quite see her there. But a year later she was
back. Znaimer had been persuaded to have her host a
magazine segment of the expanded CITY-Pulse newscast.
This was the first encounter of Gord Martineau and Dini
Petty. As she says, "We were a heavy team, right from the
start." They clicked with each other and with the audience.
Petty was obviously in her element. She got experience as a
junior reporter on the street, did studio segments with
Martineau, and found, "the more I did, the better I got, and
the more they gave me to do."

Eventually, though, she was handed too much. She had just
had her second child. (In fact, Znaimer had talked her into
allowing a close friend and CITY cameraman to film the event;
a documentary about the birth was later aired.) She returned
after four weeks to anchor the news alone; Martineau had
been lured away to Global news in her absence. This was
something Petty had never done before and it was on-camera
job training of the most harrowing sort. She was exhausted
by the experience and only too happy to help Znaimer get
Martineau back downtown.

Dini Petty has her own style and her own approach to the
news: informal, involved, and all heart. She's not afraid of
getting caught up in causes and, unlike other on-air personalities, doesn't shy away from personal contact with the
public (she takes the TTC) or worry about being deluged with
people's troubles. A wonderful combination of breezy and
matter-of-fact, Dini has no difficulty choosing among the
requests. Many of them only need to be routed to the right
social service. A while back, she helped a disabled woman
who has spent most of her life lying on her stomach because
her bones had fused together. "She wanted a cart, a sort of
banana cart that she could push about with her chin (not that

she could go far; she lives in an institution). But the cart cost $8,000 and her income is only $80 a month, so how was she going to get it? I went to bat for her, got to Frank Drea (Ontario Minister of Health) and now she has the cart and is fine."

Word gets around. Another woman called up because the Crippled Children's Centre had suggested she phone Dini Petty for help. Dini has worked with the Board of Education to get free lunches and clothing exchange programmes going for inner city kids and she's raised money for all manner of good causes, including the Famous People Players in their early days. Since writing a documentary on child abuse in 1979, she has been active on committees and panels of experts raising the issue and urging agencies like Children's Aid to deal with it. When Petty placed an ad in the news-paper that yielded 400 responses from people recounting their experiences with incest, she decided to develop it into another documentary, which was nominated for an ACTRA award for television documentary writing.

A local journalist once remarked that Dini Petty doesn't read the news, she lives it. Her zeal is infectious and it fits the image of CITY-TV cultivated by Znaimer, the street-smart station "doin' it right on the wrong side of Queen." "When Dini's involved in something, she's usually up to her neck in it," Znaimer likes to say. Dini enjoys his approval, but puts it differently, "I have power now, and that's terrific. I can actually effect change."

When Gail Scott and Kelly Crichton began working in television, the sale of contraceptives was still illegal, divorce was treated like a social disease, and no one had the remotest expectation that long hair would become an acceptable mainstream fashion for men. In 1966, René Lévesque was still a Liberal and people thought the pill slightly immoral but certainly not hazardous to health.

By the time current affairs television got rolling, the sixties counter-culture was underway. Television itself was young, didn't know its own strength, and found itself swept along by the ethos of the day. Programmes like *This Hour Has Seven*

Days and *W5* were instantly with it, involved, and dying to be part of the break with the past. If current affairs television was not on the leading edge of social change, it was certainly close enough to get razor burn. For a time, McLuhan's most vaunted "cool" medium was hot enough to burn.

For two seasons, between 1964 and 1966, about three million Canadians tuned in to CBC on Sunday night (more than the number that watched *Hockey Night in Canada*) to see *This Hour Has Seven Days*. They'd never seen anything like it before. Every week there was a new taboo subject aired, another minister confronted, another outrage revealed or committed. The fever was contagious. At *W5*, too, Kelly Crichton remembers:

> Your whole aim was to capture people's feelings — provoke them, if necessary. Documentaries were made to music; the popular songs of the time were used to tell the story, punctuated by widows sobbing, Indians denouncing, and Blacks chanting. Television was found to be such a powerful instrument that it became obvious that the emotional level had to be turned down. Those who controlled it couldn't allow it to go on working people up that way. It was irresponsible. And yet we all know perfectly well that television is most evocative when it touches feelings. It's most remembered for that little moment when someone says something from the heart.

TV was also the technology of the moment; the latest, most glamorous, and most powerful new invention — like computers today. Anyone who was young and daring wanted in. Moreover, there were fewer traditions to dismantle and institutions to defy. There were no experts and, for a while, few rules.

At the same time a generation of women who had gone to university, not to find a husband but for a degree and, if possible, an interesting job, came of age. Such bright, eager young women were readily admitted to the junior ranks of television news and current affairs — albeit more readily if they were shapely and attractive — and the men hiring them quickly found they had stumbled on a treasure. Women made superb back-up support and excellent researchers.

Studies of American television, particularly of TV drama, done by the Annenberg School of Communications in Philadelphia, have found after ten years of research that the world depicted there is vastly different from real life. TV drama is populated by dominant professional males in their thirties and forties and simpering submissive women in their twenties. "The character population in TV drama is structured to provide an abundance of younger women for older men," the experts comment dryly. You could say the same about the hiring practices of male producers in Canadian current affairs television. Were you to travel through a time-warp back to the *Seven Days* unit, you would see scores of women in their early twenties, mostly unmarried, all of them eager to please their superiors and happy to be a part of the daring experiment. *Seven Days* was more than a weekly programme, it was a cause and a commitment; the cause was crusading liberalism and the commitment was to beat out everybody else (especially the news department) to bigger and better stories. To say that the atmosphere was intense, the pace frenetic, and the hours mad, is an understatement. People willingly gave up their private lives for the show.

Merle Shain, twenty-eight years old and a divorced mother, was definitely unusual. As a freelancer contributing story ideas and occasionally writing and researching items, she recalls being called up in the middle of the night and told to get to the airport and call in for further instructions. Sometimes it was a false alarm; sometimes it was off across the country hot on the trail of "something big." "We were constantly being asked to do things that were immoral, dishonest, or absurd — it was hysterical. But years later I did realize that [executive producer Douglas] Leiterman taught us everything we knew about journalism."

For those who were part of *Seven Days* it was an unforgettable experience; for some, the high point of their professional lives. But listening to the accounts today, you can't fail to be reminded of the plot of a French bedroom farce. Shain remembers it as "an erotic zoo." No doubt, for many participants, it was also fun. Where there was no coercion or impropriety, it was all part of the *Seven Days* approach to life;

if there was a sexual revolution underway, *Seven Days* was consumer-testing it. The men commonly assumed that sex went with the territory, and that meant that some of them took advantage of any woman they could.

Shain discovered one producer's routine after a secretary came to her in tears. She had been summoned to meet the man in a hotel bar, in order (she thought) to take dictation, only to be told that he had a room and she was to join him in bed upstairs. "I was furious," says Shain, who also had some influence on the show and was friends with both Leiterman and producer/host Patrick Watson:

> I stomped into Douglas' office and told him the story. He listened, thanked me for telling him, and said that he'd take care of it. Just as I was leaving, I stopped and asked him what it was he was going to do. "Why, fire her of course," he replied, as if that were the only thing to do! I couldn't believe it. Douglas was a very intelligent, decent, and caring man. I just stood there shivering and finally said, "Do you actually think I came in here to ask you to fire her? I came in here to put an end to this nonsense." But to him, there was nothing to discuss. The producer, he said, was important to the show, while twenty-five replacements for the secretary could be found by morning. In the end she wasn't fired, but the man wasn't controlled either and I accomplished nothing.

The men on *Seven Days* were not unique, though perhaps they set a standard for shamelessness in chauvinist behaviour. Behind closed doors and off the record, the odd one will now and then be candid about the folly and unfairness of his own conduct. Says one fifty-ish television news executive:

> Remember that television was very new and still growing up. We were filled with our own importance and really thought we were hot-shots. Those young, pretty gals would come in to see us and it was great for the ego. You were flattered and free advice is the cheapest thing in the world so you'd flirt outrageously with them. I did it,

and so did everybody else. You didn't think of the fairness or unfairness of it or anything else.

He continues, warming to the confession, "Some cupcake would walk into my office and I'd sit there staring into her eyes for hours, and the news would just have to carry on...You just don't have time for that sort of thing now; it's too serious a business." It doesn't go on today, we're told, because there are laws; the industry has matured, and men are more secure. Well? "Well, it's still true to the extent that an attractive, intelligent girl is going to get more of an executive's time than an intelligent, homely girl." And if it's a choice between an attractive, intelligent woman and a good-looking, intelligent man? "The woman gets the edge; the man will get the job."

Not all television executives are that blunt or honest, and not all women in broadcasting would perceive that there is such rank discrimination in the profession. Most believe that, in an equal competition between a man and a woman, the man will not always get the job. It is true, however, that discrimination for most women journalists is hard to detect in their own lives, especially now that it is not supposed to happen (and is illegal) and especially in a field where there are no standard career patterns or expected promotions. The sins against women in television journalism have been sins of omission rather than commission; they consist of opportunities not offered and chances not given, rather than promotions or pay denied. There is a consensus, though, on one thing: women have come a great distance in television and have filled the producers' ranks in a way that would have been unthinkable in the swinging sixties. Beyond that, the statistics on women's participation are disappointing. Seventeen percent of the CBC's staff producers in television are women (thirteen percent in the English service and twenty-one percent in the French service).

There is, however, one area where women are dominant both in numbers and the length of time they spend there: research. Television programme research has been turned into a female profession like teaching or nursing, and is duly conceded the lowest pay and lowest status on the editorial floor. For a great many women and some men, television research, particularly in current affairs, has been a perfectly acceptable route into production — a place to learn the basics while working up some skills and experience. But it is generally understood that if you are serious and talented, you must move on.

Whether or not they enter the field with the same qualifications as women, men certainly do not often enter at the same level, as a glance around the various establishments shows. On *W5*, all six researchers are women and seven of the eight field producers are men; on *The Fifth Estate,* all four researchers are women and thirteen of the sixteen field producers are male; at *The Journal,* two of nine journalist/ reporters are women, all but two of the general producers are women, and all but one of the documentary producers are men. Of the six senior editors, one is a woman.

For the past couple of years, *The Journal* has been the centre of attention, the talk of current affairs/news circles, and the subject of gossip from one end of the CBC to the other. There was the usual mixture of fear and jealousy when it began, but most people had to admire the spirit and the intent of the enterprise. There were comments about the way other shows and regions were being "bled dry" or at least anemic, as more and more talent and money migrated to *The Journal.* But what really piqued everybody's curiosity was the selection of two women to anchor the new show: Mary Lou Finlay and Barbara Frum. According to *The Journal*'s chief, Mark Starowicz, "There never was a decision as such to go with two women. We decided there would be two jobs: host/principal interviewer and co-host," and they wanted Barbara Frum in the number one position. Then the planning team began casting around for her co-host. "We also wanted a clean break from existing CBC television personalities. Mary Lou, who came from *Take 30* and [CTV's] *Live It Up,* had an entirely different image from Barbara and was experienced in the studio. I remember the meeting when we realized that we had two women; we assessed the positives and negatives, but didn't really spend too much time on the issue." He continues, while he wanders about his office looking for a match to light his umpteenth Rothmans of the day, *"The Journal* was born out of fear: it could have been the next *90 Minutes Live* and been cancelled after six months; and the hostilities were already there in the press. We didn't need to take on any extra problems. In the end, we didn't think there were too many risks involved."

Journalistically speaking, they were right. Audiences weren't driven away by the sight of two women anchoring the news. They were driven instead to writing in, in startling numbers, to complain in detail about Frum's and Finlay's appearance. Never, says Starowicz, had he heard so much about hair and blouses and earrings and lipstick. He was shocked and amazed that so many people would bother to write in with such opinions. "It was damn sexist," he says, thankful that the tide has subsided. Even Finlay, who has been on television since she joined CBOT in Ottawa in 1970, was staggered by the quantity and the "almost offensive" obsession with her hair.

Before *The Journal,* Finlay had never given the cosmetic side of her work much attention — and hadn't needed to. The custom in Canadian television seems to be to leave clothes and grooming up to the individuals (clothing allowances are customary), with make-up provided at the station for everyone, guests included. The ground-rules are well known and oft-quoted: stick to the basics, don't wear anything distracting like checks or sequins, and come well groomed. There are few attempts to repackage people or mould them into images, though it is often assumed, when major changes are made in a host's appearance, that she is being manipulated by some unscrupulous image packagers lurking off-camera with colour charts and wigs. While interference is common, it is rarely conscientious or organized.

The Journal, however, was determined to leave nothing, least of all looks, to chance. Finlay recalls wearily:

> There were meetings with make-up people and hair people and they poked and prodded and said that we ought to do this with our hair and that we should wear

interesting necklines. And the only remarkable thing about it all was that none of it was right! We went out and bought twenty frilly blouses apiece (on the experts' advice) which we both hate and have hardly worn. We do, of course, have to co-ordinate what we wear. It really could look ridiculous if one of us turned up in a plain brown t-shirt and the other in a fancy, pink blouse. That part of it is a bit like dressing a set.

Now, three years into the show, the angst about looks has subsided and Frum and Finlay have got it down to a routine.

There were other aspects of the high-profile job that Finlay has found disquieting. She has always resisted the notion of being a TV star. In 1975, when she moved to Toronto to replace Adrienne Clarkson on *Take 30,* she told reporter Margaret Daly, "I see my function as a television journalist is to convey as much information about the subject at hand as possible, in a way that intrigues the viewers. I know not all CBC public affairs hosts have worked that way, and I'm not saying I don't think there should be stars in public affairs. It's just that I don't see myself in that role."

Working on a highly visible programme like *The Journal,* being on-air every night, as she was at the beginning, has had an impact that Finlay can't escape. "You do become a Somebody, not by virtue of anything you have accomplished, or by any particular thing you are doing, but because you're there. If I were on television committing axe murders, I daresay I'd be just as popular." Finlay still finds that strange and she allows that it creates a great pressure to become something else, to start thinking of yourself as a personality, to believe the image. She is still trying to figure out — the disadvantages being obvious — what the advantages of the high profile might be:

If I go somewhere in Canada now to do a story, it is diffi-cult because people want to come and interview *me* — in-cluding the very people I've come to interview. Being this visible also means you might be recognized by someone at the grocery store when you're looking like a perfect shrew. So you actually find yourself putting on lipstick

and mascara and brushing your hair to go down to the
corner for a quart of milk. On the other hand, if I want to
see or speak to someone, that visibility gives me better
access because people know who I am. That's an advantage, I guess.

Finlay's first job in television, co-host of an afternoon
magazine show, mercifully brought her almost no visibility.
She had previously been working at the War Museum and
had applied for a research job at CBOT in Ottawa. To her
surprise, the producer suggested that she audition for an
on-air position. She did, despite a terrible attack of nerves.
"It was terrifying, but it was also fun right from the start. I
knew I was going to make an utter fool of myself because I
didn't know what I was doing. But I realized in order to
learn, I had to risk that, and I also knew I would rather take
the risk and lose than regret not having the nerve to try."
  The transition from local television to network and *Take 30*
had its lumps. Comparisons to Adrienne Clarkson were
inevitable and, she felt, invidious. Her biggest headache,
however, was not her image or tart-tongued local journalists:

> If you start on a local station, you get to do everything in
> production because you have to. When you get to a
> bigger show which has more money and more people,
> they assume you don't know how to do anything. At *Take
> 30*, there was a producer who did this and somebody
> took care of that and I was supposed to be the mouth,
> that's all. Yet I probably had more production experience
> than all five producers put together. It was hard because
> those producers were also men.

She was having problems as well with her executive producer
("We didn't see eye to eye on much — on anything really"), so
she left after just two years. In the interim, she freelanced,
appearing regularly on *90 Minutes Live,* and spent some time
at home with a new baby.
  Finlay was just beginning to think she should worry about
getting a good job again — "if you're gone long enough,
people forget you exist or think there's a reason for your

absence, that you've hit the bottle or lost the knack" — when Jack McGaw called from CTV. She instantly loved the concept of *Live It Up,* which was to be a light-hearted, rapid-fire consumer and lifestyle programme, and took the job as co-host with Alan Edmonds. She was delighted at the prospect of getting back into production, though somewhat apprehensive too. "There is that tradition in television whereby producers make their names by creating on-air images. If you are somewhere in between Barbara Walters and a neophyte you could be in trouble. It could be that nobody would want to 'discover' you."

After three highly successful seasons with *Live It Up,* Finlay was approached by the people planning *The Journal* about returning to CBC and joining the new show. It was flattering to be asked, Finlay concedes. She had assumed she was outside the mainstream at *Live It Up* and would not be considered a serious interviewer. It was an agonizing decision to make, with pros and cons on both sides. She listened to friends and mentors, didn't sleep for two months, and in the end, for better or for worse, she decided to go for it.

For most of the first year, it looked as if it were going to be mainly for the worse. Some women on *The Journal* felt the decision to hire Mary Lou Finlay as co-host with Barbara Frum was wrong to begin with, because her role was not clearly defined. Ann Medina, who was in on some of the planning sessions, said as much to the brass when asked for her opinion. "It was a ridiculous decision. Mary Lou couldn't win; she would look lightweight because there was no reason to have her there. It was pure crass on their part. She was someone attractive to bring in an audience and they sold her a bill of goods."

It is readily apparent that Finlay was put in a bad situation, as second among equals in a glorified announcer's role. Starowicz admits they calculated badly; he had originally thought the show needed not one, not two, but one-and-a-half anchors. After several months on the air, he decided that the right formula was four. Besides Frum, *The Journal* needs three part-time anchors to spell each other off while putting about two-thirds of their time into reporting or production. This arrangement makes the job creatively interesting. "But we didn't know that at first," says Starowicz, "and it's hard to predict."

In other words, it is not accurate to describe *The Journal*'s anchor team as two women; it is, rather, Barbara Frum and three co-hosts, only one of whom is a woman. Still, the impression lingers that the program is dominated by women, and this has obscured the facts of women's participation there. Mary Lou Finlay is forthright about what she has observed: "Having got the two broads on the air and made the statement, you know — 'We're daring and bold; we're the future and we're feminists and for women's rights' — no other woman appeared. We have rows of perfectly capable women and yet there are five men acting as co-hosts. There was Ann Medina — top-flight, one of our best reporters — and she was never asked.

Medina was offended and angry as she watched every other *Journal* reporter and several from *The Fifth Estate* being offered the chance to anchor. It's considered useful for a reporter to have studio experience, and most TV journalists of her age and stature have it. But Medina says tartly, "They were dragging in people off the street — but never a woman." Finally, in the spring of 1984, after much pushing, she was allowed her two-week trial. Then the routine reverted to an all-male cast of replacement co-hosts.

There is no doubt that *The Journal*'s female image was a momentous breakthrough as far as the public was concerned. It did not, however, represent a breakthrough in the treatment of women as professionals. Although *The Journal* began with a clean slate and, in putting together a production unit from scratch, had the opportunity to institute a truly egalitarian unit, it didn't. Within a short time it became evident, at least to the women on the show, that among *The Journal*'s producers some were undeniably more equal (and better paid) than others.

According to Starowicz and his senior staff (all men), there was to be no distinction between producers, but in reality the labour was divided between the general producers, who are the people who chase down the interviews for each day's show and prepare the material for the interviewers, and the field producers. The "chase" producers are tied to the office and on call all the time. Their work is invisible and anonymous, even though it contributes the nuts and bolts of the daily grind where all the pressures and tensions are focussed. Their work is closer to that of a researcher than a producer, for while they have great responsibility, they don't really have the editorial authority as the field producers do. The field producers, who produce the show's documentaries, work outside the office and are not supervised. They have the creative satisfaction of realizing their own items (working in editorial tandem with the reporter) and getting the on-air credit for their work. From the very beginning, it was clear that "chase" production at *The Journal* was considered women's work. Most of the people hired for it were women, while most of the people hired as field producers were men. Though Starowicz and company have had three years to make adjustments, the statistics have scarcely budged.

The frustration felt by the women of *The Journal* does not come from being denied opportunities that would be inappropriate, but from being denied the same opportunities given to men in their positions. And it has not escaped their notice that when it comes to opportunities to break into field production, once again, the men have an edge. "The male 'chase' producers are now doing almost nothing but documentaries," says one woman, who has since left the program:

> They have not had the same problem proving themselves, and are almost never asked to do daily work. I used to think that the biggest step in my career would be moving from secretarial ranks into production, into jobs normally held by men. Now I realize that was only the first step. You have to fight the whole way along, because you don't get promoted the way men do. If a man and a woman of roughly equal skills are both given a tough assignment, and supposing both do a good job of it, the senior editors will say of the man, "Wow, this guy's really got potential; he's going to go far." Of the woman, they'll say, "Wow, she did a terrific job, we never thought she could do that." They would see it as the top of my ability and the bottom of his. They imagine whatever they see us doing is the most that they can expect from us. The

fact that we are not stupid bimbos is a pleasant surprise to them. So it never occurs to them to push us up, or give us challenges, or to expect more than we are giving them now.

Indeed, Starowicz does not believe he has any trouble recognizing talent in women. When asked why there is more prestige attached to documentary production and why daily producers are anxious for a chance to get into the field, he replies, "Regrettably, most people in the daily unit attach more status to field production for the wrong reasons; the wrong reasons being a perception of liberty in the field and the romance of being in Beirut." He shrugs off the issue and redefines the problem as one of numbers. There aren't enough women around to fill out the proportions of his unit equally. "I can't reform the industry from *The Journal*," he pleads.

Times have indeed changed since *Seven Days* and the sixties. *The Journal*'s office does not abound in rambunctious sexist behaviour; but it has earned a reputation (and a nickname — Pig's Paradise) in certain quarters. Inching his way towards equality, Starowicz has made two appointments of women to senior positions in the past year: Maxine Crook as the arts editor and Beth Haddon as the deputy managing editor. They have made a difference that is appreciated by the women on the program. But the essential problem remains, here as elsewhere, and it is a problem for which the men in charge — even the best of them — still don't really believe they are responsible.

SEVEN

Winners, Losers and Celebrity Wives: Coming to Terms with Sex Appeal

MERLE SHAIN lives in a cosy, downstairs apartment in one of those once-stately homes on the outskirts of Rosedale — just a bit too close to Yonge Street and the subway tracks to be pure Establishment. The best-selling author of *Some Men Are More Perfect Than Others* and *Hearts That We Broke Long Ago* is one of the few Canadians who's made a good living from writing. It wasn't easy. Shain didn't achieve her international reputation without labouring through some lean years, taking risks, working inhuman hours, and raising a son on her own with one hand while tending her career with the other. Now she is at a stage where she can choose to write when she wants. The son has grown up and left home ("the rewards are starting to come in") and Shain's only domestic responsibility is a shaggy white poodle named Chutzpah, who wears a red bandana and though female is referred to as "he." "All dogs are male," says Shain.

Aside from being famous, pretty, and the woman whom Ralph Lauren once asked to join his design team, Shain is a genuine character — a true eccentric who has always cut a path for herself far off the beaten track. She was a feminist in sentiment and deed before the women's movement staged its comeback in the mid-sixties.

When her son was eighteen months old, Shain left her

husband (refusing alimony because she didn't believe in it), and set out, full of enthusiasm, on a new career, counting on her native good sense and determination to see her through. Twenty years later, she is still happily single, though hardly alone. Her life is full of friends, lovers, companions, and streams of interesting people encountered on her travels, whom she collects like treasured books. Though not far short of fifty, Shain has an impish quality about her, an effervescence and lithe physical grace that a twenty-year-old could envy.

It's easy to see why she makes such an impression on people, with her offbeat mixture of fashionable elegance and quicksilver wit, her bohemian outlook and high spirits. If Shain has arrived, though, she didn't pull up in a chauffeured limousine. She drove herself with a combination of energy, brains, nerve, and luck. "My career is a mystery to me. I've been lucky. People say you make your own luck; I'd say it's a little of both." There have been times in her life when luck kept her alive. For instance, when she was commuting between two jobs at opposite ends of the city, one at the *Toronto Telegram* and the other at CFTO, she often wondered why in her exhaustion she didn't drive herself right off the expressway.

If life seemed insecure and slightly mad during her days in television, Shain was at least right there in the middle of the chaos, exactly where she wanted to be.

> My ambition in the very early days was to be where the action was. I had just come out of a marriage that was quite confining and a career in social work. I really wanted to be where things were happenig and where life was exciting. I knew I wanted to get somewhere, but I didn't know where somewhere was.
>
> When I started in the early sixties, it was very easy to get in. I did my first radio series in 1963, for a programme called *The Learning Stage*. I had heard they were looking for a girl to edit tape at the CBC and wandered down one day, passed by their door on the way, and casually asked someone there what a tape editing job might entail. In the course of the conversation, I said I thought I had a

good idea for a radio series on the changing role of women, and I outlined the idea off the top of my head. They were interested; they had used architects for programmes about architecture and it seemed perfectly logical for them to use a social worker on this one. So that's how it happened. It was very easy; no one even asked me if I knew which end of the tape recorder to talk into.

The series, which explored male and female attitudes (and found them already hardened into rigidity among kids as young as twelve) was very radical for its time; it was before Betty Friedan's *The Feminine Mystique*, and Shain became infamous overnight. "A lot of people got very angry because of it; perfect strangers gave me shit at parties." It also attracted the attention of higher-ups in the CBC, who suggested she make herself known over at TV Current Affairs, which was gearing up for its new blockbuster, *This Hour Has Seven Days*.

Shain had originally left social work to have her baby and, while at home, had discovered two things: that she disliked domestic life intensely and ached to get back to work; and that her husband, who liked the arrangement, did not want her to go back. It was not exactly conventional in 1963 to resolve such marital differences by leaving your husband (it was called desertion), and even less common for a woman to strike out on her own with every intention of supporting herself and her child while working out an amicable way to co-parent with the child's father. Nor was it cautious behaviour to pick that moment to switch professions. "It was, perhaps, less a sign of confidence than foolhardiness. If any young person came to me today with the idea of leaving a job in social work to freelance in the media, I'd say, 'Wait, hold on, have you thought about this?'" Merle, however, went out, hired a nanny, and then started job hunting. For safety's sake, she did keep a seat warm in social work for a couple of years, but in 1965 she "sold the candy store" and dove into current affairs television, where there were opportunities aplenty but no guarantees.

I had been told to make myself available to *Seven Days*

and had a letter of introduction in hand. But I couldn't get near the place for the line-up of journalists from all over who were trying to get on that show. I was standing in the hall waiting, when Beryl Fox, one of the show's producers, came by. I was actually standing beside Larry Zolf and Beryl, from Winnipeg like Zolf, stopped to talk to him first. My radio series had just been aired and she asked what I was doing there; like everyone else I was hanging around hoping the producer would see me. "Oh, come along with me," she chortled, and shoved me into Douglas Leiterman's office.

Leiterman was on the telephone talking to Russia, trying to arrange permission for a cameraman to enter the country, while absent-mindedly cutting on a piece of meat that looked about four days old. Without stopping, he looked up and asked, "Are you tough?" I said "no," having no idea what the question meant. And he said, "Then we have no need of you." That was it. I'd been out in the hall for two days and I was so outraged I shot back, "And I have no need of being tough." And he said, "Sit down." Which has got to be the most efficient interview process in the world; he was so insolent it brought out the tough in me. That was how I started in television.

Back before I did the radio series, a friend had sent me to see Eric Koch (it was he who told me about the tape editing job in the first place) and I remember his words of wisdom about television: "There are lots of pretty girls around," he advised me, "and none of them will get on television unless a producer falls in love with them, and that won't happen because producers are all in love with themselves."

These were prophetic words, as it turned out.

Shain was also hired that year to interview artists for a TV programme called *The Observer*, so she was put on-air immediately, without any preparation or training. Before long, she discovered serious flaws in the magic medium:

Once I made the jump from radio to television, I found

the emphasis was put on very different things. Radio really was interested in content and thoughtfulness. But in television, I found I was often being hired for all the wrong reasons. A producer who might have a yen for me would hire me without ever acknowledging his feelings. I guess I was lucky, for by the time he put his cards on the table, I'd usually shown that I could do the work required. Otherwise I'm sure I would have been fired at that juncture for not living up to the producer's fantasy.

That sort of thing happened continually in early television, although I have to blame myself for a lot of it. It was the era of the miniskirt and I don't think I was aware of the response I was producing. Today I'd say that kind of behaviour may, in the short run, get you somewhere, but it costs you dearly in the long term and isn't worth it. In the end, I found it all a terrible annoyance and switched to writing. There I knew I could control my product and I wouldn't have to cope with producers' egos and their absurd interest in producing my clothes. Many of those guys had Svengali fixations and wanted to "create" you. I was "discovered" repeatedly. Every producer who ever hired me claimed to discover me. Where did they discover me anyway? Down the hall working on somebody else's show. It was a popular mental set, nevertheless, and they'd give you the old line about "stick with me, baby, and I'll make you a star."

Shain did once find herself inadvertently caught up in someone's fantasy life. The incident almost scuttled her career and abruptly ended her chances for serious work in TV public affairs. It happened when she was hired as the host for a current affairs programme in its first season by one of the show's senior producers. This was a high-profile job and a big gamble for Shain, who had reservations about taking it. It meant putting her job, her future in television, her nanny's salary, and her child's security on the line. She threw the dice, jumped to the new station, and landed in terra incognita, the uncharted territory of a man's inner imaginings and "menopausal urgings" which even he didn't know how to control:

> It was all in his head, a fantasy life I knew nothing about and he would advance and recede according to his own guilt. So he would hire you to be host, then feel terrible and guilty about what he was thinking, and then refuse to let you go on-air for weeks and ignore you.
>
> I had two opportunities — exactly two — to go on-air. The first time was when I had lined up an interview with Hugh Hefner, assuming that I would be doing the interview. At the last minute, the producer decided that he would do it and I was to cue the item dressed in a nightie and holding two bunny rabbits. I learned about the changes just before air-time, when somebody came into my dressing room and handed me a box containing a nightie and instructions from the producer that I was to put it on. They had assigned me a hairdresser and clothes designer for the show (that's all he ever talked about, dressing and undressing me), so I knew what clothes I had been assigned to wear that day and I thought the nightie was a joke. When the producer came in about ten minutes to air he was furious that I hadn't changed yet; he pulled rank on and *ordered* me to get into the nightie and onto the set. To my everlasting discredit, I did. Close to tears by this time, I was ushered to a huge circular bed and handed these two rabbits, one of which peed on me, while the other made a run for it. There was a tight shot of me and then cut to the interview.

The second time she didn't even get that close to her interview subject:

> It was the interview I'd lined up with the Maharishi Mahesh Yogi, who was a big cult figure and a coup to get an interview with in those days. This time the producer decided I'd do it wearing some kind of moslem costume, sitting in lotus position. I, of course, could not get my legs up under my earlobes in twenty seconds, so he had someone push me into the position. He'd also got this

wonderful idea that he'd shoot me through a mirror, with my head tilted back and my knees framing my head. So there I was bent in an unbelievable position, expected to deliver my lines even though I couldn't clear my throat properly. He flew into a rage and fired me from the set, saying that I couldn't project, that I was an amateur, and that he was sending me to a voice coach. (I did go and the coach wrote the producer saying no human could do what he'd asked me to.) This was all just before air-time and Barbara Frum, who was doing a piece for the *Toronto Star* about the new programme, happened to be in the control room. She called me the next day to say not to worry, that she wasn't going to write about any of it. "But," she said, "you are in trouble — I guess you know it. I'd bail out if I were you." She was right, but it took me six months to do it.

For most of those months I cried all the way to and from work. The atmosphere around the office was horrible. I was ignored by the staff, who really didn't know what to do with me anyway, and they all thought I was there because I was sleeping with the producer.

About half-way through the season, I realized he had not even told the other producers on the show why I'd been hired. At one point, when I asked one of them what I would be doing the following week he asked me why I was asking him. "I don't have anything to do with you," he said. "How can you not have any interest in what the hostess of the show's going to do?" "Who's the hostess of the show?" he asked, to my amazement. I told him *I* was, and he said, "Well, that's the first I've heard of it." So I promptly drove all the way home, retrieved my contract, and drove back with it to show it to him, and to give him his due, he was much nicer to me after that.

The whole thing was too awful for words. Macabre. But eventually, I had won over the whole staff so that when the producer would try to manoeuvre me out, they would manoeuvre me right back in. It was wonderful, but also quite hopeless. I was simply going to walk away from it all when it suddenly came to me that I could be bought out of my contract. The deal I made with the network required only that I return all the clothes and never speak of the incident to the press.

Now returning the clothes was terribly funny, because when they'd hired a designer, I'd chosen the girl who made clothes for me regularly. They were supposed to give her credit on-air and when I didn't appear, they had had to pay her for them. However, returning them meant that I was left with no winter clothes.

It was 1968, and looking for distraction from her awful situation at work, Shain had become involved with a group of people who wanted to draft the then minister of justice for the Liberal leadership race. Pierre Trudeau had agreed to meet his admirers in Toronto on his way back from a trip, though he was not at all enthusiastic about their proposition. "We were gathered in a room at the Royal York and he said to us, 'Where will you people with your fancy jobs be should I finally accept the nomination? You're going to be busy and I'll be up there alone.' So I had made a mental note to myself that should he ever declare, which seemed quite unlikely, that's where I'd go." When Merle Shain left television, she immediately got on the train and went up to Ottawa to join the Trudeau campaign team. She was one of the first to arrive. It was late winter, still very cold, and she turned up wearing summer clothes.

Years later, she ran into the producer who caused her so much grief. To her astonishment, he started reminiscing wistfully about the show. "It should have worked out. I realize that you have considerable talent, but you do understand that I was in danger of falling in love with you?" The "confession" was delivered with the expectation that it would be taken as a compliment; Shain was nonplussed but not speechless: "Do you realize," she retorted, "that you couldn't have done me more harm if you'd planned it?"

Barbara Frum recalls the incident with some disgust:

Merle was hired to be a courtesan on-air, to make the show glamorous. Even more appalling was the costume — those gauzy pantaloons. She was mortified, and understood perfectly what was going on. I interviewed the producer and he went on about how mesmerizing she was and how mesmerized he was by her. I'm sure he'd be embarrassed today. At that time, though I hadn't done any television myself, I did realize that this was a ridiculous use to make of anybody. If she wasn't a journalist, she should not have been hired for a journalistic show. To put her in a harem get-up demeaned everything, not just her. The whole process was injured.

The experience put Shain through an emotional wringer and battered her reputation. When she was being considered for a job at CFTO, John Bassett inquired whether she wasn't the "girl who hadn't worked out." The offer wasn't withdrawn (Bassett was set straight by another producer/reporter who'd been there) but Shain feels her career was badly hurt. Her move had been advertised as a big event, the press was alerted and waiting and then, nothing happened.

Merle Shain's misadventure happened almost twenty years ago, when men wore their chauvinist attitudes like badges and television was too hot not to cool down. Since then, says Shain, men have learned the dialogue of liberation. Are women still being compromised, given that men still do most of the hiring of on-air talent? There are many, Adrienne Clarkson and Dodi Robb among them, who believe the real pros can spot the elusive magic or at least recognize the right "broadcasting chemistry" when they see it. They admit that the choices often look idiosyncratic and whimsical; hiring on-air talent, even for the news, has an element of casting to it that defies rational definition. Putting the right personalities together requires intuition and imagination. So mistakes can and are routinely made with the purest of intentions.

For women, just knowing that whether they will be hired or not has something to do with their looks, their appeal, can be disconcerting. Chances are you will never know what was going on in the producer's head, or how much you owe your job to sex appeal and how much to your professional merit. For those who already have some status and a reputation, there is less ambiguity; they are able to rise above their looks. No one suspects Barbara Frum or Quebec's top journalist

The face has become as familiar to Canadians as the voice. Barbara Frum, anchor of CBC's flagship, *The Journal*. (CBC)

Gail Scott and Norm Perry in a story meeting, on location for *Canada AM*. Scott was one of the first women hired as an on-camera TV news reporter in Canada. (CTV)

Pamela Wallin, at the 1983 Progressive Conservative convention for *Canada AM* and CTV news. (CTV)

Ann Medina interviewing a Muslim holy man at the mosque in Kirdasa, west of Cairo, for a documentary report on Egypt under Mubarak, 1982. (CBC)

The sixties in private radio. Dini Petty, CKEY traffic reporter and her pink helicopter, in the station's coy official publicity shot (left) and Petty the pilot at the controls (right). (COURTESY DINI PETTY)

Mary Lou Finlay on the set of *The Journal*. (CBC)

W5's interview of the decade. Carole Taylor and Margaret Trudeau at 24 Sussex Drive, 1975. (CTV)

Suzanne Perry, Global news anchor for one week. (GLOBAL)

Christine Pochmursky, the ''Moon Goddess of Bay Street,'' as she was called by the news director who put her on the air covering the business beat for Global news. (CBC)

Denise Bombardier during the heyday of her immensely popular television show *Noir sur Blanc*, with mayor Jean Drapeau of Montreal in October 1981.
(JEAN-PIERRE KARSENTY/CBC)

Bestselling author Merle Shain started out in current affairs television in the sixties and barely survived the experience.
(COURTESY MERLE SHAIN)

Hana Gartner, *Take 30* alumnus and host of *the Fifth Estate*. (CBC)

Doris Anderson in her office at *Chatelaine* in the mid-sixties. With her arrival, the women's page tradition took a new lease on life. (NORMUNDS BERZINS)

Shirley Sharzer, associate managing editor of the *Globe and Mail*. One hundred years after Sara Jeannette Duncan led women into the editorial offices of the *Globe*, Sharzer is the highest ranking newspaper woman in Canada. (HANS DERYK *THE GLOBE & MAIL*)

Marge Anthony, CTV's vice-president for network relations. (TORONTO STAR)

Trina McQueen, executive producer of CBC's national news, on the day her former boss, Knowlton Nash, took over as the *National*'s anchorman, 1978. (CBC)

Margaret Lyons, now vice-president of network radio, has been a powerful force in the shaping of CBC radio service. (CBC)

Dodi Robb, the first woman of her generation to break the gender barrier in senior management at CBC television. (CBC)

Denise Bombardier of trading their way to the top on the basis of glamour. But they form an elite among women journalists, very few of whom are able to discount their appearance and what men think of it. This means on-air women are dealing in the world's most unstable currency — subjective male opinion about female beauty. The judgments may not be directly linked to an executive producer's private fantasy — though the rumour mill still churns out racy stories about women who were hired because a producer fancied them — and women's careers may not necessarily rise and fall with the bosses' libidos, but nevertheless, sex appeal is still a quirky and unpredictable factor.

The people who are most vulnerable are, naturally, the young and inexperienced. It doesn't help that the television industry buzzes with tales of overnight sensations, lucky breaks, and women who walked onto a set into the waiting arms of fame and fortune. It also doesn't help that it is a job hardly anyone studies for or is even coached for, before being hustled in front of cameras and lights. In many cases the only training is the audition itself. So, like it or not, any woman taking an on-air job in television is entrusting her success to the producer's casting ability, and she has to take it on faith that his judgment is not being distorted by purely personal considerations. Are women still being hired for television jobs for all the wrong reasons, as Shain was? Apparently so. Take the unpleasant case of Suzanne Perry and Global News.

In 1980, Perry was hired away from her job as press attaché to the prime minister, to anchor the news at Global. She had attracted media attention because of her blonde good looks and that volatile combination of beauty and brains that often intrigues men. In addition, there was the cachet of her proximity to the prime minister. Had she or hadn't she? No one knew for sure, but Global News Chief Bill Cunningham was counting on thousands of viewers tuning in to get a look. Perry had no experience in television but, says Cunningham, since there are people who do take to it instinctively, it wasn't

unreasonable to expect that she might. Her Ottawa connections, moreover, were "tangible journalistic assets" and, he
gloats, her audition was excellent.

Ray Heard, who replaced Cunningham as head of news at
Global just before Perry arrived and was privy to the
decision, is even more eulogistic. "Perry's qualifications were
intelligence, attractiveness, contacts and recognizability, and
the best television test I've ever seen in my life. It was
absolutely her first time in front of a camera and when the
corporate guys saw it, they said 'grab her.'"

What happened then was that Perry went on air as
co-anchor with Gord Martineau (recently lured from CITY-
TV) and — before a hungry audience of celebrity watchers
— bombed. Her audition was her best performance, which
was beginner's bad luck in her case. Once on air and in
trouble, though, Perry apparently was on her own; even the
adoring male newshounds abandoned her. The publicity
surrounding her swift, dramatic exit after four days was
unprecedented and appalling. One scurrilous *Sun* reporter
unearthed photos, taken by a friend, of her sunbathing
topless on a beach in France, doctored the picture, and
spread the word that she had been performing in a porno-
graphic movie. All this would have unnerved wonder woman.

Perry had the added difficulty of having to anchor, not
with Peter Trueman, as originally planned, but Gord
Martineau, who plainly wasn't pleased with the environment
at Global or with having to work beside a rank amateur.
Martineau wasn't long for Global's world anyway. Heard
disliked flashy good looks and thought his style smacked of
"disco journalism."

If you can talk about on-air chemistry, Martineau and
Perry repelled each other. Martineau, the debonair charmer,
is fabulously at-ease on camera. Global News producer
Wendy Dey was awed: "He could walk into a studio two
minutes before air-time and look like he knew everything
that had happened in the world." Perry seemed shy and
reserved beside him, visibly on edge, with her eyes darting
about and her body held rigid. Christina Pochmursky recalls:
"Perry was a very telegenic, but under the lights and in the
set she was lost. In a sense, she was too vulnerable for the

medium. She thought about things, and it was almost as if the camera caught her ruminating. Cunningham saw her as glamorous and sexy...but she was frightened and her fear showed."

The consensus on Suzanne Perry is that she wasn't ready and was never properly prepared for television. Heard admits he should never have put her on the anchor desk right off, that he should have started her reporting. Indeed, once she was pulled from anchoring, she did go off to get some experience reporting at a safe distance from the limelight. So she was able to turn a disastrous year to some personal good by learning to edit tape, to put stories together, and to conduct interviews. But it was too late. Perry's credibility had taken a terrific tumble and whatever hopes she may have had for becoming a television journalist were mired in gossip and sexual innuendo.

From Perry's point of view, Ray Heard and Global News never had any intention of using her as a serious newscaster, let alone training her to become one. "My impression from the moment I set foot in the place was that a decision had already been made to focus on Martineau and to exploit me for the maximum possible publicity. The message (from Heard) was very clear; it was 'I didn't want to hire her so let's get what we need out of her in the first week.'"

The worst part for Perry was not the first week but the other eight and a half months she spent at Global, when she was constantly being undermined by people around her. They took pains to remind her how badly she was doing — making sure, for example, that she saw all the worst comments about her phoned in by viewers. The atmosphere was treacherous:

> Heard would be kind and supportive privately and then publicly be just the opposite. For instance, once when I cut my foot very badly I arrived in for work on crutches, and he insisted that I go home and rest. On my way home I dropped by a store for some books and the next morning a memo was delivered to my home, copied to all the brass around Global, saying that a member of the staff had seen me at the bookstore when I was supposed

to be off sick, and that I had better have a proper explanation.

Perry had not gone to Global TV thinking it would be easy. She knew enough about anchoring to know that acceptance might take time (she also knew people were saying she got the job through political influence and her pretty face) and that credibility would only come as she proved herself. She was excited and prepared for that challenge. What she wasn't prepared for was the backstabbing. "Coming from a political milieu I shouldn't have been so naive. What's so insidious about that kind of situation is that it destroys your self-esteem and you begin believing you are as bad as they say you are." When she finally left Global (to return to Ottawa, where she now lives with husband and *Journal* co-host, Keith Morrison and their two children) she withdrew for a time to lick her wounds. The recovery was a long one. "I felt I had destroyed myself and that I actually deserved everything that had happened. It was two or three years before I fully rebuilt my confidence."

What is the lesson in Suzanne Perry's story? That even smart women with ambition can be conned by dream-weaving news executives? That there are genuine no-win situations that no amount of intelligence, talent, or guile can overcome? Obviously television can be shamelessly exploitative, and the effect on those caught up in it can be psychologically devastating. The strong, like Perry and Shain, learn the hard lessons, and go on to other things. (In Perry's case, back to communications work and on to consulting.) We can only speculate about the women who do not survive the experience, who are used, abused, and then thrown away.

If Pierre Trudeau had an inadvertent influence on Suzanne Perry's short television career, his victorious bid for the Liberal leadership in 1968 gave Merle Shain the escape route she needed out of television. She had arrived in Ottawa to find a couple of men in an empty office and stayed on through the convention as hundreds flocked to the Trudeau banner. For a time, she travelled the country with him (partly as counter-propaganda to rumours of his homosexuality.) It soon became clear, however, that female company was the last thing the campaign needed; with Trudeaumania sweeping the country it really required a quarterback from the Toronto Argonauts to handle the crowds, and that is what Shain told her candidate before returning to headquarters. The leadership campaign was like another *Seven Days* experience — madness. And at the end of it, Shain returned home, lay down on her bed, and wondered what she could possibly do next. Work on the upcoming election? "Well, John Roberts dropped by the house one day," she recalls, "and pointed out that the kind of work we'd done in the leadership campaign would now be done by ad agencies and big professionals. Why not get on the press plane and write about it, he suggested. So I called up Doris Anderson at *Chatelaine* and suggested a profile. She said 'Sure, go ahead' and then I thought I should warn her that I had never written anything before. Her wry response was only, 'Don't tell me your troubles.'"

Shain was a novice again. Out on the high seas without a lifeboat. She didn't even know how to type, let alone how to splice an article together, but she did know how to get herself on the press plane and how to get along with the press gang.

Once she had the article drafted she asked a friend, David Cobb, who was a feature writer for the *Toronto Telegram*, to vet it for her. "Your spelling and punctuation are about as poetic as your writing style, but I think you've got something," was his verdict, and he encouraged her to send it off to *Chatelaine*. The following day, Anderson was on the phone to say, "Well, you're a writer." She then offered Shain a job.

About two days later, when I was still reeling from that, David called and asked me to meet him at the *Tely*. When I got there, he told me, "Now this is what you're going to do. See that man in there? That's Ron Evans, the editor. Now you go in and apply for my job. I have just resigned and he's still in shock." He shoved me towards the door whispering, "Go for it." I just sort of stood there, feeling absurd. Apply for David Cobb's job? I had written one thing in my life and it hadn't yet been published. But I went in, introduced myself to Evans, and said David told me he was looking for a feature writer and perhaps he would consider me. "Well, tell me what your background is," he said. When I explained, Evans just looked pained and kindly told me he thought he was looking for a more senior person. "I'm as old as David," I told him — I didn't even understand that part! In desperation, he asked if I'd like a freelance assignment, and offered me $50, no doubt to get me out of his office.

A day and a half later, Shain returned with the piece and went out to lunch with Cobb. By the time she got home, the phone was ringing. This time it was Evans and John Bassett offering her not only Cobb's job, but also a theatre review spot on CFTO.

That was like on a Monday and Wednesday of the same week. I was knocked out. I didn't understand why it was happening, and I couldn't really believe it. But I also knew that obviously I wrote well, because I had had these two quite separate reactions to the same piece. It was very exhilarating for me, because I'd been working all this time in television where I had the feeling men were hiring me because I was cute. I always wondered what they were really up to. In fact, when I had the choice between the *Tely* and *Chatelaine*, I told Cobb I was sorely tempted to take the latter, because I'd had it working with men.

But Shain didn't go to *Chatelaine*, at least, not right then. She wrote for the *Tely* and began freelancing magazine articles. About five years later at a social do one evening, Ken Bagnell asked if she would be interested in doing a companion piece in the *Globe Magazine* to an article written by Toronto artist Harold Town about women and what he liked about them.

I was quite thrilled with the idea because I thought I wouldn't have to research it; I could just write it. Six weeks later I was wringing my hands and wondering if I was in menopause, because I was having hot flashes and anxiety attacks. Usually when I write, it comes in long fell swoops and this was coming in syllables rather than pages. I couldn't get anything written at all. I found myself locked into a dialogue with every man I'd ever tried to explain myself to. Then the *Globe Magazine* folded. Martin Knelman called up to tell me the good news: "Merle, this will make you happy. You can throw the goddamn piece out and get on with earning a living." In the end I took the piece to Bagnell, praying I could get it in under the wire so they would have to pay me a kill fee if it couldn't make the last issue. I'd get my $350 and be off the hook.

But they published the piece and the phone calls started coming at ten-to-eight the next morning. Then came the letters from all sorts of people: philosophy professors, teenagers, old people, psychologists and rabbis. I've got a suitcase full of them. People also started mailing the article around the country. I heard about a woman in a steel industry library who copied it and mailed it out in bulk. It got as far as California.

When the book came out, the same incredible response happened. People came knocking on my door from all over the world and movie producers came up from Hollywood. People stuck roses in my mailbox and called in the middle of the night, so I had to get an unlisted phone number, a business manager, and a whole lot of other things. Finally, I went to England to write my second book in relative quiet.

Ten years later, *Some Men Are More Perfect Than Others* is still going strong in three editions and her books sell in several languages all over the world. Shain calls her genre personal philosophy, comparing it to the French *belles lettres*, a literary tradition which takes in essays, criticism, and even biography (and the likes of Proust, Apollinaire, and de Beauvoir), but which English literature no longer recognizes. In the New York publishing world they call it the "Merle Shain book." All three of Shain's books have been enormously popular and

runaway hits with both men and women. The first time it
wasn't fun; no one, least of all the author, was ready for the
avalanche.

> It was very confusing to me and I didn't enjoy it. It was a
> remarkable thing for a writer, but I was completely
> baffled by it. I would open my door and total strangers
> would walk in. A psychiatrist from Montreal, who'd been
> entreating me for weeks to have dinner with him,
> walked in with flowers and a bottle of champagne.
> People were mau-mauing my house; men were leaving
> their wives and phoning me from hotel rooms. I found
> I'd become a lightning rod for other people's pain.
> Psychiatrists wrote to tell me I'd written the book they'd
> always wanted to write and numbers of people asked me
> to take them on as therapy patients. Eventually I learned
> that you have only so much emotional currency and that
> you can't afford to give it out on a first-come-first-served
> basis. I guess the book linked me up with more people
> than my heart could hold. And who has experience with
> that sort of thing? It just doesn't happen to people.

A lot of men wanted to meet Shain. They'd write, demanding private meetings, and some would get a bit nasty when
she turned them down. "When people responding to you are
in crisis you tend to draw out the crazies." Even those who
were sane could be annoying, for there is something irritating about people who expect an outpouring of friendship
from a stranger, on demand. On the other hand, there were
people who merely wanted to thank Shain and return the
favour her book had done them.

> That response was very touching. But overall, I was
> really very troubled because here I'd written a book
> about letting your defenses down and making yourself
> available to others and suddenly I was having to put
> mine up. I just kept thinking it was all absurd. Besides
> which, it was interrupting my work. I was lucky in those
> days to have my clothes on by mid-afternoon, because

the phone would start ringing first thing and keep me sitting around my bedroom in my nightclothes.

All stereotypes are difficult to live with; some, however, are much harder to break out of than others. One of the trickiest is the gilded trap of beauty. Carole Taylor would have had a hard time in any profession, but it is possible that television has been kinder to her than most would have been. Television is obsessed with looks; it's a surface-loving medium. It pays to be narcissistic in television. It doesn't, however, pay to be *too* beautiful, for it makes too many people uncomfortable; men and women find themselves distracted, intimidated, even tongue-tied in the presence of a real Beauty. Once they recover, they may be inclined to dismiss the mind and the feelings of the person inside the lovely exterior. Why would anyone that gorgeous want to do anything or be anyone? When you have a face that can launch a thousand ships, working for a living has to be a come-down.

In Carole Taylor's case, the circumstances that conspired against her in the beginning turned around to help her in the end. Hers is another story of chance propelling a young woman into television, of well-meaning friends and teachers pushing her into the right place at the right moment almost against her own wishes. Her high school entered her in the Sweetheart of Metro Toronto pageant, which she won easily. Not only did she go on to win other contests, she defied the odds (beauty pageants are typically won by bright-eyed, naive women who are has-beens the moment they are crowned) by going on to make something of herself.

Two early decisions separated her from the pack. In 1963, when she won the Miss Toronto title, she took the paid university education instead of the $1,000 in cash which winners had always taken before. Then in 1964, when junior broadcasting tycoon Johnny F. Bassett offered to make her host of the daily after-school teen show on his daddy's television station, she accepted but didn't give up her studies. She graduated from the University of Toronto in 1967, still thinking of television as a neat part-time job and an easy way to finance her education, and still expecting that a light would soon go on and she would suddenly know what she wanted to do with her life. Graduate school? Teaching? Business? Eighteen years later, the light has still not gone on.

Meanwhile, Taylor had taken to television and, with no training whatsoever, had mastered the studio, the technical paraphernalia, and developed her own style. She was among the advance guard of women who got themselves onto television as real people: not dancers, singers, or actresses playing parts but hosts, interviewers, and reporters. Taylor had her own show at seventeen, when Adrienne Clarkson was still doing book reviews for *Take 30*. So she was there through the salacious sixties when television was at its exploitative worst, though she herself was not actually exposed to the bad behaviour.

Despite the fact that she was young and pretty, Taylor was starting out at the top, under the protection of the boss's son. Because she kept her nose so close to the grindstone, she didn't see what might have been going on around her. She had an ailing mother to help care for and books to crack for university. She was also, for several reasons, spared the meddling of producers with delusions of creative genius. None of them could "discover" her, because that had already been done. Further, what man can tell a Beauty Queen how to fix her hair and still keep a straight face (not to mention his job)? Because she started so early in the business, Taylor had status in her early twenties and no producer would dare to tamper with her.

Having eluded the horrors and pitfalls, Taylor was still saddled with an image that took more than a decade to dispel (if, indeed, you can ever completely dispel a fairy tale that others fabricate for you and want to believe in for themselves). It is tiresome and demeaning to be cast as the Princess of Perfection in a mindless little story which isn't bedtime reading for youngsters, but your own life. Yet that is what happened, and it began when a Toronto newspaper dubbed her "the absolutely perfect teenager." From there, she went on to be the Absolutely Perfect Television Host and when she married campus football hero and star surgeon-to-be Bryce Taylor, the two became the Absolutely Perfect Couple.

Through the sixties, she continued at CFTO, doing day-time television, moving to *Canada AM* as co-host with Percy Saltzman in 1972 when the show first began. By this time, she had become the Absolutely Perfect Mother (of a son born a few months before she took on the early morning current affairs beat), and it was hardly noticed that the move represented an important shifting of gears in her career. *Canada AM* was network television, which meant national exposure and the opportunity to develop her journalistic skills. Taylor had auditioned for the job with thirty-five other candidates in a contest that was designed to test, not on-camera poise or mental agility of the thinking-on-your-feet variety needed for interviewing, but knowledge of economics, politics, and the stuff of current affairs. Taylor won not only the job, but the admiration of CTV news boss Bill Cameron, who had no qualms about shifting her to *W5* after one season on *Canada AM*. (She had quit in frustration because of terminal incompatibility with Saltzman, who was in the invidious position of being the upstaged star of the show.) It didn't, of course, stay the tongues of cynics, who went on carping that she was a "no-talent."

At *W5*, Taylor was lucky to form a partnership and friendship with the unit's only female field producer, Joan Donaldson. Donaldson was a seasoned veteran who had had a brilliant career in radio news before she moved into television news for CBC. Close in age, though diverse in talents and experience, the two women had a lot to learn from each other. Says Donaldson:

> Carole's special quality is being a good journalist; she really loves a story and will go after it and wrestle it to the ground. She's the one I liked to travel with on *W5*, because she worked as hard as I did. And she supported me; we were a team. It wasn't a matter of who got to write the script: if we were on the fly, one of us would write it and we trusted each other; we vetted through each other as part of the process. She was one of us; we were us.

Both women were a decade into their careers by this time and tentatively starting to reassess their lives, their work, and their working relationships. *W5* gave Taylor journalistic experience that she had not had much of before. Working in the field was an eye-opener; reporting on events as they were happening and witnessing the filth and chaos of war (Chile after Allende, the Middle East after the Yom Kippur war) was exhilarating but often unpleasant. The death and destruction she saw there had a powerful impact on someone who had only seen dead bodies in funeral parlours up till then. There was one very memorable day spent in the Syrian desert interviewing Israeli soldiers and being strafed by MiG jets. Driving back, watching the sun set in magnificent splendour over the wasteland of destruction and human decay, and listening to the strains of classical music over the car radio, "The contrast just crashed in on me. It was one of those moments you never forget. I don't want to sound superficial, but I came back and cleaned out my life," she said in an interview later. House-cleaning entailed liquidating a marriage that had already ended, doffing the Perfect Woman stereotype, and embarking on a personal odyssey that many women of her generation were taking. It meant taking charge of her life and reassessing old decisions. "I had never asked myself if I wanted to get married; it was what I was socialized to do." She had done it at twenty-one, when "you are too young to know what personality you will be or where your interests lie."

Like Donaldson, Taylor had spent most of her working life working with men. She had never really had a woman friend until her late twenties, so it was fortuitous that such a friend should turn up in her life at just the right moment. In those days, says Donaldson, "It was really hard to define your role. You always had to swing between being very aggressive and trying to be decorative. It was just hard to be yourself. Carole and I found allies in each other." And Carole found not only support but some relief in a situation that allowed her to work with women. She is, today, hosting a CBC television show, called *Vancouver Life*, with a mostly female production team. "I really like this experience. There is a much more relaxed atmosphere with women. You don't have to worry about sexual innuendos or whether anyone is coming on to anyone else, or about travelling together. There just aren't those old worries you have with men about hurting their egos. With women, I find it a much straighter working relationship."

Taylor managed to get her life back together after her marriage ended in relatively short order and without the prolonged angst that her most famous interviewee on *W5* suffered. The 1975 encounter with Margaret Trudeau on the lawn of 24 Sussex Drive was a national political sensation, because it revealed the prime minster's wife hanging out the family's emotional laundry. This was not going to be Camelot on the Ottawa and P.E.T. was not as endearing and gallant a husband as he had been a bachelor. But the interview may well be remembered for something else entirely — it's a social documentary recording the meeting of two troubled, middle-class married women who'd lived through the sixties but had been strangely untouched by the personal and political questioning going on around them. Instead of emancipation, they signed themselves into traditional marriages at the age of twenty-one. Now they were both trying to dig themselves out from under the role and the image, while mighty forces of disapproval were ranged against them.

Trudeau had a much tougher fight (including the tacit and insidious assumption of those closest to her that it wasn't the marriage that was coming apart, but her own mind). To the delight of the media vultures, she took to flaunting her rebellion in public. Taylor's burden was an adoring public who wanted to script her life for her. When she took up with the mayor of Vancouver, Art Phillips, a married man with five children who was then separated from his wife, they invaded her private life, writing letters chastising her, advising her, even threatening her. The press loved it; living in sin was "in", spicy but acceptable enough to write articles about. And what could be better copy than the romance of the country's trendiest mayor and its loveliest television star?

Maclean's dispatched Marci McDonald to Vancouver, where Taylor was living, while commuting to Toronto on first class air-fares ("You make concessions for stars," said CTV) to continue her work as solo host on *W5*. McDonald wrote a sympathetic piece, titled "Carole Taylor Doesn't Want to Be Perfect," which drew a sensitive portrait of the superstar dilemma but was then unabashedly trivialized by the people who write the headlines and captions: "She was the Prom Queen who married a Prince and Lived in Golden Places. Then she ran off with the mayor of Vancouver." "Sweethearts of the Seventies — rich, beautiful and liberated, and discovering that it's lovelier the second time around." "Beautiful winners believing in all the right things, taking life on their terms, creatures of their time." So not being perfect had, through the perversion of the media lens, become the perfect thing to be.

Being a celebrity is another word for living in a fishbowl, where everyone can see in and then write in to tell you how to do it their way. Through sheer endurance, with the help of shifting attitudes and social mores, Taylor has succeeded in beating the Perfection rap. She has also avoided being permanently type-cast as a brainless beauty and has acquired the experience and skills of a first class broadcast journalist, wresting an interesting career in her unintended profession from the jaws of cosmetic success. She even defied the powerful centripetal force of the media industry when she moved to the West Coast. She was warned her career would not survive the distance, but it did.

Taylor hasn't quite beaten the public's obsession with her, though. With a sigh, she acknowledges that particularly good-looking women attract more of the lunatic fringe, more obscene mail and threatening intrusions on their privacy. It makes her think she would be happier on the other side of the camera. "But it happens that what I do best is on camera. When I took a break a couple of years ago, it was mainly because I craved some privacy, a chance for some time out without people watching, writing, and telling me what to do." A sabbatical from the fishbowl.

There could hardly be a more poignant example of a woman trapped in an image than Margaret Trudeau, the flower-child wife of the nation's first minister, who grew up to resent being the flower in his lapel. Often, it seemed she was participating in the gossip swirling around her. But her predicament and the public's view of what was happening to her was the creation of a large group of people who surrounded her and structured her life down the smallest detail. They included powerful, important men from the inner-most pantries of power in government and the Liberal Party. In Margaret's case, there was very little room for swimming inside the bowl. Unlike Taylor, who also drifted directionless through her twenties, Trudeau had no market-able professional skills of her own to fall back on.

When Trudeau did flounder in the role of celebrity wife and mother, there was no outpouring of public sympathy. People found it hard to summon compassion for someone whose main problem in life seemed to be the burden of too many servants. After she separated from Pierre Trudeau and began looking around for a career, she had a difficult time overcoming the image long enough to get the training she needed and a place to start. She settled on television, which at first seemed like masochism, or at least a case of compulsive foolhardiness. Why take up with the very trade and the same types who had burned her so often? What made her think she wouldn't be used again?

Trudeau hasn't changed her mind about the media and the people who practise the profession; she still distrusts journalists, especially those who work in print. But she has learned a thing or two. In 1982, when she took a daytime host's job on CJOH TV in Ottawa, she was perfectly aware that her entrés were a pretty face and her name, probably in the reverse order. She gambled, though, that she could trade these in for a guaranteed audience, at least long enough to get some training. Suzanne Perry's experience at Global served as a lesson:

> I felt Suzanne Perry was badly used the way I'd been often — exploited for the publicity. I was offered network television right away. But I was not going out there without some expertise behind me. What I'm doing is taking time to learn, so that if I do have a career in television I'll have the training. I was not going to try out in front of a national audience; it is quite different with a kind, local audience that forgives your mistakes in the beginning.

Ironically, television gave Margaret Trudeau the chance to

settle down and get some solid experience. Other television pros who were interviewed by her say that she was thoroughly professional and very competent. She and Carole Taylor are examples of women who got into television because they were already well known and could pull an audience; women who were able to use their fame as a lever to get training and opportunities on which to build. But as a strategy it can be tricky, because it's hard to discern if you are attracting people or are merely an attraction, and because it is such a temptation to the base commercial instinct of broadcasting executives. Nevertheless, it puts the famous names and faces in a class apart from most other women in the media, who have only their individual native abilities to negotiate with.

Sexist attitudes don't just trap the young, the beautiful, and the inexperienced. Very capable women at the top of their performance have occasionally run aground on it. That is what happened to Denise Bombardier.

Bombardier has been called the Barbara Frum of Quebec, not only because she occupied the chair opposite Frum on *Le Point* (Radio-Canada's equivalent of *The Journal*) during its first season, but because, like Frum, she made a name for herself with a little programme that fooled everyone by becoming a runaway, popular success. This programme, which propelled her to stardom as a television journalist, was called *Noir sur Blanc* (Black on White). It was an hour-long, low-budget interview show that focussed on books, writing, and criticism. By its fourth season it was commanding an astounding audience of half a million, even though it was stranded in the backwaters of the schedule on Saturdays at 6 P.M.

Noir sur Blanc was Denise Bombardier. Her interviewing style and her demanding, incisive intelligence were her trademarks. She was the first woman to have such a show of her own and the first since Judith Jasmin to participate at a senior level in the making of current affairs television. The public took awhile to get used to the novelty. "I was interviewing all these politicians and I am supposed to be a tough interviewer. Yet women in our society are not raised to question authority figures that way. So here was a young woman who was not timid or afraid to ask questions the politicians couldn't answer. This was very new."

Bombardier went to *Le Point* partly because everything in Radio-Canada's TV current affairs was being moved or cut back to clear a path for it. But her career also needed a change. For their part, the producers planning the show needed a reliable, top-flight journalist with star status to draw an audience. Bombardier was ideal. The assumptions both she and producer Michel Beaulieu (*Noir sur Blanc*'s co-creator who went with her to *Le Point*) made at the outset were that the style and tempo of television journalism they had developed would become a prominent element of *Le Point* and that the show would focus on Denise.

Bombardier was paired with Simon Durivage, who came from Radio-Québec and had many years in radio current affairs behind him. Although he was well known, he had neither the track record nor the status of Bombardier, and capturing the anchor job on *Le Point* was a much bigger career advance for him. Long before *Le Point* hit the air, there was speculation about how these two would get along. When the show finally appeared, everyone watching could see at a glance that there was little rapport between them. Each evening they appeared side-by-side in stony formality, looking for all the world like the gingham dog and the calico cat ready to devour each other on the stroke of midnight.

With hindsight, it seems logical that people would wonder how someone used to making her own decisions and working with a small, tightly knit team would take to working with a unit of sixty. Would she like sharing the limelight? For that matter, why did no one consider whether Durivage, a man roughly Bombardier's age and just as ambitious, would willingly play second fiddle to a woman. If one of the co-anchors had to be in charge, would he cede to her expertise?

Bombardier had her answer within days. "I knew from the beginning I'd been burned. I knew that I could not continue. I had thought the journalistic approach would be different and I disagreed with almost everything they put on the air. But I had no say in it." She had expected the isolation, being the only woman at the top of the hierarchy, but she had not expected the dismissive treatment she was given in a unit headed by a band of men who "clearly didn't want me there." Bombardier is circumspect about describing her ordeal. "You can say that there are men who cannot stand being in a situation where they have to defend their opinions to a woman. At meetings they would tell me I was talking rubbish, philosophically what I had to say was shit. I think Barbara Frum is well treated; she has told me she is. That was not my experience."

It quickly became an open secret that Bombardier was not happy and that there was a "personality conflict" between her and Durivage. Less well known was the fact that a rift had developed between Bombardier and the senior editors of the programme. Word leaked out through professional circles that Bombardier was the problem; that she was difficult to work with and an intellectual elitist. The critics joined in the fray, and when they saw *Le Point* staggering through the week, turning off more and more viewers (ratings fell from a kick-off high of 550,000 to 180,000 by spring) they blamed Bombardier for the cold, hard tone and the "wall-to-wall interview" format. Even her own boss, the Director of Information Programming, Pierre O'Neil insinuated publicly that her approach to journalism was responsible for *Le Point*'s lacklustre performance.

It was all a rude awakening for Bombardier. Her sense of professional power as a journalist faded. Even so, she made some useful discoveries about herself. "I discovered that I am not a woman of power in the male sense; I am not willing to play the game myself. I am fascinated by people who will sacrifice everything to power — love, family, everything — to a myth. I am fascinated because I don't understand." She continues "I have been a fighter all my life but I found out I could not fight that kind of battle" — by which she means the squabbling with Durivage over position and who would lead off each evening with the first item and the Machiavellian games being played by the men around her. She didn't appreciate having to jockey for position, to argue for recognition and the right to be heard, and when she realized that the winner would take all she knew she would not come out ahead — no woman would be allowed to.

So Denise Bombardier chose discretion over vain valour and made the most important decision of her career. She quit *Le Point* and left current affairs. In so doing, she found that she could walk away from the lights and the cameras and the accoutrements of media stardom; turn her back on the seductions of prime-time television. She has since taken on two programs in another department where, she says thankfully, a woman is the assistant director. The score-keepers might claim the move is a retreat to a lower status department and that she has been defeated. Personally, Bombardier feels she has gained more than she has lost, even though her career has certainly been set back. It is also true that most of the egg flung at *Le Point* stuck to her, and she was tagged as a Difficult Person in the same way that Lise Bissonnette was when she took a strong stand as editor-in-chief of *Le Devoir.*

Listening to Bombardier, reading the press accounts of *Le Point*'s turbulent first year, one realizes how difficult it is to broach the subject of chauvinism in a professional setting. Personality conflict, as everyone knows, is a euphemism for a multitude of sins including sexism. And it doesn't take a radical feminist to recognize that Bombardier was a woman alone at the top and that the guys were playing hardball.

Getting along and making it possible for the on-air journalist/host to do her work is the responsibility of senior direction. At *Le Point,* they reneged on this responsibility and turned Bombardier into a scapegoat. All the while, the press studiously avoided speculating on the male-female dimension of the conflict as if it were a nasty family secret. Clearly the situation traded on negative stereotyping and on attitudes consciously and unconsciously held, conspiring to bring out the worst in just about everybody. It is hard to imagine a male journalist of Bombardier's stature, say a Patrick Watson or Pierre Nadeau (her replacement on *Le Point*), being subjected to such behaviour. It is hard to imagine such a situation happening without sides being taken and protests made. And it's hard not to be cynical about Denise Bombardier's experience, not to see it as a straight case of the boys closing ranks against a woman with too much ego for their comfort.

One thing that is certainly needed for working on air in television is an ego: not necessarily a mammoth one, or one that's pathological, but an ego large enough to support the weight of public attention. It is therefore remarkable how often on-air personalities will tell you in hushed and earnest tones that they are really very shy and private people. Such assertions are, perhaps, more accurate in some cases than others. It is true that some people — Mary Lou Finlay, for example — are quite at ease in the studio in the company of the crew and fellow workers, but nervous in front of a live crowd, even a small one. Others (Gail Scott and Pamela Wallin, for instance) see themselves first and foremost as journalists, and bury their egos behind a smooth professional manner.

Assertions of shyness or modesty may, of course, be defensiveness against the presumption on our part that anyone who would choose to put herself in front of a camera and in the public eye *wants* to be in the spotlight and must have an inflated opinion of herself. Some do; the television industry has its share of prima donnas and superiority complexes. The fact is, being on air can be an ego boosting experience. Some personalities get a bit drunk on it, begin to believe their own PR and become addicted to the daily "fix." Others who have tried hosting back off. Jane Fairley, now the production manager for *The Journal*, started out at CITY-TV "as a cameraman in the days before there were camerawomen or camerapersons." She found on-air work, which she flirted with briefly, a very heady experience. "The need for feedback from others is extraordinary and it may distort some people. It may take a certain kind of personality, I don't know. I do know it didn't do great things for my ego. 'How was I? How was I? How was I?' was all I could think of."

To be an on-air host does require motivation, something to drive you in front of a huge, anonymous, and seemingly imaginary audience. The motivation could be intellectual or ethical, the job being a means of serving some other end besides self-gratification: the desire to find out the truth, a naked curiosity about people and events, the desire to help right wrongs of the world. Yet, however honest and altruistic your motives, the ego is still the vehicle for realizing them. At the best of times, one can only guess at the underlying psychological or emotional reasons people have for wanting to work on air.

Hana Gartner's reasons seem complex and somehow enigmatic. She began in private radio in Montreal as a student fresh out of Concordia's communications arts programme — ready, willing, and bursting with enthusiasm to "use me. I wanted to use me." For three years, she had carte blanche from station CJAD to provide items of her own invention to a daily show hosted by Andy Barry. Following her instincts and roving eclecticism, she took a trip with a trucker on a short haul to Toronto, tape recorder in hand, to explore the "psychology of the road"; went sky-diving at the invitation of an instructor who called up looking for some good publicity ("I wanted to decide for myself"); and even had "the gall" to share her favorite poetry with the audience. She was fascinated by other people's lives, and had a feeling "for the Studs Terkel kind of thing." She got herself to India and Israel and reported back about what she saw.

She had fun:

> I had a good time and I put my heart into it. Nobody could have had a better start. Without knowing it, the station manager gave me the opportunity to inflict more pressure on myself than he ever could in a million years. He just gave me air-time and a 50,000 watt radio station to play on. What I did defied any job classification, and had I started with the CBC and a job spec I probably would not have gone on as quickly as I did.

CJAD was followed by a stint covering the 1974 federal election and then came an offer to get into television on the local evening news. There, she was spied by Ross McLean, who liked her and was impressed with her jovial calm in the face of a loss of sound (he was watching a feed in his Toronto office). Subsequently, he invited her to Toronto to host a light current affairs programme called *In Good Company*, which followed the six-o'clock news. It was not a success, however, and when the show was dropped, Gartner found herself reading the news and liking it less and less.

Gartner felt her career was drifting backwards, so she quit. By her own account, she then spent the better part of a year "very much unemployed," living on her savings doing the rounds in a city she found didn't like to hire people it didn't know. "It was my first professional setback," she says, "ten months of 'I'm a failure, I can't get a job,'" and wondering if she was being hurt by rumours suggesting she'd been fired. In the end she went to Robin Taylor, the new head of TV Current Affairs at CBC and, with his recommendation was passed on to the executive producer of *Take 30*. Mary Lou Finlay had just departed and the producer was looking for a new female co-host. Gartner's stay lasted five years, during which time she had opportunities to pick up other shows in between seasons in the summer (*This Half Hour*, for example, in 1978) and broaden her interviewing skills.

Robin Taylor was there again at the next juncture in Gartner's career, this time as executive producer of *The Fifth Estate*. As usual when a host's position comes up on a premier show, the grapevine worked overtime guessing who would be appointed to succeed Adrienne Clarkson. Gartner was not thought to be the strongest candidate, but she did have some seniority and the stalwart support of the man doing the hiring. "I guess Robin Taylor always had faith in me. I know I'm better in a situation where people have faith in me and I have to live up to their expectation, rather than my going out to prove something on my own." Now on her fourth season, Hana is thriving and more than holding her own with the two male hosts.

Among media women who have made it into the winner's circle, Gartner is something of an anomaly. For one thing she has never freelanced or developed projects on her own. You could not describe her as a career journalist who happens to be doing television; rather, she has become a television personality and she seems to have few other ambitions or interests. Concerning the possibilities she explored during the period she was "between engagements" she jokes, "I don't know, a correspondence course in brain surgery?"

Almost by a process of elimination, you come to the realization that it is the medium itself that intrigues her most; the
experience of being out there on an electronic limb, with
stopwatch ticking and heart thumping. She talks a lot about
"being thrown off the deep end" in jobs and how she likes it.
"I have always been nervous and frightened. I mean, I like
the feeling; I like that feeling when I put that foot out of the
airplane at 5,000 feet and feel it flop around like a wet
noodle with someone telling me to get out on the strut
because I'm going to fall away from the plane. I like that. It's
perverse!"

Despite her unemployment experience, Gartner isn't perturbed by the faddishness of the business or television's
gluttonous appetite for new faces. "I have no insecurity
about that. I don't worry about what's going to happen to me
tomorrow or about getting older. I'm not worried about what
will happen the day they don't want me. I'm more worried
about the day I don't want *it*. I've thought about this, about
the fact that I don't play around the way I used to at CJAD
radio. It's different, and the adrenalin rushes are fewer and
fewer."

As a youngster, Gartner was attracted to the theatre, and
actually applied and auditioned for the Yale Drama School.
She didn't think of television at the time but she did know
definitely that there were elements of live performance that
she thrived on. "I liked being on stage; I liked the relationship,
that creative exchange between audience and the people on
stage. I also liked the attention, being centre-focus. But I
didn't know specifically what I wanted to do."

To this she added a free-floating interest in people,
especially those involved in dangerous or oddball activities. A recent *Fifth Estate* item on organized crime had
Gartner interviewing a retired hit-man, which appealed
strongly to her taste for the bizzare:

> That day was wonderful. All we had was access to the
> man (and he had changed his mind about it a couple
> of times); no research, nothing. He was under police
> protection, as there was a contract out on his life, so we
> did the interview in a motel hideout. It took a lot out

of me but I loved it — getting to dabble in a lifestyle you would never want to get close to. I had that same tingly, nervous feeling, a little tickle in my lower digestive tract when I was with the killer, just like when I was making a parachute jump. He got very mad when I asked tough questions and suggested he was a stool-pigeon. "You've killed and now you want to change?" I didn't want to be a bleeding heart *or* accusatory and getting the right balance is difficult. Most of the letters we got were sympathetic to the murderer, and called me a bitch for not believing people can change!

To other women who have worked with her, Hana Gartner is aloof, though not unfriendly. She is utterly dedicated to her work; it consumes her life and, unlike her predecessor, Adrienne Clarkson, she does not insist on having a circle of friends outside the business. Gartner studiously avoids office politics (work keeps her on the road a good deal, in any case) and does not cultivate friendships there. "The people at work are not my buddies, they are the people I work with." She is, in short, a loner. Although she has perfected a good-natured "one-of-the-boys" bonhomie with the crews, she keeps her ideals and her emotions to herself, concentrating her energies on the work at hand. She is, understandably, uneasy about being interviewed and being asked to be introspective with strangers.

Perhaps a lot about Hana Gartner goes back to the immigrant experience, coming to Canada as a three-year-old with parents who had given up a secure existence and comfortable life in Czechoslovakia:

They lost their property and the plant (which manufactured comforters) to the communists and then left the country, following the DP route to Austria. For a year they tried to find a country to accept them and then Canada allowed them in. I don't remember the trip but I do remember one of the first places we rented. At the time, Canadians didn't understand immigrants and if you didn't understand English people spoke loudly to you as if you were stupid and treated you as some kind of peasant. They were explaining to Mummy what a light switch was and what happens when you flush the toilet. My parents went through a lot; had to redesign their lives and start over. But they never talk about how much better life was in the old country.

The family didn't move into a Czech community, but settled down to learn English and make good in their adopted country. "We talk about the loss of the language and once I tried to pick it up. I feel some guilt about losing it, but it was natural too. For a time I was an only child (my brother was born here, eight years after me), and Mummy thinks it was all a very wrenching experience for me. I hated school from kindergarten; I didn't speak English and I didn't want to be around other kids." It was the same through high school; she had few girlfriends but basked in the warm, supportive friendship of her immediate family and lots of encouragement from her parents to be an individual and have pride in herself. Her family remains her community and the mainstay of her life.

If Gartner keeps to herself and does not have close relationships with the women she works with, she does get along well with the men, in particular the executive producers at *Take 30* and *The Fifth Estate*, Ain Soodor and Robin Taylor. This is something of an achievement, as both men have well-earned reputations for being hard on women. But Gartner has an ability to screen out the nonsense, concentrate, and get her own job done. As a veteran who has worked her way into the heart of a man's profession, Gartner is aware of the barriers but not particularly sympathetic to the plight of "fellow female travellers." "I don't have any more obligation to someone who wants into this business because they're female. If a man and a woman come to me for advice I wouldn't feel, well I should help the woman. I don't think like that." This is because she believes that nobody gives you your rights and, human nature being what it is, individuals simply have to stand up for themselves. Thinking about how her own mother overcame hardships on arriving in Canada she explains, "I don't think a situation stops you from expanding. I think you stop yourself. When we did a documentary on battered wives, I never understood what it is that makes a woman who's humiliated and beaten stay in that situation. I wanted to hit those women. People get used to good and they get used to bad and become complacent."

There are other contradictions. Beneath the self-assured exterior, she claims it is a lack of confidence which propels her; a shy insularity that others read as self-absorption or egocentricity. There is one thing, however, which everyone agrees about: the camera loves Hana. She looks fabulous on air, and consequently, has had few of the usual hassles from her producers. She has had far more trouble with the press and the people who assumed when she cut her hair and got contact lenses before joining *The Fifth Estate* that someone was making her over into a "sexier, chic-er Hana." Then there is the preoccupation of "everyone who's ever interviewed me" with her predisposition to gain weight. "Television can't tolerate it and I decided to make a consolidated effort. Even though I have a high energy level, I don't burn calories. But all the interviewers get into that; it's boring, it drives me crazy."

Whatever qualms Gartner may have about herself totally disappear on-camera. Inside she may be quivering; outside she glows with well-being and sociability. As an interviewer she's outgoing and affable and visibly enjoys what she's doing. It's tempting to wonder if she isn't most alive, most at home with the world, and most at ease with herself when the lights go on.

EIGHT

"Women's World"

EIGHTEEN EIGHTY-SIX was a red-letter year: the year Canadian women broke through the heavy brocade curtains of Victorian decorum and became working journalists. It was the year Sara Jeannette Duncan returned in triumph from the United States and resumed her newspaper career in Canada, not as a "lady journalist" sending in delicate dispatches from some gilded perch away from the day-to-day hurly-burly of putting out the paper, but as a regular member of the *Globe* staff. She was the first woman given a desk and a place among the men in the newsroom and the first woman employed in an editorial capacity by a leading city daily. When she inaugurated her column "Women's World," she inadvertently launched a tradition.

The debut of a separate page in the newspaper dedicated to women's subjects and women writers was symbolic, evidence of the gathering strength of women in society. Originally, the women's page was not a ghetto but the exact opposite: it was claimed as a platform from which women could address the general public and voice their own opinions. It represented a step out of the domestic shadows onto the public stage and was a declaration of female emancipation. The first women's pages were not treated as second-class sections or as a playground for not-quite-professional journalists. They were often widely read by men as well as women and, on occasion, the women writing for them became better known than male reporters plying their trade in other sections. During the suffrage campaigns at the turn of the century, moreover, the women's pages became important politically. They were a natural forum for airing views on the subject of the vote and the role of women in society.

Over time, however, the original spirit and energy that inspired the women's pages slowly dissipated. They ceased to be a window on the world, lost the cosmopolitan outlook of the early years, and turned inwards. There were ups and downs in this history but, by the time the women who would take part in the second wave of feminism were coming of age in the 1950s, the women's pages supported the most conservative attitudes of the day. They took part in the effort to entice women out of the workforce and back into the cocoon of food, family, and fashion. From radical roots, the women's pages had grown into a thoroughly reactionary tree. Professionally, they had become institutionalized dead-ends and any woman with real intentions of becoming a journalist avoided them.

In 1963, Donna Logan graduated from university with degrees in political science and journalism and the clear determination to practice her profession. Those being the days when employers cruised university campuses brandishing job offers, she had five to choose from. She selected the Halifax *Chronicle-Herald,* primarily because she was about to marry a man who lived there. It was a lucky choice, though Logan didn't appreciate it at first. At the *Chronicle-Herald* she was allowed to try her hand at almost everything, starting with the police beat, "a fairly rough-and-tumble thing for a woman," and including sitting in occasionally for the vacationing editor. Thus, when she decided to move to Montreal two years later, she was already a veteran. Still, she was not hopeful of getting work in Quebec because she was not then bilingual. Before she left, her boss offered to call a friend at the Montreal *Star* to put in a good word for her. Both of them were surprised by the response: her lack of French wasn't going to be a problem; being female was. All the same, the recommendation got her an interview with the *Star*'s managing editor, who was disposed to bend tradition a bit. Although two women in the newsroom was unofficially considered "enough" at the *Star,* Logan became the third.

The *Star* was going through a bad spell at the time. A new editor-in-chief named Frank Walker soon arrived and quickly decided to shake the place up. He appointed a new managing editor, who in due course approached Logan with the proposal that she take over and revamp the women's section. "At first I said no. I wasn't at all interested. But he insisted they wanted to change the section and needed someone to do it who hadn't worked in the department before." Eventually, Logan took the job. She redesigned the women's page, calling it "Lifestyles," and proposed a thorough-going reorganization that would involve the dese-gregation of the women's section and its complete integration with the rest of the news department.

As Lifestyles editor, Logan sat on the city desk with the other editors and all assignments for all departments were handled together. The change, she admits, was chaotic. "We knocked down the walls around the women's department and all the women's reporters, who had been hived off behind glass in a separate world of their own, were put out onto the general floor. It was unreal. I was used to it, but the other women weren't and a couple of them fell by the wayside. They just couldn't hack it."

Mercifully, the changeover was not protracted. "I quickly got a couple of new reporters to replace those who'd left. I hired a graphic designer and redesigned the section. Once we got it really zinging, the reporters were coming to me with stories and ideas they wanted to do for this section. I felt like an orchestra conductor. All I had to do was direct." Logan is a bit embarrassed about admitting she was the first to use the term "lifestyles" in Canada, but by any name, what she did with the section was bold. At the Montreal *Star* women took a giant step out of the ghetto.

Logan was twenty-four when she masterminded all this. Of course, it was not a one-woman job, as she had neither the authority nor the clout to pull it off on her own. Frank

Walker wanted sweeping changes. He liked Logan's concept and backed her. "The editor-in-chief trained under E. Cora Hind at the *Winnipeg Free Press* and believed that women could do anything they wanted to do in the newspaper business."

Walker did more than smooth the runway for Logan. He took her on as one of his protégés. "Walker made a career of being a mentor to people he thought had a spark and he was prepared to spend endless amounts of time with them." He spotted Logan, groomed her for the spectacular career he saw in her and gave her responsibilities, room to be creative, and all the support necessary:

> All the news content decisions were centralized. There were no preconclusions about where a piece would go in the paper unless, like a fashion shoot, it was obvious. After general assignment, the copy would come back to the city desk for sorting, and the material for Lifestyles would come to me. I immediately found myself faced with what I call "the abortion-Lifestyles mentality."

It first happened with the Henry Morgentaler story. The city editor looked at it, read abortion and thought, "Ah, Lifestyles." Logan looked at it and read "Page One." "The city editor told me there was no way that story was going on the front page. So I went to Frank Walker and though he was a Catholic he backed me. Having won the battle once, however, didn't mean it would not have to be fought again. Every time that story came up it happened. For me, it was grit-your-teeth-and-don't-blow-up time."

Under Donna Logan, the women's page entered a new era and found a new audience. "We were looking for a different readership, younger and of both sexes. It was no longer to be a page for women only, although there were some items which would have interested only women. When we did fashion and beauty, we did it for both sexes, and everything was approached that way." Slowly, over the next decade, the women's sections of other Canadian newspapers started opening up. Sometimes only the name was changed — to the

Leisure, Family or Life section — and sometimes newspapers had to be badgered into going even that far. The *Globe and Mail* retitled its women's section the F Section, which, as managing editor Clark Davey said at the time, could stand for family "or whatever." The old-style women's sections had come to be seen as quaint vestiges of the past, insulting to women.

Today, while familiar women's page material is routinely included, there are also human interest items and coverage of social policy issues. As we are heading for this century's *fin de siècle*, it is fitting that the women's page has survived in its originally intended spirit by expanding its outlook. Once again, it is sometimes possible for the women writing there to broaden their scope and deepen their analysis. The reason is that newspaper executives stumbled on the discovery that men could be attracted to the section too. A bigger readership breathed life into Lifestyle because it also fed dollars into sagging advertising receipts. Despite the prejudices against "soft" news, the section has acquired new lustre and a bit of prestige within the profession.

Michele Landsberg grew up wanting to be a writer. More accurately, she grew up fully intending to be one; from the age of four, when she remembers writing her first poems, she constantly practised. As a small child, she was precocious in several other ways. She was exceptionally pretty, and began modelling at four and acted professionally on the stage and on radio, contributing to the family income, by the age of nine. "At twelve, however, I completely rejected the female role. I became a raging feminist, read Simone de Beauvoir and wore blue jeans to school, which was strictly forbidden. Boys' jeans, with fly fronts!" No one could understand it, least of all Landsberg's "dainty, lady-like" mother. For some time, Landsberg had been silently rebelling to herself in her writing. Now she openly expressed her interest in things intellectual. It was while reading the French existentialist philosopher Jean-Paul Sartre that she came across a reference to Simone de Beauvoir's seminal work, *The Second Sex*.

Without knowing why, Landsberg knew it was a book she had to read; she sensed that it would have something to say about the malaise she felt.

But it was easier to read Sartre at his most abstract than to get *The Second Sex* out of the library. The book was kept in the adult section, and none of the librarians would let her borrow it, so Landsberg had to mount a campaign. She had a whole string of neighbourhood libraries she visited regularly on her bike (each would lend only three books a week, a starvation diet for a intellectual in training) and she hit every one of them. "The St. George Street branch had the book behind the desk. I begged and pleaded and put in a request slip for it, but they thought it was about sex and wouldn't give it to me. I just kept pestering them until someone finally did." It was worth it. Her instinct had been right: the book was a revelation. "I'll never forget the thrill of reading that book. Someone finally was saying what I knew to be true, and that transformed my life."

After she graduated from university but before she had figured out what she wanted to do next, a job with the *Globe and Mail* landed in her lap. She had written a piece as a favour for a friend who was the paper's crime reporter (it was a story about poets breaking the Sunday by-laws by giving readings) and his editor had been very impressed. Though she had never contemplated going into journalism, she decided to give the job a whirl.

For the next two years, young Landsberg did general news, entertainment, and some investigative reporting. Then she cottoned on to the fact that in the women's section she could take a month or so to research a series, which was impossible on the news side. Eventually she made the shift, and found it to be a great job. She had all the leeway she wanted and she learned to work efficiently and to write clear, crisp prose. Things went smoothly for quite a while; her pay was raised regularly and her assignments were good. Only gradually did it dawn on her that she had stopped progressing in her work, that she was treading water professionally. She knew she needed new opportunities, but she didn't know how to make them happen. "I was not aggressive about my career," she says tersely. But then, no one expected her to be.

"On my first day at the *Globe*, I was sent down to run the bureau at the CNE with Geoffrey Stevens. He was being groomed by the *Globe*; I was not. He was expected to have ambition; I wasn't." Stevens is now managing editor of the *Globe*, which is not necessarily what Landsberg aches to be doing, but she does wonder what would have happened had someone higher up likewise praised her writing and fed her ambition with phrases like "we have plans for you."

Stymied by the situation and weighed down with advancing boredom, Landsberg waited. In the meantime, she married Stephen Lewis, and in due course nature solved her problem. "I think I got pregnant because I was bored," she admits a bit sheepishly. Three Lewis children arrived in quick succession and Landsberg took the next five or six years to be with them. After her husband became leader of the Ontario New Democratic Party, a job which inevitably affected the family's finances, Landsberg had to go back to work.

> I phoned the *Globe* because the two men in charge, Dick Doyle and Clark Davey, had told me when I left to come back anytime, that the *Globe* wanted me. When I called Davey he was extremely insulting. He listened, and then after a long pause said to me, "Have you thought about trying the *Don Mills Mirror*?" I hadn't expected trouble like that; I was naive perhaps, but I had taken those men at their word.

Landsberg began making the rounds, wondering if she was going to find full-time work anywhere. She put out feelers to the *Star*, and word came back through friends that managing editor Martin Goodman's response had been to the effect that he wouldn't touch the wife of the NDP leader with a thirty-foot pole. Everyone hedged because of her political connection until, with desperation creeping up, she went to see Doris Anderson. Landsberg had written some freelance articles for *Chatelaine* before; now she proposed that Anderson hire her as a staff writer. The trouble was that the position was already filled and there was no room in the budget for another. Instead, Anderson offered to guarantee Landsberg eight freelance articles over the year and give her office space at the magazine. "It was a lifesaver. Of course, she was no fool. She was getting a staff writer cheap. But she never said one word about my political affiliations and she was the only person who treated me like a writer whose work was valued." It was, she says, a good lesson about discrimination against political wives.

Over the next seven years, Landsberg was a staff writer and later articles editor for the magazine. Then Bonnie Cornell, with whom she had worked at *Chatelaine*, moved over to the *Toronto Star* to edit the Family section and began coaxing her to come and write a column for her. Though dubious about returning to newspapers, Landsberg gradually let herself be persuaded. Once again, she went to work for a woman who was blazing trails. "Bonnie was the first in the daily press to make women's issues, feminism, and equality an absolute focus. She doubled the size of the section, initiated the food and fashion sections, hired me and lots of others and beefed up the writing."

Never having written a daily column before, Landsberg didn't know what she was getting into, but she hoped it would be good for her writing and she believes it was. "It forced me to be lucid, to make strong, clear arguments without empty rhetoric, to be vivid, concrete, and humane. You don't set out to write like that, but you just know what you want the column to be." The formula? Follow your own instincts and be prepared to work like a dog: eighteen-hour days, seven days a week, with no clerical staff to help with the research or even the correspondence; getting along on three to four hours' sleep a night for three years. That was Landsberg's way. "The first years I would rewrite things eight times or more until it was perfect. I am an insane perfectionist compared to most newspaper people, who can write off the top of their heads. I would polish even the inconsequential pieces."

The column which arose from this ferment was wonderful:

> From the very first column, I got tremendous, enthusiastic response from people at the *Star* who cared about good writing, and right away it became clear that there was a huge audience out there for real talk about

women. To my astonishment, I found that I could be strongly feminist; I could say things I had never thought of putting into print before. Perhaps this was a holdover from my childhood when I thought of my convictions as mine alone — ideas that no one else would understand. But the women's movement had come and gone while I was having babies and I hadn't realized how widespread these perceptions had become.

There were men at the *Star*, though, especially older men, who were resentful of things I said. For example, when I wrote a column about rape in marriage (after the case in Oregon in which a man was charged with raping his wife) some of them went berserk. They came over and banged on my desk, thundering "How dare you!" I thought they were crazy. They seemed to be saying that the right to rape your wife is the foundation of marriage.

Landsberg had her supporters (the publisher Beland Honderich was a "champion"), and her detractors. Gary Lautens disparaged her opinions, but as editor-in-chief he could also read a balance sheet, and he was not about to can the paper's most popular columnist.

Michele Landsberg is the very picture of ebullience: vital, energetic, exuberant, vivacious, although these adjectives don't convey the quality of forbearance underlying her optimistic outlook, or the quiet anger that has settled like ballast in her character. She is short and broad, a soft, motherly figure of a woman who defies all the commercial conventions of femininity and still embodies its elusive essence. She greets you at the front door of the family home and ushers you through a large vestibule bearing the familiar scars of teenage traffic. She pads briskly out to the kitchen (recently renovated into a beautiful, airy room that reaches out to the back garden), comes back bearing mugs of good strong coffee, and settles in at the large dining room table.

Landsberg remains an intellectual, but her lifelong romance with ideas has not removed her from people. Down-to-earth and practical, and fuelled by a flame of rage at injustice, especially injustice to women, her perspectives on society and politics never sink into abstraction. In real life, she is just as she appears in print: clear-eyed and generous, a woman's woman. She is an includer and she speaks with the collective "we," locating herself within a community, as part of a movement that touches all of us. Her sense of solidarity is infectious and, as someone who spent long years in the wilderness as a loner who didn't fit in, she relishes belonging to a crowd. That consciousness, however, wasn't won without tears.

Writing a column in a major daily newspaper gave Landsberg automatic credibility as well as a platform. Building on that, she attracted an astonishing following, which she credits modestly to two things: honesty and the willingness to admit being wrong. "For instance, I told people I have had a lifelong, humiliating experience with fatness. Very few people will admit such things, and it wasn't easy for me either. I think people trusted me a little more because of that and perhaps were more willing to entertain what at first may have seemed to them outrageous views." She was also willing to be corrected by her readers, like the women who wrote in furious at her dismissive reference to housewives.

One of the most painful, yet instructive, clashes Landsberg had with her readers occurred in 1979, when the Toronto-based feminist paper *Broadside* brought out its first issue:

> It included an excoriating attack on the public press and dumped on the *Star*, along with everything else, without ever acknowledging there was a sister, a feminist voice there. At the time, I was feeling pretty lonely, all by myself, so I wrote an attack on *Broadside*, which was very wrong of me. I let my hurt ego goad me into writing a column that should never have been written. Here was a brand new baby put out by a bunch of feminists and it shouldn't have been attacked by someone with my powerful position in the daily press. Except I didn't *know* I was powerful.

Landsberg sighs when she speaks of it. "I learned the hard way, by bouncing off people I would have hoped to consider my sisters in feminist struggle, that I had more power than I realized." It took Michele Landsberg a while to assimilate that incident, to see it for what it was — a clash of vulnerabilities. "I'd hurt them without intending to and they hurt me without thinking they could, because they didn't know they were strong enough to injure someone who had a column in the *Toronto Star*. I learned a great deal from that about divisions among women." Bouncing back and forth between the radicals and the housewives in her audience, Landsberg began redefining herself. "You throw your views out into the world to rub up against all the other views and you get a clear picture of who and what you are. You see, I never wanted to see myself as a bourgeois housewife — which in reality is what I am."

"From 460,000 to over a million." The phrase follows Doris Anderson around like a mascot. It symbolizes her achievement as the doughty editor of *Chatelaine*, the magazine she ran for twenty years with the cunning of a master mariner racing under sail in open ocean. Doris Anderson guided *Chatelaine* through the 1960s and most of the 1970s, two momentous and turbulent decades for women, doubling the magazine's circulation as she did it. Actually, the achievement was even more dramatic than the statistics make out. Anderson took over as editor in 1957, and within two years the paid subscriptions had shot up from 397,000 to 719,000, and continued to climb at a steady pace in succeeding years. She turned *Chatelaine* into the most lucrative magazine in the Maclean-Hunter empire, a consistent and dependable money-maker that carried other, less successful publications (like *Maclean's*) along on its surplus. This situation once prompted *Maclean's* editor, Ralph Allen, to refer to himself as "Anderson's kept man."

Anderson had inherited a magazine founded in 1928 (the year the Supreme Court of Canada ruled that Canadian women were not persons) as a consumer magazine for Canadian women, the majority of whom were housewives not working outside the home. It had been launched with a nation-wide campaign to find a name for the publication and the first issue promised to tell the true story of "how the winner thought up the $1,000 title."

The first cover was a period piece of stylized design,

depicting a woman in a magnificent floral patterned frock that billows across the page, obscuring the two little children to whom she is reading from a gigantic book. The content of the magazine is encompassed in that one picture and, as you might expect, inside were features about home planning, fashion, gardening, and cooking, accompanied by general articles, profiles, and fiction.

All, however, was not macaroni and cheese. Women in 1928 had had the right to vote and hold public office for ten years, and the excitement of that victory was still palpable. Some of the momentum carried on through the twenties, buoyed up by irreverence for the past and passion for new styles and new attitudes and everything modern. The roaring of the twenties was the din of speakeasies, radios, model T's and vacuum cleaners; the sound of social customs collapsing, old morality colliding with new. *Chatelaine*, true to the *zeitgeist*, burst onto the newstands with a modern, forward-looking confidence.

From 1929 until 1952, *Chatelaine* was edited by Byrne Hope Sanders (cbe) who championed the twenties version of up-to-date womanhood while sticking closely to old-fashioned ideals about woman's primary role as *materfamilias*. By the fifties, *Chatelaine*'s orientation was firmly directed inwards, celebrating the housewife/mother who had by then moved to suburbia, was marrying younger, and getting divorced more often. Articles stressed the care and feeding of the male sex and, as the readership expanded to include teenagers, included advice on how to catch your man as well as keep him. Typical titles were "How to be a Good Listener," "What You Don't Know about Your Husband," and "How to Cook for a Man."

From the beginning, the nuts and bolts of *Chatelaine* were its service departments: Fashion and Beauty, Housekeeping, Meals of the Month, Needlecraft, and For Chatelaine's Young Parents. The advertisers followed suit, cramming the pages with pictures and praise for food items, household appliances, and cleansers of every description. When Anderson became editor, the staples were retained, but the tenor and tempo of the magazine changed immediately. She recalls:

We redesigned the whole magazine, giving it a more

modern look with lots of white space and contemporary graphics and layout. I started columns on mental health, on activities for women in their communities, and on politics. I was trying to open up the whole magazine. Occasionally I would get a letter from a woman saying I was trying to entice women out of the home, but not often because this was the sixties and things were loosening up.

In short order, Anderson devised a matchless combination, maintaining *Chatelaine*'s tradition of service to the readers and garnishing it with solid, provocative journalism. She ran feature articles on current issues, extensively researched pieces on divorce laws, trade unions ("how they let women down"), baby beating (as child abuse was called in 1960), poverty ("why the real poor are women") and a comparative analysis of salaries in several fields. Conventional wisdom about women's lives was challenged rather than coddled in Anderson's *Chatelaine*. She treated homemakers as professionals and gave them expert advice and detailed information covering the entire range of housekeeping and child-rearing topics. The emphasis was less on how to keep hubby happy and more on how to lighten the housewife's load and improve working conditions inside and outside the home.

Anderson's single most significant innovation was her editorial. Inside the front pages and under the masthead, she set the tone and staked out the territory *Chatelaine* would cover. It was a perspective that was feminist and woman-centred but outward looking. The view may have been from the kitchen, but it reached as far as world politics. Month by month, she elucidated the women's issues of the day, advocated reform, cajoled governments and policy-makers, and incited her readers to action. Ten years before the contemporary Women's Movement was born, Anderson was arguing for enforcement of equal pay laws, for women's right to a free choice about abortion (1959), for opting out of the Happy Homemaker's role if it doesn't suit (1963), and occasionally taking dead aim at a stubborn myth. "Do Women Really Dominate Men?" she asked in 1959. Throughout the sixties, Anderson's editorials were patiently tilling the soil of public opinion, politicizing two million or so Canadian women about their rights and the need for programmes and social legislation to protect them and their children. Behind the scenes, she was also pushing for the appointment of a royal commission inquiry into the status of women. When that came to pass, she followed the commission's deliberations and became a self-appointed "national nag," tracking the fate of its 167 recommendations.

To the women who wrote for *Chatelaine,* the magazine was irreplaceable. It was the place where they could write on subjects like politics that would never be assigned to them by other general interest magazines. For Michele Landsberg, "It was a place where you could ask, 'Why aren't there more women in parliament and what the hell's going on with pensions?' and get paid for it *and* get support and encouragement from Doris."

Anderson assembled a group of writers of differing political persuasions and ages who were at different stages in their careers. When Michele Landsberg went to work there, she candidly confesses:

> My feminism was there but it was not the burning issue for me that children were. Doris fought me every step of the way on that. When I wanted to write a piece on breast-feeding, she would insist that I balance it and not overemphasize the importance, in case I made other women feel guilty that they had to wean their babies and return to work. I didn't understand their point of view then; I had contempt for it. But Doris was sensitive and was always on the side of choice for women.

Landsberg soon joined with the other *Chatelaine* women who would gather around at editorial meetings once a month to complain that yet another nameless model was being put on the cover. It wasn't feminist. "It sells copies," Anderson would growl. End of the monthly debate.

Landsberg was an editor at *Chatelaine* in the early seventies, when the Women's Movement was in full flower, visible, articulate, and quite unaware of the progressive tradition harboured in the bosom of the media mainstream. At *Chatelaine* Landsberg felt she was part of a pioneering effort, that *Chatelaine* was doing things no one else was doing and that it had been playing a significant role in tending feminism for a decade or more. But the young feminists didn't want to know; they assumed she was part of the problem:

> I remember when the Women's Centre on Dupont Street opened. I was thrilled. At last other women were getting interested, were going to gather information about women in Canada and lobby for change. I went high-tailing over there, and their reaction was more or less "drop dead, we're not interested in the bourgeois press." I didn't understand that they were like the American student movement in its iconoclastic resentment of anything establishment and in its fairly diffuse rebelliousness. Now I also think there was an age gap. *Chatelaine was* (and *is*) a bourgeois magazine; it *did* have ads for cosmetics and bras. It was middle-of-the-road, and if it published a pro-choice article it would also print the opposite point of view. I think it was hard for younger women who didn't have children or care about recipes to get past those trappings which were there for the ordinary reader and see the valuable things *Chatelaine* was doing.

The surprise was not that differences existed between Landsberg and these young feminists, but that the younger women were so categorical in their rejection. But if *Chatelaine*'s radical history was not recognizeable to them, it certainly was understood in Maclean-Hunter's boardroom. On a couple of occasions, Anderson came perilously close to sinking the boat, and the ship's owners were not amused. "The piece on abortion almost got me fired. It was the first article (in Canada, anyway) which suggested it might be sensible to have legal abortions if a woman's life were in danger, if she had been raped or was carrying a grossly deformed fetus. Two years later, I was still getting letters."

Anderson used to joke about the fact that one in three Canadian women read *Chatelaine* and that they all wrote back to her. But she counted on those letters. Through them, she kept her finger on the pulse of the rank-and-file readership, gauging the moods of large, usually quiet segments of the population — rural women, for instance. She responded to their opinions and criticism and watched for openings to advance the debate. Anderson did lead, but she always listened. Her editorials never harangued the unconverted or talked down to the unliberated. From her first editorial, she assumed that there was a common cause among women, based on a shared experience, and assumed there was work to be done to improve the situation for all women. She was able to be as forthright and as radical as she was because she mixed her prescriptions with generous respect.

Still, one wonders. How could the publishers and board of directors countenance detailed articles about equal pay when they themselves were guilty of discrimination? (The editor and senior writers at *Chatelaine* were paid well below their *Maclean's* counterparts — as much as $10,000 below.) Anderson is matter-of-fact about that. "They didn't want me to push articles on feminism or inequality or anything like that, but I was already doing it before they realized what was going on and the magazine was *very* successful." She could trust the board not to stand in the way of a good profit margin.

Doris Anderson grew up in Calgary, the only daughter (and middle child of five) of an apparently mismatched couple. Her mother married twice and, notes Anderson with a grin, seemed fatally fascinated by handsome, n'er-do-well men. Her father was a man of ideas and an atheist who wanted to change the whole system; her mother, a fervent Anglican, was a traditionalist. "It was an interesting household to grow up in, though, for there were two points of view being presented most of the time."

Anderson has often talked about her early impressions of marriage, which she gleaned while looking around at her own family: a grandmother abandoned on the prairie with six kids to rear and aunts similarly deserted by wayward husbands. There was one exception, the aunt who "married well," but to young Doris she seemed to be living a cloistered and boring existence. The message she got was not against domesticity or even children, but it did warn against marrying young, and against marrying without training or one's own means of support.

On one thing Anderson's parents did agree: she wasn't over-protected or kept away from the games her brothers played. She was encouraged in her independence, and she began to claim it early. At school, she discovered there were restrictions on girls that didn't affect boys:

> I must have been a feminist even then and thought it was wrong that women weren't given more of a chance. I remember being taken aside by a male teacher who told me I was a good-looking girl and I should marry a nice boy. "Don't fret so much," he told me, "it won't get you anywhere." The women teachers were bluestockings, suffragettes, and what I got from them was their great expectations. They truly believed that they were teaching a generation of young women who would achieve things they had not been able to do.

Anderson started writing soon after she learned to read. She produced a book at the age of ten that she bound together with string and presented to her family, who passed it around admiringly. The relatives were less impressed with other traits she displayed: the hyperactive imagination of a future writer which led her to embellish the truth. Once out of high school, she sold her first story to the Calgary *Herald* for five dollars. And at university she worked as a stringer for an Edmonton paper that later offered her a permanent job on the society page. "That seemed much less interesting to me, because as a stringer I had been covering everything from football games to fires."

Anderson was a high-spirited adventurer. She wanted to go places and do things, to write novels and work for the newspapers. She soon concluded that this meant leaving the West. With a train ticket, eleven dollars, and the address of the WCTU women's residence in her pocket, she took off to Toronto. Her first jobs were at the *Star Weekly* and in Eaton's advertising department, writing ads for thread and pincushions in the notions department. After a while, she landed a job writing and researching scripts for Claire

Wallace — which was more interesting but no picnic. Wallace was a tough boss: "She went through a whole string of people because she was difficult to work for. I wasn't a protégé of hers in any sense. But every time I quit my pay was raised, and when I left I was making a rather phenomenal $75 per week."

Anderson saved her money and with proceeds from the sale of three short stories to three magazines (including *Chatelaine*) she took off to Europe, spending three months in Paris and longer in London.

Back in Toronto in 1951, Anderson got a job on *Chatelaine*'s advertising staff. For some reason, she hadn't tried to pursue her writing as a full-time occupation even though, after publishing her short story, Byrne Hope Sanders had invited her to come in for an interview. Anderson had taken it as *pro forma* politeness. Her stay in advertising was mercifully brief. Sanders soon had her working on the editorial side. Then, in 1952, Sanders resigned as editor and two short-term replacements ushered in a period of change. Anderson had the opportunity to try all sorts of things (though she resolutely resisted the efforts of higher-ups to turn her into a copy-editor) and eventually got the chance to write features. From there, she jumped into a senior position managing the service department, a responsibility which made her the boss to several old-timers, "some of whom," she recalls, "did resent taking orders from an upstart" in her late twenties.

When the managing editor left, Anderson took over his job and ended up essentially running the magazine. Finally, she was in direct line for the top job when the editor left to work at *Homes and Gardens*. She was also just about to get married, and to her humiliation and chagrin all the men involved assumed she wouldn't be interested in the job.

> Floyd Chalmers (the publisher) won't admit it happened, but it happened all right. He dropped into my office one day with the news that he was going to make Gerry Anglin the editor. "Well, I'll resign," I told him. He was stunned. "But you're getting married and you're going to be a hostess" — I loved the priority — "and a mother!" My future husband didn't want me to take the

job either. He thought it was fine being married to a managing editor but he didn't want to marry the editor — which was *the* big job. Damn it all, I'd worked for it.

Anderson knew that she was better qualified than Anglin, the man she had succeeded as managing editor and who had, in fact, taught her a lot about the business.

But I really didn't think he knew as much about women and women's magazines as I did. So I gave my husband a choice: either I'd stay at home and write short stories and he could support me, or I would take the editor's job. Reluctantly, everyone agreed; they decided to give me a chance, though I didn't get the title for a year or so. As 'managing editor,' I completely redesigned *Chatelaine* and had a baby while I was doing it. *Then* they made me editor.

It is easy to see, now, that Anderson was merely twenty years ahead of her time. She spent her young adulthood travelling and experiencing the world and then settled down for a stretch of concentrated apprenticeship in a chosen profession. Only when that was well under way did she take on marriage and family and neither caused her work at *Chatelaine* to skip a beat. By the late seventies, women's magazines were chronicling the new professionals and late motherhood. But it was Anderson who field-tested the formula. Aside from everything that she wrote about from a feminist point of view, she was herself a role model who made it possible for other women to see themselves as successful writers and editors.

The 1950s saw the women's pages sink to their lowest; those years might well have witnessed the demise of a tradition, had not daytime radio breezed in just at the right moment. In 1952, Helen James became assistant supervisor of the Women's Interests Section of the CBC's Talks and Public Affairs Department. It was she who oversaw the launch of an innovative programme called *Trans-Canada Matinee*.

Matinee was a magazine show, so-called because its format was borrowed from the general-interest magazine.

The broadcasting day was carved up into much smaller bits in those days. Fifteen minute programmes were common, and even shorter ones, mostly commentaries, were sprinkled through the CBC schedule. The magazine show was a revolutionary concept, both simple and ingenious. Public affairs producers were handed a large chunk of airtime, but instead of presenting a programme on a single subject, they programmed many small items, varying style and pace with music, short drama series, mini-documentaries, commentaries, and interviews. They broadened the appeal of the programme while rendering it more flexible and accessible. For one thing, listeners could now come and go as their domestic routines dictated: it was possible to join the programme at any point and quickly catch up. It was altogether a more entertaining approach to current affairs and it was as liberating for the producers as it was for the audience. Without having to sell the brass on new programme ideas, rally the budget to get them produced, and wrangle a slot in an overtaxed schedule, they were free to try them out on *Matinee*.

Since it belonged to the Women's Interests Section, *Trans-Canada Matinee* never amounted to much within the CBC, never mind how popular it was with audiences. The recognition wasn't there and neither were the resources. Helen James was willing to put up with the situation, as Elizabeth Long had been before her, for one excellent reason:

> Since we were a daytime programme, the members of parliament were not listening and neither were the senior officials of the CBC. We were, therefore, able to deal with subjects and use words that could never have been used in the evening. We broadcast an eye-witness account of the birth of a baby in 1952 with Allan Anderson right there in the delivery room.

Other taboos were breached: birth control was discussed on air and contraceptive devices were mentioned by name; subjects like homosexuality and masturbation were dealt with. Most of these feats were accomplished without fanfare. *Matinee* was never hauled over the coals for impropriety, though it is true that the childbirth documentary was never re-broadcast. "Women's College Hospital," James explains, "happened to be in the middle of a fund-raising campaign and the wives of several of the men on the board of directors were furious about the programme and said they wanted nothing to do with a hospital that would allow a man with a tape recorder into a delivery room."

There were other "indiscretions" that passed without notice. *Matinee* continued to use women as political commentators and often in its consumer items mentioned products by name. There was probably a rule against that, James admits with a twinkle in her eye, but it didn't prevent Dr. Janet Robertson from telling listeners what she thought of Lipton's Soup. "She advised mothers that Lipton's Soup only filled up children's stomachs with water as it had scarcely any nutritional value. The company protested and we offered them the chance to come on the air to reply, which they never took."

Helen James herself was a convert to Women's Interests. Although she worked there from the beginning, she had gone out of her way to avoid being identified too closely with women's programmes, sensing that it would limit her own horizons. Six years later, she was boldly using Women's Interests to pioneer a new kind of radio programme while opening up the field of current affairs to a female audience:

> I was tired of hearing the refrain of women saying, "I'm just a housewife." To me it is a very great job and I wanted to give it prestige. We all talk about our own work among our peers, so *Matinee* talked about home-making as an occupation. We introduced a weekly "Matinee Quiz" and brought in outstanding experts in psychology, nutrition, medicine, textiles and so forth and invited the audience to send in questions that would be answered on air. My motive was to recognize the complexity of the job, to give it some status.

Trans-Canada Matinee could deal with controversial subjects because the programme was sheltered from the glare of the public eye, and because the CBC was a public broadcaster. Programmers like James were not required to kow-tow to the wishes of advertisers or conform to their notions of community standards. "We were not trying to please everybody. What I was concerned about was demonstrating that women had broad general interests and a knowledge of the world that corresponded to men's. I didn't like this ghetto business or the suggestion that women's interests are entirely different."

With this conviction firmly in mind, James set about changing the name of her section to Daytime Information, although she's realistic about the effect the name change had on CBC brass. "I'm sure the hierarchy went right on thinking of it as Women's Interests." As head of the department, James was similarly treated as the ladies' auxiliary by management. "I always had the feeling that I was included in meetings as a token. I'd be the only woman and I disliked it very much. I disliked the way men fell over themselves at the door, letting me in or out, and I disliked the patronizing way they would suddenly come to and realize I was in the room and ask for my opinion."

In her turn, Helen James was succeeded as head of Daytime Information by one of the great pioneers of TV production in Canada, Dodi Robb. All was not well at CBC Current Affairs when Robb returned in 1965, after fifteen years in the private sector. Television and radio were still coupled administratively, to the general detriment of radio, and the place was churning in the aftermath of the *Seven Days* mutiny, which happened when the CBC brass canned the much-watched but controversial Sunday night prime-time TV programme in the name of good taste, employee discipline, and corporate policy. Robb still can hear James' words to her as she prepared to take over:

> The only thing she said to me was, "Dodi, I'm glad you're tough." She didn't say anything else but that chilled my blood. I think part of her frustration was not being

allowed to do the shows she wanted and I think she was painted into a corner by an arrogant group of people who essentially told her to go away and write memos. I had to tell them I was not going to accept that role, that I hadn't been doing what I had been all my life so that I could write memos.

Trans-Canada Matinee, in the meantime, had been joined by a sister programme on television. At first it was called *Open House*, with Anna Cameron as host, and it debuted in 1955. In 1962, *Take 30* came along. Under Robb, *Take 30* became what *Trans-Canada Matinee* had been under James: a place where women were favoured and where women producers, broadcasters, researchers, and freelance journalists were given a chance. There was nowhere else in the corporation, with the possible exception of children's programming, where women were so welcomed.

Both Robb and James considered it part of their mandate to develop women and, as a result, over its twenty-two-year lifetime, *Take 30* raised two generations of eminent women broadcasters. Its alumni include Adrienne Clarkson, Hana Gartner, Mary Lou Finlay, and producers Madrienne McKeown, Margaret Fielder, Donnalu Wigmore, and Cynthia Scott. Robb glows with pleasure when she thinks about the talent she watched pass though *Take 30*'s studios.

> The show had a very good reputation and I was proud of it. Particularly when I had the alliance with Adrienne, with Donnalu Wigmore (who has since won several Golden Harp awards for her documentaries), and Cynthia Scott, who won an Academy Award for her short film, "Flamenco at 5:15." God, I could scarcely believe it. There she was in front of 500 million people; accepting the Oscar, the best in the world, and I remember talking with her about her decision to stay in television or go into film. That's pretty heady wine.

Robb's approach to television production is the team approach. Her recipe for success is simple. "You have to do things the very hard way. I always demand that you go that extra mile, to get the visuals, to work with the performers, to define who your audience is and what we should be broadcasting and when. I guess we were all imbued with the desire for excellence." Being wily and wise in the ways of the corporate world, Robb knew how to protect her programmes; and she was blessed with a boss "who was always pushing and defending *Take 30*" in the upper councils of the corporation.

On one thing Robb never compromised; *Take 30* was a women's programme. That was why it was always most strongly identified with the female host by the public and not the male co-host. "The executive producer liked to think there were a lot of men out there watching, but I always felt that fuzzied up the thinking." *Take 30* had a female audience and Robb had an unerring sense of exactly who that was:

> She is a woman with two kids, perhaps three, who are under five, and who lives in Willowdale and it's February and she has no car and she's going crazy. I've never seen her, but I can feel her. For half an hour every day, there was a programme which treated her as an intelligent, sensible person and someone worth talking to.

Robb's male colleagues, she vividly recollects, were quite content to believe that all the afternoon audiences wanted were soap operas and game shows. No doubt some did, but, she maintains fiercely, "there was another group and I had half a million of them tuning in by the end. That would fill the O'Keefe Centre or Place des Arts three times a day."

Like Helen James, Dodi Robb was acutely aware of the stigma attached to daytime programming. Children's and so-called women's programmes were treated with benign contempt by corporate potentates and her own colleagues in public affairs. *Take 30* was, in their view, amateur current affairs that would never be ready for prime time. But Robb was equally aware that, basking in the shadow of neglect, she had a freedom unimaginable in the evening hours.

"We were avant-garde. If you are sly enough, you can do things when people aren't paying attention. We were doing stuff on birth control before anyone had decided on the corporation's policy. We didn't only talk about it, we showed the devices." While prime-time current affairs was busy being flashy and controversial, *Take 30* was quietly dealing with topics the mainstream would not have the courage to address for a decade, such as interracial marriage, television violence, legalized abortion, and teenage sexuality. All of these were discussed in *Take 30*'s first year. Subsequent seasons high-lighted items about prescription drugs, the alcoholic's family, a series on the family (the generation gap, the empty nest, parents without partners, remarriage), and women and depression. *Take 30* talked about forbidden subjects and more important, as far as Robb was concerned, it talked about feelings. Ordinary, everyday, convoluted, contradic-tory human feelings. In 1968, the show did a series called Women Alone, comprising interviews with women about their lives, about aloneness and loneliness.

In typical women's page fashion, *Take 30* combined cur-rent affairs with Mme Benoit's cooking lessons. Its curious eye roved as far afield as a ruthlessly husbanded budget could be made to stretch — to Japan, Eastern Europe, or North Africa. If the show specialized in anything, it was probably the celebrity interview, *Take 30*-style, for the celebrities included eggheads as well as actors — Jonathan Miller, Margaret Meade, and Betty Friedan along with Agnes Moorehead, Harry Belafonte, and Carol Channing.

Take 30, together with *Matinee* and *Chatelaine*, set out to explore the shifting conditions of women's lives and the murky depths of relationships between the sexes and within families. They looked at the personal and the political, studied the repercussions of the sexual revolution and the Women's Movement, and checked back to see what effect it was all having on the family, marriage and monogamy. Together, they assembled a unique social document of an extraordinary era.

In the 1960s, the women's pages took a new lease on life. New women were recruited and a new script written. In Quebec, in the French language publications, the same thing was happening. There too the women's pages have a long and venerable history that reaches back to Gaëtane de Montreuil and the debut of the *page féminine*. In the French media we can also detect the existence of a "women's page" tradition, similar yet in some particulars quite distinct from the one that has evolved in English Canada. It too lies half-buried, awaiting its historians, and, for the last twenty-five years, it has also been busy remaking itself.

The career of Michelle Lasnier spans those twenty-five years, following a path from the women's page at *La Presse* to *Châtelaine* to Radio-Canada's long-running television success *Femme d'aujourd'hui*. A career such as Lasnier's would not have been possible earlier, because the programmes and publications simply didn't exist. Apart from the popular "advice to the lovelorn" shows on radio and the obligatory section in the newspaper, there was no place to go. There was no women's page dedicated to presenting female audiences with anything more challenging.

Lasnier came to journalism in 1956 out of ignorance. At twenty-six, she had spent her entire adult life at university (including four years at the Sorbonne in Paris), in a closed and protected milieu a long way from the mainstream of contemporary Quebec life. She chose journalism because she wanted to learn something about her society and she figured that daily reporting would give her a crash course.

As luck would have it, the first person she encountered upon returning from France was an old family friend who was then the drama critic for *La Presse*. He blithely invited young Lasnier to give him a call at the paper, suggesting that her opportunities were good. A week later, he was on the phone to tell her, while apologizing profusely, that *La Presse* didn't actually hire women except for the women's department, where there were no openings. Odd as it may seem now that the hiring of women has become a political flashpoint, many men were oblivious to the fact that women weren't to be seen at their workplace because their own employers had strict rules barring them.

In due course, an opening did come up: Lasnier applied and was hired in the department begun by Gaëtane de Montreuil fifty years before and joined the team of women in discreet, if not splendid, isolation next to the president's office on a floor separated from the rest of the editorial department. The arrangement, Lasnier recalls, was meant to "protect our morality."

After a couple of years, Lasnier applied for a transfer to general news. Management deliberated and did finally agree to the move, but she elected not to go through with it. Some other women had preceded her into the "men's" department and what she saw happening to their work cooled her ambition:

> I saw their reports appearing on page fifty-two of the paper, hidden among the 'petits annonces.' So I decided to stay with the women's page where *we* decided what stories to run and where to place them, and where the concept was very open. We covered all sorts of stories which you would find in the general news section of the Montreal *Star* or the *Gazette*. We were also well-placed in the first section of the paper near the editorial page and the international news.

In 1960, flush with the success of Doris Anderson's *Chatelaine*, Maclean-Hunter decided to introduce a French edition. They approached Lasnier and Fernande Saint-Martin (her boss at *La Presse*), and the two became editors of the new enterprise. For Lasnier and Saint-Martin, it meant creating something that hadn't existed before — not, at least, in living memory — a woman's magazine that treated women as sentient adults, not merely consumers of romance novels and soap operas. *Châtelaine* adapted Anderson's serviceable formula, twinning traditional women's information with articles on current affairs. It was speaking to a readership that belonged to a more traditional society than did their sisters in the rest of Canada. Quebec women were not granted the vote until 1940, twenty-five years after Nellie McClung and Cora Hind triumphed in Manitoba. But it was also 1960, the inauguration year of the Quiet Revolution, and every aspect of Quebec society would be open to question in the decade to come.

Lasnier stayed with *Châtelaine* for its first four years and then struck out on her own to freelance. For several months she filled in for an ailing Louise Simard, the creator, host and producer of *Fémina*, a fifteen-minute daily interview show, broadcast to a mid-morning, primarily female audience. Simard had built this into an institution in Radio-Canada's schedule. Lasnier, who had never worked in radio before, was immediately delighted with the programme. It allowed her to range freely across a widening spectrum of interests, and "every Wednesday was politics," she says triumphantly.

Lasnier's stay with public broadcasting was supposed to be temporary but in September 1965 Radio-Canada launched a new afternoon show on television, called *Femme d'aujourd'hui*. A few months after it went to air, Lasnier was drafted as executive producer and thus began a sixteen-year association that eventually placed her at the head of "émissions féminines" for the French network.

Femme d'aujourd'hui followed *Take 30*'s magazine format, presenting a mix of women's page material — food, fashions, and fads — plus many topical items and interviews. As the years progressed, its thrust became less exclusively women's interests and moved more into current affairs programming. Since *Femme d'aujourd'hui* was not authorized as an information programme within Radio-Canada's structure (as was *Take 30* in the English network) there had to be some rules: the programme was to keep its nose out of politics in general (unless women were significantly involved), and political controversy and union conflicts in particular. For some women, the stricture was intolerable. Lisette Gervais, the programme's first host, quit at the end of the season. In 1981, she told the Women and Information Conference why she left.

> I was terribly frustrated with the way we had to treat all information from a female angle, which around Radio-Canada meant an obtuse angle. If we were doing a current affairs story on any subject, we had to stipulate how many women were implicated and so forth. I found it intolerable that an equal value should be attached to this year's hem line and the plight of the women in Viet Nam. Voilà, the ghetto, I said to myself; the ghetto of dull, tame programming.

When Lasnier arrived at *Femme d'aujourd'hui* in December, she found that there was no topical edge to the show. She was troubled by its penchant for items about the proper crystal in which to serve vintage wines and flower arrangements using long-stemmed roses.

"The producers were doing the programme *they* wanted to do and it did not speak to viewers about their lives. It was not informed by a larger vision of what it was to be a woman." *Femme d'aujourd'hui* was out of focus, and what would bring it into focus was listening to the audience. Lasnier had learned a thing or two at *Châtelaine* about how to tailor a programme to an audience. She applied the same principle to television, inviting the audience to send in story suggestions so that the programme was able to thrive with few researchers by using the ideas and tapping the knowledge of its own viewers. It was a "participatory programme," Lasnier notes, adding that "the audience's appetite for current affairs kept the programme on the move. They really wanted something from us; they wanted to learn something during that hour and were quite determined about it."

Lasnier and her colleagues kept off the holy ground of hot political debate, "but," says Lasnier, "we did everything else." The ghetto, from Lasnier's vantage point, became a bastion:

> We had one full hour of airtime a day, which is fantastic power when you think of it; it is more time than the news gets. Moreover, in the afternoon we were able to treat extremely delicate subjects; we discussed vasectomies, for instance, years before it was an accepted method of birth control. The mentality may have changed a bit since then, but in 1970 what we were doing was out of the ordinary.

The internal arrangement that kept *Femme d'aujourd'hui* bureaucratically sectioned off was deeply symbolic. Even if journalists like Lasnier found their way around the limitations, there were drawbacks they could not overcome. Lasnier was not naïve and any illusions she might have had at the outset were completely cleared away when, at the end of her first year, she went to her superior with her annual budget. She requested the usual increments in salaries and several merit increases. "He hemmed and hawed and hesitated. I was very generous, he said, but, after all, the programme wasn't *that* important and the responsibility of its producers wasn't that great. So I told him, 'If you want to talk about responsibility, we spend one hour every day talking eyeball-to-eyeball with your wives. I don't believe anyone has a bigger responsibility than that.' " Management was not moved — not then, anyway.

Propelled by the whirlwind of social change that caught up everyone in Quebec and by the second wave of feminism simultaneously sweeping the continent, *Femme d'aujourd'hui* gradually became more radical in its coverage of women's issues. In 1976, a special two-and-a-half hour programme celebrating the 2,000th edition of the show was mounted and almost became a *cause célèbre* when businesses all over the province discovered women were refusing to work on the thirtieth of March unless there was a television set around. It was a nation-wide production, linking up seven studios and two hundred guests across the country in what was a technical first for the corporation.

It was through such events as these that Radio-Canada slowly became conscious of what was going on during the day on *Femme d'aujourd'hui*. By and large, management wasn't enthusiastic about the trend it saw. The tone was becoming too feminist, or so it was said later. Disapproval translated into slow death by starvation; budgets were cut back and the production team was not revitalized. When Lasnier was herself promoted off the show (lured by the Director of Information into a management position) she had come to accept the fact that "they wanted that programme dead." A few months later, the show was gone from the airwaves for good.

In some ways, Lasnier was philosophic; she had often mused that the success of the programme might kill it, for if women chose emancipation its audience might disappear, leaving home to take jobs outside. Officially, that was the reason for pulling *Femme d'aujourd'hui* in 1982. There was no longer an audience out there demanding programmes for a female audience. Still, Lasnier says, "I cried when it was cancelled because I realized something would disappear. Radio-Canada would no longer have what I describe as a preoccupation with cultural values. I was right. A certain reflectiveness and depth on a whole range of topics have completely gone now."

What happened to *Femme aujourd'hui* was not unlike the fate of *Take 30*, which was also reaching its peak in the mid-seventies. The "long, slow slide" of *Take 30* was characterized by perfectly competent and worthy current affairs programming; but the events of the world, and in particular the female world, were passing the programme by. It could no longer play an avante-garde role or be particularly controversial because the issues, which were its stock in trade, had migrated to the mainstream. Moreover, behind the scenes, the programme had ceased to be a training ground and had become instead a dumping ground for (mostly male) producers. That is what happens to a programme when it loses its verve as well as its pull within a broadcasting operation.

The existence of women's programming as a separate entity provided Lasnier with a measure of autonomy she believes she would not otherwise have had; that is a common theme among women's-page programmers, whatever the medium. Low profile and low status means less interference from the guys managing the "real" stuff. Unlike *Take 30*, though, *Femme d'aujourd'hui* was never a mecca for women journalists, and for much of its life there were more male producers attached to it than female. But comparatively speaking, its record was not too bad, for Radio-Canada has acquired a reputation for being far less receptive to the advancement of women than English CBC.

The career of Lise Payette is a case in point. Payette worked for twenty years in radio and television as a journalist before she resigned to run for the Parti Québécois in the 1976 election. She won, and became a cabinet minister in René Lévesque's government. Payette had burst onto the Radio-Canada airwaves in the fifties, with an irreverent opinionated radio show called *Interdit aux hommes* (No Men Allowed). Through the sixties and seventies, she piled success on

success with a series of different programmes (for both
French and English CBC networks) and ended up hosting a
radio programme called *Place aux femmes* (Women's Place).

Appelle-Moi Lise not only established Payette as the best
all-around interviewer in the country — the most acerbic and
entertaining wit on television — but she proved that, in
Quebec at least, late-night interview shows could attract an
audience. She broke the mold in yet another way, for when
Payette took on the show she proved that a frankly big,
middle-aged woman could be a glamorous celebrity. There
was, however, one barrier she never broke. Although Lise
Payette has been a major figure in broadcast journalism for
years, she has never worked in current affairs. That is a
staggering fact — and one she herself is convinced is not
happenstance. She told *Le Devoir*'s Renée Rowan in 1982:

> I never had access to the domain of information and
> public affairs. Judith Jasmin had it, but she remains an
> exception. She is the *only* woman who has had access.
> Denise Bombardier *may* have it, but in my own case I was
> summarily dealt with by being relegated to the Variety
> department. They never so much as asked whether I
> could do anything else. When I was doing *Appelle-Moi
> Lise*, I often said that if Radio-Canada had been able to
> find a man capable of doing the job, I would not have
> been there at all.

Ghetto or bastion? The women's pages in newspapers,
television, and radio have been both. They have harboured
some, cloistered others. They have nurtured talent that
otherwise might never have seen the light of day. Journalists
like Michelle Lasnier and Michele Landsberg came up
through what might be called a women's page "system," save
that the word lends an air of formality to something that was
highly unstructured. Long before anyone thought of using
"network" as a verb, or using it to describe human relations
instead of television stations, a women's network existed in
Canadian journalism, a network in the sense of there being a
few intersections where women were concentrated, and a few
larger-than-life figures who looked out for female talent and

were in a position to nurture and promote it. These individuals, among them Helen James, Dodi Robb, and Doris
Anderson, have had an enormous influence, greater by far
then the sum of the people they helped or the intercessions
they've made on women's behalf with public opinion.

In broadcasting, only the CBC has a continuous history of
programming directed to a largely female audience and
produced largely by women. For the better part of forty
years, it dedicated budgets and airtime to such women's
programming, and only in 1984 was that objective abandoned when *Take 30* was cancelled. Such a development
could be taken as a positive sign that "women's interests"
need no longer be treated as separate and special, that they
have penetrated the mainstream and can now be regarded
simply as human interests. To some extent, that is true.

The definitions of news and newsworthiness have been
broadening, moving further afield, and yet there are some
who would argue that there will always be a need for women's
programming, not in order to compensate for discriminatory practices elsewhere, but because there is a demand for it.
They would postulate the existence of an audience with
distinct interests in certain subjects (like men have in sports)
and certain styles of programming. It is clear that there is no
consensus about which direction to move in: CBC's two national
television newscasts have taken opposite approaches, for
instance. *Téléjournal* has a reporter, Danielle Levasseur,
specifically charged with the women's dossier, who is responsible for news dealing directly with women and social issues
mainly affecting them. *The National* appointed Marguerite
MacDonald as its national reporter on social affairs, but her
responsibilities aren't confined to women and she doubles as
a parliamentary reporter.

So the debate continues over the justice and justification of
the women's page: whether, as a concept, it is a positive or
negative thing, a ghetto or safe haven, a professional dead-
end or a greenhouse for talent. The tradition has undergone
many a metamorphosis in a hundred years and seems to be
passing through yet another. One thing is indisputable.
Media women would not be where they are today had the
women's page not been invented.

NINE

Women at the Top: Working Alone with the Male Point of View

WHEN THE Honourable Judy LaMarsh was setting up her royal commission on violence in the media, so the story goes, she arranged a meeting with Dodi Robb, who was then head of Children's Television at the CBC. "I have heard of you, Dodi," said LaMarsh when the two women met, "and they say that, had you been a man, you'd be vice-president of the CBC by now."

"Hell," retorted Robb. "I'd be president."

The story, as it happens, is not apocryphal. Those were Robb's words. "It was a very arrogant and cheeky remark to make," she says now, yet she makes no apology. She knows, as do the people who have admiringly quoted her, that a man of her generation, armed with her qualifications and achievements, would certainly have attained high office. More than once in her life, she has reached the door marked vice-president, only to find, etched in discreet letters underneath, the words "Men Only." Now nearing retirement age, Robb has been around television from the beginning and has spent her life creating good television programmes. Finally in the seventies, when social custom had budged enough for some of the men's rooms to open their doors to selected women with escorts, Robb pushed into senior management at the CBC.

True to her Scottish background, Dodi Robb is a woman of strong opinion who doesn't mince words, hates wasting anything, especially airtime, and has a strong liking for unlikely challenges. "Show your Scotch independence, girl," was one of her father's favourite expressions, and she still hears it ringing in her mind's ear. She never married and, in a curious way, her father may have prepared her for that. "He meant that we should stand on our own feet, that we didn't need a man, though he never came out and said it that bluntly."

By the time she completed university, Robb was already determined to become a writer. She got a job as a columnist for the *Star Weekly* but the war was on and her sense of duty called. Unable to get overseas, she settled for a year's assignment with the U.S. engineering division, then constructing the Alaska Highway through Northern B.C. and the Yukon. Although hired for secretarial skills ("I didn't have any, so I practised typing madly all the way up on the train"), she was soon writing for the service newspaper.

Three years later, back in Toronto, Robb was anxiously wondering if she could revive the infant career she had left behind, now that the men were returning from the war and reclaiming their old jobs. CBC radio needed continuity writers, though, and she soon found work writing scripts for disc shows, occasionally doing the on-air commentary between records herself. This gave her a chance to design the entire show, an interesting task which was also technically outside her job specification. "We drove the corporation crazy," she fondly remembers. She also began writing entertainment programmes for people like J. Frank Willis and Gisele MacKenzie.

In 1950, Robb was lured away from the CBC by MacLaren Advertising. "So away I went down to the Bay Street world of advertising, riddled with concern about "going commercial." We were well indoctrinated with the public broadcasting ethic in those days at the CBC. MacLaren's, of course, had all sorts of big accounts: Imperial Oil, the Liberal Party, and General Electric. I came on as chief writer-producer."

She started with radio, writing for shows like *The Leslie Bell Singers* and *Howard Cable and His Orchestra*, which were sponsored by MacLaren's clients. When television arrived, she was ready and waiting to make the switch. (Having seen it coming, she had had MacLaren send her for technical training.) Robb got in on the ground floor, and she soon was writing for the top television variety shows in the country. After ten years, however, she came to a standstill professionally and MacLaren's didn't know what to do with her. Robb relates the story without rancour:

> The men I was working with were all eventually made vice-presidents and acquired fat portfolios of MacLaren stock. I saw younger men coming in and being given positions with more influence and power than I — though never with more creative responsibility. So I suggested they make me vice-president, which was the last thing they would contemplate. I fought it, but not the right way. I am not a belligerent person or a political scrapper. My only defence has always been my creativity, which no one can take out of my head. So I would rebel by holding back on an idea or slacking off work, which was dumb. Nowadays, I advise women to go in and be straightforward. Back then I guess I was too frightened they would say no.

In 1960, she resigned and left advertising for good. The CTV network had just been licensed and was looking for talent to help fulfill the promises it had made to produce thousands of hours of original Canadian programming. Robb was offered a position as chief writer of daytime programmes. The money was good, the opportunity unprecedented, but it was a mistake. "CTV was a slave ship." For five years, she worked sixteen to eighteen hours a day keeping CTV's Canadian programming on the air and its owners in the good graces of the Board of Broadcast Governors. For a very long time, she believed that if she worked hard enough for the company, especially when the entire effort so obviously depended on what she was producing, eventually she would be rewarded. But that never happened. Moreover, she was involved in an energy-draining conflict with a male colleague that finally became unendurable:

I had never resigned in a huff, but one day I did just that. Within half an hour, John Bassett was on the phone booming, "What's all this about your leaving? We think you have a big future with this company and we want you to stay." So I reconsidered and I stayed. Six months later, nothing had changed. I had been there four-and-a-half years with the same salary I had when I walked through the door. So I wrote Bassett to remind him of what he had said and asked for a raise. He wrote back to say he wouldn't think of it, that he felt I was overpaid when he hired me and if he did raise my pay that would mean I'd be making as much as the senior men in the company. He probably didn't realize what he was saying.

Robb quit and rejoined the CBC as head of Daytime Information programming. The decade 1965 to 1975 was one of expansion for the CBC and for women working there. New shows, new ideas, and new people were floating around current affairs, and Dodi Robb's unseen hand was behind many successes. She loves telling a story about one encounter with two young radicals, Maxine Nunes and Deanna White, about 1970.

Those two tigers came stomping into my office in their capes and boots one day and said they wanted to do a series on The Women's Movement. "Tell me about it," I said, and they described a show which would have Kate Millett and Irving Layton fighting it out and discussions about the myth of the vaginal orgasm. "Whoa...say that again!" I said. You can imagine the old lady ricochetting around at this! But always being one to take a chance, I told them, "Yes, that would be spendid, ladies," and so, long before the Burning of the Bra, we had this wonderful series called *Women Now*, which was on at 2:30 in the afternoons.

Eventually she was made executive producer of a new programme called *Market Place*, an unassuming little consumer's show that went to air in 1972 and sped to the top of the charts with an audience of two million. *Market Place* was

Dodi Robb's greatest hit. What was brilliant about the concept was the unexpected homespun style which was far more
imaginative than it looked. Drawing on her show-biz savvy,
Robb cast Joan Watson as host, with Stompin' Tom Connors
singing the intro to the show — low-keyed, careful consumer
and rough-cut country singer — just the "ordinary folks"
touch needed on a show that would be handling highly volatile information. "It was David and Goliath out there all the
time. We were tangling with big guns like G.M., and you have
to be dreadfully careful and very right. If once you fall off,
the whole show would go, so we had to have extremely rigid
standards. It is a miracle it's still going without lawsuits."

The stress of running such a show eventually becomes
unbearable. Robb was happy to make her next move, to head
children's television. From there, her route has taken her
through senior postings as director of television in Winnipeg
and director of the CBC's Maritime region. "Those last three
jobs I took deliberately because no women had ever done
them before. It may be a perversity in my nature that I
wanted to prove something and blast a path where others can
follow."

Just as the air becomes thinner when you scale a mountain,
Robb found the environment thinning of women the higher
she moved. She had been used to working with lots of them
around, and now she found herself going into room after
room where she was the only woman. "Frankly, you get tired
of the all-male point of view, even if you get along with men
as I do." Among all those men, the atmosphere could be
strained:

> There is one thing men are nervous about in women:
> their intuition and character-assessing ability. We can
> look right through the mean-spirited, the puny, the
> inept, the irresponsible. We see it and they don't like the
> look in our eyes when we do. It is what a good wife does
> for a pompous man. Men who are all facade and no
> substance are frightened by it. For women it is a plus.

Robb made a feature of being the lone woman at the table.
She reached into the depths of her womanly strengths and

hauled out the best in herself, her sense of humour and her robust friendliness:

> There is a jocularity that occurs because they don't take you terribly seriousy, which I never actually minded. Humour is a great tool. So is being personal. Asking how little Johnny is can transform the mood of a person who walks into a meeting. I think there are many endearing qualities women have that should be used in business. I can't stand the jungle ruthlessness of men fighting their wars; I loathe the power plays and the way that when the powerful and successful get in, everyone forgets the person who has just been beheaded. I believe there has to be a suitable time for grieving and regret.

At the same time, life at the giddy heights of senior management was not quite as deadly dull as she expected, "so long as you don't take it too seriously or go by the rules instead of walking around them as I have always done. I have one criterion which keeps everything crystal clear for me. Is it about programming? If not, let's make it short; if it is, I have lots of time." Yes, men do engage in political games around the table, which can frustrate a straight-talking person, but, says Robb, "I don't think I am as straight as my reputation has it. I put things off too, when I know they are going to be unpleasant, even if I know it's better to face the music early."

Robb's last job (before she went back to children's television again in 1984) was without doubt the hardest of the lot. Network chief Peter Herrndorf, who was detemined to have her become the first woman regional director in the English CBC, knew he was sending her into one of the more "traditional" (meaning chauvinist) CBC territories by sending her to Halifax. "Dodi had to think long and hard about whether she wanted to be a Jackie Robinson among regional directors. She was going in cold; she hadn't grown up there professionally, and had no family or friends there." In making the appointment, though, Herrndorf knew Robb had qualities the situation demanded that he could rely on:

She had to be able to establish herself right off the bat and Dodi has a set of programming *bona fides* that no one can challenge. She was able to go in (and there is no way round this sounding pejorative) and be an earth mother to that operation so people could respond positively. It would have been very difficult for someone with a more macho style of management.

If Robb's driving force was her "Scotch independence," her colleague Margaret Lyons' drive came from immigrant's determination. "My career was atypical," Lyons cautions. "As the first-born of immigrant parents, I was raised to be an achiever. My mother insisted we all do well. And my father, who had wanted a son, treated me like a boy and assumed I would be interested in all the things he was. I was very lucky in that combination of circumstances."

The next stroke of luck for Lyons was the arrival of the war. Along with hundreds of Japanese-Canadians, Lyons' family was removed from their farm and sent inland to the prairies.

This is not a popular thing to say, but for young women like myself who wanted to break loose from the conventional Japanese mold, the war offered a chance — and I seized it. Mother wanted her daughters to take up ladylike pursuits and not intellectual ones, and I was forbidden to go to university. She had, in fact, decided I needed finishing school. Had the war not come, I'd have been shipped off to Japan to learn flower arranging and things like that.

But young Margaret Lyons had her own plans:

I always wanted to be a journalist. I don't remember a day when I didn't. Young people often dream of being creative writers but I was too interested in things around me, politics especially, and international history. Neither of my parents read English with great facility, so from the time I was very young I read them the Vancouver newspapers.

With a sharp eye on the future, Lyons worked as a domestic in Winnipeg, where her family had settled, and saved enough money to send herself to university. Thinking she might go into international journalism, she studied political economy rather than history or literature as she might have preferred but which would have "put me at a competitive disadvantage because those are the courses young ladies were expected to take." Upon graduation, Lyons married and with her new husband left on a world trip that ended with an eleven-year stay in England.

Once in London, Lyons set off for the BBC. Crashing the British Broadcasting Corporation took patience. She tried the front door, retreated, and then, trading on the secretarial skills she had shrewdly acquired in Canada, she got a job as a dictation-typist in the foreign newsroom.

> I was only there a few months when they needed a senior clerk to assist the editor of the French newsroom. Being Canadian, they assumed I was bilingual. I said, "sort of" (I had two years of university French) and bluffed my way through. Then they needed a production secretary in the Japanese section and seeing I was Japanese-Canadian, figured I could speak Japanese. Again, I said, "sort of," which was a bald-faced lie. My Japanese was primitive, certainly not up to broadcast standard, though sufficient to explain texts to people who were broadcasting in Japanese.

From a standing start, it took Lyons eighteen months to make production. For six years she was a producer in the Far East Section of the BBC's prestigious overseas service.

> Radio was much more interesting than print, I thought, and it was a very exciting time in London for an international affairs expert. I covered all the constitutional conferences going on at the time. Malaysia was becom-

ing independent; India was going through the final stages of its independence and the African nations were just starting.

In 1960, however, she left it all and returned to Canada, partly because of a comment of Lester Pearson's. "I happened to interview Pearson when he was on his way back from collecting his Nobel Peace Prize in Stockholm. He asked me what I was doing working in London and lectured me about Canada needing all the talent it possessed at home. Well, I thought he was just talking, but I did think about what he said."

Back in Toronto and by now the mother of two small children, Lyons decided that she would take some time off before going back to print journalism. Before she had even started looking around, cbc public affairs radio was on the telephone pleading with her to apply for a producer's job with them. Lyons held back. She wasn't sure about the job and she definitely didn't like the salary. When negotiations were concluded, cbc radio gained a top-flight producer, and Lyons came on with the highest producer's salary in the department.

Over the next twenty-five years, Lyons served as head of Radio Current Affairs, director of the am service and, in 1983, became the vice-president in charge of network radio — cbc's first woman vice-president and the highest-ranking appointment since Nellie McClung was named to the first board of governors in 1936.

Lyons took the great leap from production to management in 1971, at the behest of programme director Peter Meggs.

I was invited to realize some of the wild and woolly notions I had been feeding Meggs, which I could only do from management. I did miss production, because it is satisfying to be able to think up a project and execute it immediately instead of having to work through a lot of other people. My job is to create an atmosphere to encourage others to produce, and there is much that is satisfying and fascinating about that too.

Lyons is very different from Dodi Robb in personality and

style. Nevertheless, she has also achieved notoriety around the CBC, first as a gifted producer and then as an imaginative and controversial programmer. She has never been afraid of change or, for that matter, highly vocal resistance from listeners and CBC watchers to some of her innovations. She is not intimidated by large-scale egos or difficult personalities, and she has made something of a practice of collecting genius shitdisturbers and turning them into brilliant producers. She is admired, respected, and also known far and wide as radio's "dragon-lady," the owner of a savage temper that some say has her eating people for breakfast.

She is partisan and passionate about radio, and candid about her management style. "I consult with people. I usually have a plan in my mind and when people have other views I first try to persuade them, then I'll hector them, and then we have big fights." Margaret Lyons sees winning the argument as part of her job as the woman in charge. So the stories flourish; Margaret Lyons standing almost obscured in a thicket of men, shaking her finger at them as she rounds off an argument. She concedes the reputation but is unrepentant. "I know I was a sore trial to some of my colleagues, who would tactfully suggest that I could achieve my ends without being so bull-headed. I'd listen but it didn't change my approach much. Even if people don't like it, there is a point when you must express your views — silence is taken as consent, and I'm never going to have that mistake made about me."

Lyons gives fulsome credit to the three radio chiefs she has worked for over the years. "All of them," she says, "were truly gender blind," which is an apt description of Lyons' own attitude. She was only vaguely aware of discriminatory attitudes and practices in television in the sixties and never encountered any in radio. "You see, because I have not suffered discrimination personally, and because I saw women around me accomplishing as much as they wanted to — or if they did reach an impasse I could see clearly that some of it was due to their own behaviour or attitudes — I didn't think women were discriminated against."

Then along came the inquiry into the status of women at the CBC. Lyons was ambivalent, at first. "I have to say, about halfway through, I became a convert. I had been living in a sheltered environment and felt that action was unnecessary if women only asserted themselves. When Kay MacIver's findings began to come in, I went to some meetings and saw how the women became shrill because some of the men forced them to be." So Lyons tempered her opinion. "From the mid-seventies on, I began to encourage women consciously. I saw the need to groom women for management and I made sure I spoke to women I saw had potential."

Dodi Robb and Margaret Lyons belong to the same generation but their experiences in broadcasting have been different. This can be partly explained by the fact that public radio (CBC English services radio, to be exact) has been a shining oasis of opportunity for women. Unlike Robb, who has often been painfully aware of the road-blocks (attitudinal and institutional) and of her own singularity in senior management circles, Lyons has not felt alone in the meeting rooms she frequents. Nor has she felt called upon to be an activist leader the way Robb has. Gingerly, though, she has come to believe that affirmative action is sometimes necessary: "I'm not in favour of it on the creative side, because I'm inclined to think you get better people if they are motivated enough to seek advancement and do better if things aren't handed to them. On the management side, however, I think we need some, simply because it will take too long otherwise."

But she has been disappointed with the poor showing for her efforts to boost women into management positions. Many have refused to leave production, either because that is where they genuinely want to work or because they have seen too many people disappear upstairs, becoming detached from programming and eventually losing touch with the very purpose of public broadcasting. Says one, "They might as well be managing Pepsi." What has irked Lyons especially is women's refusal to accept important promotions if they compromise personal and family life.

Robb, on the other hand, has made a lifelong practice of helping out other women, being a mentor, and steering women into job openings. She is well known as a sympathetic ear and the path to her office is worn smooth by secretaries wanting to get into research, and executive producers contemplating a career in management. Among her fellow executives, she is known as a programme activist, and indeed she is a moving centre of energy that draws out the creative sparkle in others.

The appearance of women in senior management in the last six years at the CBC happened because of the effort of a few men at the top: Peter Herrndorf, when he was head of the English division, and Al Johnson, who was the CBC's president from 1975 to 1982. Both of them were magnanimous under the pressure of changing times and the recommendations of women's groups. It has to be said, though, that the CBC's French services don't merit a very honourable mention here. Not one of the top-level women in the corporation has come up by that route. For years, the only senior level woman in Montreal has been Betty Zimmerman, the director of Radio-Canada International, the CBC's foreign service.

Outside the confines of public broadcasting and beyond the reaches of public or government pressure, newspapers and privately owned radio and television have manfully resisted including women in the upper chambers of management. There are no female equivalents of Ken Thomson, or John Bassett, or Superchannel's Doc Allard, or cable-TV's Ted Rogers. Nor are the presidents, chief executive officers, or publishers running these media empires ever women. Over the years, a few women have appeared on their boards of directors, usually because they were related to the owners or, as in the case of Carole Taylor's appointment to the board of Rogers Cablesystems, because of a high-profile professional background. Their experiences seems to indicate that it is best to come in at the top with rare qualifications no one else can match. Working up through the senior ranks tends to be a futile pursuit, unless it is done with the sponsorship of one or more powerful men.

The sign on the door reads "CTV Vice Princess." Marge Anthony sits in a comfy armchair at the head of an elegant hardwood table filling up half her office. Other chairs float around it in a casual circle. The air is informal, and it takes a second or two to recognize the famous faces winking out at the visitor from photos on the wall — Hollywood celebrities, four-star entertainers, the occasional prime minister. Marge Anthony is vice-president of network relations for CTV; and the sign on her door — a joke from her staff — was meant, she says, "to soften the blow." Still, there is something of the princess in Marge Anthony, and a self-made Cinderella quality to her life.

She was the small-town kid with a gleam in her eye who dropped out of nursing, talked her way into a television studio in Moncton, New Brunswick, and with unswerving nerve made it all the way to Hollywood as the personal manager for the Smothers Brothers. She was the woman who "took care of business" for the comedy duo throughout their years of super stardom. When that relationship ended, Anthony went on to work for Neil Diamond, likewise handling publicity and coordinating production of television specials and recordings. Then, in 1978, with her marriage ending and the glitter wearing off tinsel-town ("though I was never part of the seventies craziness, I saw friends destroying themselves on coke"), she decided to come home.

Very quickly she was picked up by CTV as director of promotion and within two years was a vice-president — the first woman to capture the title in Canadian broadcasting. But if acceptance was not automatic or effusive, Anthony was willing to be patient. She is still the only woman in the CTV boardroom, and over the past four years has watched approvingly as some of the "old school" have mellowed enough to bury old habits. "They don't stand up for me any more," she says proudly.

Discussions about discrimination make Anthony uneasy. When she was delegated by CTV to serve on a CTRC task force reporting on sex-role stereotyping in broadcasting, she found the experience baffling and annoying. "The other committee members got very angry because I didn't identify men as the oppressors, and I didn't see everything as a struggle for women. For me it is a matter of commitment, and maybe women do have to work a little harder and prove themselves. I have seen a lot of women who have done it and succeeded." Like the network she works for, Marge Anthony is a firm believer in "hiring for talent and advancing on ability." Affirmative action is not part of her lexicon. "You can't say that because there are only two women doing a particular job, we ought to get another. I don't think that way and neither does my boss."

Shirley Sharzer also has been blessed with success. One of the country's most accomplished newspaperwomen, Sharzer started young, entering university at the startling age of sixteen. By the time she was twenty, she was city hall reporter for the *Winnipeg Free Press*, and later was the first woman ever assigned to cover the Manitoba legislature. There followed a ten-year career hiatus while she raised two children. In 1956, she returned to newspapers, working first for the *Toronto Telegram*. When the *Tely* folded in 1971, she was offered a berth at the *Toronto Star*, and three years later she was made features editor. Then the motor stalled. She watched and wondered as she saw others passing on the inside lane, taking the city editor and assistant managing editor jobs that she was in line for and wanted. Finally, when managing editor Martin Goodman told her she had not been promoted because she lacked administrative skills, she knew that she had been passed over deliberately.

It was at the *Star* that Sharzer became aware of other women's experiences and learned how they were (and still are) being systematically held back. "I took pride in the work I did on the newsdesk at the *Tely* and I knew I was paving the way for other women; but I was not consciously analysing things then. You'll find that about my generation, even those of us who were pioneers."

Today she is the associate managing editor of the *Globe and Mail*, the most senior woman in the business. (Only one woman in living memory has been made managing editor of a big-city daily — Dona Harvey, who was briefly with the *Vancouver Province* and left in 1984.) But in that title lies a story which has caught the attention of younger women journalists. Sharzer is understandably ambivalent about such attention, since it casts her career in a quasi-tragic light.

It was editor-in-chief Richard Doyle who lured Sharzer

away from the University of Western Ontario, where she had gone to teach journalism. Doyle would later crow that hiring Sharzer was "one of the most brilliant" decisions he made. It was Doyle, nevertheless, who passed her over in appointing executive editor Cameron Smith as managing editor. Two years later, Smith was moved out and Geoffrey Stevens was given the job. Once again, Sharzer stayed where she was. On the first occasion, she was given a new title — associate managing editor; the second time, her office was enlarged and outfitted with carpeting and executive furniture. When asked whether these trappings were a form of compensation, Sharzer hesitates; she doesn't consider herself a victim of discrimination at the *Globe*. The victim of circumstances, perhaps (Stevens and new editor-in-chief Norman Webster go back a long way together) and bad timing. But she doesn't take these decisions as a comment on her own abilities; nor does she believe they have led her into a professional cul-de-sac. On the contrary, her job carries great creative and managerial responsibility and she openly enjoys it. She has been influenced by the young women around her who, she says, have done more to sensitize her to feminist concerns than books have. "I have to give credit to the women here. I appreciate the way they express themselves and complain to me about sexism in the newsroom or in "Your Morning Smile," expecting me to speak up on their behalf. They've been good for me and I hope I've been good for them."

Sharzer accepts, nevertheless, that the story of her double by-pass at the senior level has become a symbol to other women and is regarded as symptomatic of the difficulties women still have gaining acceptance and recognition. In her own case, colleagues have suggested that her warm, conciliatory approach in dealing with people has been seen in the male world as a weakness, rather than as the strength it is.

In the United States, where equal opportunity is the law, women have been able to launch suits against employers to force them to eliminate barriers. The *New York Times*, the *Washington Post*, AP, NBC and the *Detroit News* (among others) have all been sued in recent years and settled out of court for huge sums of money in compensation, while disclaiming the charges of discrimination. American women have also jumped at the chances offered by new developments such as pay TV and have used their entrepreneurial skills to capture the leadership of new operations rather than waiting around for invitations to arrive from the big established companies. In Canada, that has occasionally happened too. And that is the story of how Joan Schafer became vice-president of programming for First Choice Pay TV.

Joan Schafer began her career as a floor director at CITY-TV in its feverish heyday and, by grabbing every opportunity that whizzed past, was executive producer of *The City Show* by 1976. She established a reputation for sleuthing down talent in odd places and slipping it on the air. She also became known for her preference for hiring women. Her first unit was, in fact, all women. "We were called the Schaferettes and we were all fairly strong people. We didn't walk around, we pounded around," she says with glee. When she was asked in interviews at the time why, given an equal choice between a man and a woman, she would choose a woman, Schafer retorted, "Because I like working with women. I like their enthusiasm, and in my experience they work harder and care more."

During her years at CITY, Schafer lived and breathed television production. She was responsible for three shows a day and two on weekends for six years, churning out an incredible 9,000 programmes in that time. She thrives in a super-intense work environment. A lively, wiry person who exudes confidence and high-octane energy, she is also a practical person who doesn't shirk the distasteful tasks of management. For instance, when she took over *The City Show* and began to refashion it into an entertaining news package, she had to jettison some of the team, who vociferously opposed the up-tempo, downtown image she was creating. In one awful day she had to fire thirteen people.

Schafer was originally asked to join the group planning a pay TV proposal because of her knowledge of the CRTC (the federal licensing commission) policies and procedure. She helped put the application together and appeared before the commission as the team's vice-president for programming.

When First Choice won its licence, Schafer became, over-night, the most sought-after woman in Canadian movies. With Canadian content quotas to meet and a production fund of $29 million to invest (over a period of two years), she was automatically on every producer's, screenwriter's, and di-rector's A list. Until First Choice's financial bubble burst in 1983, she was logging sixty-five calls a day.

Clearly Schafer is at home in the world of movies and money. She looks and sounds right for the fast-dealing part. In her mid-thirties, Schafer cuts a dashing figure. She sashays about in large, man-tailored suits with extra-wide padded shoulders. The look is lanky and ultra-sophisticated, but the talk is salty and animated. Working for First Choice removed her from the fray of production and deposited her in another sphere, where movies and money are called properties and profit pictures.

She joined the board of a major communications enter-prise with seventeen high-level financiers and businessmen representing millions of investment dollars. "I asked to become a board member and lobbied to get on. I would not have been there otherwise," she tells you. This much she had learned about the laws of the business world — you have to insist on your *quid pro quo*. If she was going to be used as the front person for Canadian Programming (and therefore First Choice's lease on respectability with the CTRC), then she was going to extract her return for it: a good meaty contract, a slice of the shares, and a turn in the boardroom.

Once in that door, she realized she had to bone up quickly on the fundamentals of "boardroom decorum": Robert's Rules of Order, and the intricacies of what must be put on the record and what must not be talked about. She had to figure out where information was available and work out her own lines of communication with other directors. It was a major revelation to find out that board business doesn't always take place at meetings. "I'd get calls at 11:30 at night to come down right away, and at first I would go. I had to learn not to be available on demand or my time was squandered — which is a popular corporate game."

Early on, Schafer also hired a corporate lawyer whom she kept supplied with blind copies of company memos. "With major blocks of money moving around, I needed help interpreting what was happening." Then she went out and assiduously acquired some "number skills." "In my first budget report, I put in all the zeros — not done. It took me a long time to get over the fear of big numbers."

There were other gaps to contend with, too — lifestyle gaps:

> I used to tell Peter (my mate) I felt like I had landed in from outer space. There were so many things I knew nothing about. I became very careful about how I walked into the boardroom, when I left, what I said, how I said it, and what I wrote. To make the other directors feel more comfortable, I took to wearing more expensive suits. I don't think I ever relaxed on the job.

The fact was that in their "very straight" milieu she was an embarrassing anomaly. Not having a socially accepted term for one's live-in lover was tricky; not having the wherewithal to seat twelve for dinner was a disadvantage, and not having the wife to cater the party and pack the suitcase for sudden trips to New York was a hassle. "I did, at least, keep the same address throughout. It may sound strange, but that sort of thing was actually important."

Having worked with women exclusively and with an all-male board, Schafer finds the difference in men's and women's working style to be huge:

> We think differently. We take bigger risks. I've seen women do swan dives into space that take your breath away. Not knowing the system or what options are possible, women often take incredible risks. A man will go into a meeting, say something for the record, and leave with three other moves up his sleeve. They think in longer terms. Most women I know, including myself, find that two years ahead is the most they can run. Which could be evidence that women really do think about the future differently, or it could be the age-old reality that most women with families or husbands cannot plan in advance for anything.

There are other factors Schafer noticed which keep women out of the boardroom. "To be at the top of a pay TV proposal required about $200,000, and I don't know many women with that kind of money to plop into a risky venture. Moreover, you have to start with the understanding that men don't want women there. So any woman who is going to get in has to have something they need and can't get anywhere else." Then she tells a story about the shareholders' Christmas "stag" at the Hyatt Regency hotel, the night it all came home to her. "It was a long dinner with a very macho menu, roast beef and so on. They were all very polite about passing me the wine and trying to be nice. Then it was cigars and cognac time, and suddenly they began talking about the women they had screwed. Not until one of them turned to me and asked, 'Do you mind?' did any of them realize something was wrong." Having observed boardroom culture at close quarters, Schafer concludes: "Typically, the men wonder why they should endure women in the boardroom if they don't have to."

In the spring of 1984, Joan Schafer pulled out of First Choice, the last of the founding members to leave.

Consciously or unconsciously, men are reluctant to let women into the boardroom. They worry about having to alter their behaviour, about whether they might end up working for a woman, and, all in all, as Peter Herrndorf describes it, "it's just easier to be good old boys together." Discussing the attitude and those fears, Herrndorf elaborates, "After a tough negotiating meeting, it is easy for two men to suddenly decide to go out for a steak and a beer to talk tactics. Many men think that this would be tricky with a woman, although in practice it works out exactly the same. The biggest change I saw among my male colleagues at the CBC was that most of them are now comfortable with their women colleagues." One thing hasn't changed, Herrndorf admits: men are not comfortable with attractive or aggressive women. "That gets in the way of men evaluating women, particularly young women. If they are attractive or difficult, a whole new set of factors is introduced to the evaluation equation, and a lot of men in senior and middle management are not good at discerning it."

In management, however, it isn't a case of women applicants being turned down; they are simply disregarded. Seated around a table discussing who ought to be considered for a vacant job, the men think of other men. In Dodi Robb's experience, "They suggest who they want and I chime in with the names of some women. If I weren't there, those names would never be considered. They don't think of women; they just don't, dear."

Since 1975, the percentage of women in CBC management has risen from ten to twenty percent. It has been a slow and arduous process. Donna Logan, who went into CBC radio in Montreal after the Montreal *Star* folded and once again rose rapidly to the top, has been Information Programme Director since 1984. She has had occasion to sit on hiring committees and watched it happen. Recently she was conducting interviews along with two men. "There was one woman candidate who was very clearly better than the rest. When the board was over I asked the other two for their reactions and both of them had chosen men as front-runners. It was *so* obvious that I wanted to blow up. Instead I went through a laborous process to bring them around. In the end they agreed — I don't think it was just because I was the boss."

Like Joan Schafer, Trina McQueen started to work when television was in an expansive mood and the opportunities for women were unprecedented in number. In 1966, she was the first woman hired as an on-air reporter for CBC local news (in Toronto) and three years later she repeated the performance when she went to *The National*. Although she adored news reporting, McQueen never cared much for the on-camera part of the job. "It's so ego-involving," she complains. So she happily traded in her mike for writing and editing assignments. Her career took its most dramatic turn in 1976, when she became executive producer of *The National*. Like all the other jobs along the way, this one was offered to her: "The last job I applied for was the one to get into the CBC." It was the move which would catapult her into senior management four years later as director of television programming for the network. One might detect from such a resumé that McQueen had a clear-eyed ambition which carefully guided her along a chosen track to the top. That is not the way it happened — or at least how it began.

"When I started out, I thought I would work for a while and then marry and have children. I never thought of my job as a career until after I had had my daughter and realized I was going to have only one child." Her daughter was born while McQueen was at *The National*, and although she was not tuned in to women's issues then, it didn't escape her notice that the rules entitled her husband, who was also in news and a member of the Newspaper Guild, to three days off with pay for the birth of his child, while she was entitled to none.

When McQueen joined *The National*, it was full of hard-nosed newshounds, yet she did not have difficulty fitting in. She kept a respectful distance, expecting the others to reciprocate. "I was never one of the boys," she explains. "I was always 'ladylike' and had no problem maintaining a coolness. Those hard-drinking types also have conservative views about women and wouldn't even swear in front of me. Some of the roughest and toughest of them were actually very friendly and supportive."

The trial by ordeal was to come later, when she became executive producer. "The trouble did not come from the macho types but from sophisticated men who resented my appointment because I was a woman and fairly young, thirty-three years old. They were the swashbuckling, foreign correspondent, commando types who live and breathe the 'we're the unit that goes over the top' mentality. They did not like my being there and refused to accept my authority."

One woman who worked with McQueen at *The National* was Ann Medina. She recalls:

> Trina took on a fairly fierce battle and won, and that gave rise to ill feeling. She took over *Newsmagazine*, pure and simple: She had the executive producer, if not fired, then pushed aside, which is a ballsy thing for a woman to

do. And she did it! There were those who said the man did it to himself, but whatever the real story, there was an intensity of criticism leveled at her no man would have had. A man would have been given, "Good for you," instead of "God! That awful woman," which is what she got.

For four years, from 1978 to 1980, McQueen was responsible for covering two federal elections, the Tory interregnum, the constitutional debate and patriation, and the Quebec Referendum. Almost daily, she was making highly sensitive decisions. She was the first and so far only woman entrusted with the crown jewel of the national news service, and all eyes were upon her. Previously, she had never given much thought to the fact that she was blazing a trail of "first woman" appointments and it didn't particularly bother her to be the only female member of the shop. Once she reached a position of real and visible power, however, people came along to scrutinize her record. As Ann Medina remembers it:

> There was a lot of buzz at the time that Trina didn't push women. I think she could have been more aggressive about hiring women, but a person's record should not be made in terms of the numbers hired. I knew when I dealt with her that she was all you could want in an executive producer. Intelligent, fair, decisive, and she could admit it when she was wrong. I felt nothing but encouragement from her and there were no games.

Stung by the accusations, McQueen checked the figures herself to corroborate her recollection that she had brought on more women than any other executive producer had before. "I really made a conscious effort to hire and promote women. But clearly it was not seen as enough by some activist women. I think some individuals and women's groups thought if I took the job that I would make it possible for women to succeed in journalism. I got a lot of criticism for not changing the world."

Trina McQueen got caught in a cultural crossfire and created controversy on both sides. To the men whose turf she threatened (by suggesting that the carefully drawn lines between newsreporting and longer documentary items be relaxed a bit) she was an unwelcome agent of change. McQueen doesn't like reciting the details of what went on, but her colleagues remember that the resistance was often underhanded, of the late-night-calls-to-her-boss variety, and personally insulting. On another side and in another context altogether, she landed in the bad books of feminists who, indeed, expected to see some visible changes on the news.

In terms of personal style, you could say McQueen had a credibility problem. She had perfected a persona for the newsroom, somewhere in between one-of-the-boys and Lady Madonna, which allowed her to be competent, decisive, and efficient. But what had worked in an all-male environment didn't work with everyone when she became the boss. To many of the women in the profession, her coolness is jarring and seems to show a lack of fellow feeling. Nevertheless, she has a shrewdness and political games(wo)manship which stood her in good stead when handling the dissidents. It has also aided and abetted her career in management. Peter Herrndorf speaks with admiration of her skill on that ancient chessboard. "She aggressively went after the job she wanted and played it beautifully, with a wonderful combination of aggressiveness and reticence, the 'I want to stay, here I am, coax me' approach."

McQueen talks about her last four years in the executive suite with unbridled enthusiasm. "I had been immersed in journalism and was suddenly plunged into the world of *Fraggle Rock*, the ballet, and made-for-television movies, taking off on trips for Hollywood. I was like a kid in a candy store. It opened a whole new world for me." It worries her that she is still an exception and that women seem to be avoiding management. "Production is seen as being really a lot of fun, but management isn't. Well I am here to say that it is creative and can be a tremendous source of excitement and energy."

She recognizes many women dislike what they've seen and heard about management, thinking of it as a den of labyrinthine politics, an alien world of cigar smoke, acronyms, and secret cabals in the men's washroom. She wants to change the image — and the reality a bit too. "I didn't think about it in the early years, but now that I look back on it, I must have been lonely. Now that I do have women friends on this floor, I see how wonderful it would have been to have had women around. But I didn't know what I didn't know." One neighbour and cohort is Joan Donaldson, who came to network management in 1983 to coordinate regional news and information programming. She shares McQueen's enthusiasm for the work. Her original misgivings have vanished; she has not found it necessary to transform herself into a single-track, memo-obsessed person. "Women don't understand much about management," she now concludes. "There is a mystique about it that often turns them away which I suspect has been there *to* turn them away."

Donaldson and McQueen want more women around for selfish reasons. It makes their own job easier. As Donaldson puts it:

> Women around here have been lifesavers for me. To be able to kick your shoes off and talk to someone about your frustrations and fears without having them categorized as female tremors! You don't really quite know how to talk with a male colleague about that. When I was a producer on the road, I often barricaded myself in a hotel room and ordered a cheeseburger because I was uncomfortable going out alone and couldn't confess those personal fears to anyone. Now Trina walks into my office to tell me about the job she is taking on, the pitfalls she sees, and the qualms she feels. I have felt it all too — and it makes me feel great to know I am not alone.

Whatever the perks in being the First Woman, it is a lonely position and doesn't change much. McQueen has an acute appreciation of the vicious circle. "You have to have more women in to change things, but until you change things you won't have more women." She continues, with intensity creeping into her voice:

> I have a feeling this is a critical time for women. The gross injustices have been corrected and the changes

needed now are both subtle and revolutionary. The research on women in the corporate world indicates that when participation reaches fifteen or twenty percent, the resistance from men hardens. Being the first was not terrible, because I was such an oddity no one felt his job was threatened or feared that I was going to have an affect on the business. The problem now is that real equality is no small thing. I can't emphasize enough how revolutionary it is. It may not seem so because it has been on the news so much, because people are sick of talking about it and think it has happened. Well it hasn't happened and it is not going to happen unless there is leadership at the top.

As McQueen and Donaldson blaze their way through a narrow pass in the second barrier, they are keenly aware that the success of the expedition depends on women helping and supporting other women. In this they are not alone. Media women generally are highly conscious of themselves as women in the profession. Although they may dislike labels, most do consider themselves feminists of one stripe or another. Even if they believe they should not, they notice the differences in the way men and women work as journalists, and they prefer the reliability and conscientiousness of women. Given the cliché about bitchy women bosses, the absence of malicious talk and catty behaviour seems remarkable. One finds instead among them a vibrant *esprit de corps* and an unsentimental feeling of solidarity with each other.

The biggest change for women in the media during this past decade has been the change in women themselves, in their own attitudes and expectations. Have they observed men and male attitudes changing in tendem? Somewhat, they say with cautious optimism. But most think that the transformation in men is skin deep, that their main achievement is an acquired capacity to forget that the person beside whom they are working is female.

The picture of media men drawn by their women colleagues is neither hostile nor flattering. It is abundantly clear that *very* few men are enough in tune with the prejudice in themselves and the system to make fair evaluations of women's work and potential. Media women, like women everywhere, have to escape the stereotypes to succeed. And there are many men around who will resist the attempt with dogged determination, derailing a career in the process if necessary. Where you do encounter a large vein of mean and nasty behaviour, ranging from simple rudeness to outright harassment and occasionally rape, is on the part of men towards women.

The women who have established themselves in journalism managed to settle the issue of sex in their work relations a long time ago. They found a way to operate and be seen strictly as professionals. If ever they had to contend with untoward sexual advances from colleagues, it was when they were young and inexperienced. Today they talk about culti-vating a demeanour which conveys an unmistakable message that "this woman is off-limits and definitely not interested." Of course, the more powerful they become personally and professionaly, the less likely men are to court their dis-approval. But no one is under any illusions that the scurrilous behaviour has ceased. Officially, sexual harassment in all its ugly forms may be condemned; in practice, it is condoned. Women are asked to be understanding about offensive male behaviour — he didn't mean it, he has diabetes, his wife is sick, he has problems with women — because if it is admitted at all, sexual harassment is treated as a private personal problem. In the few instance where women have been brave enough to make a formal grievance, senior management has closed ranks against them, protecting the man's career and compounding the injustice towards women.

For this and other reasons, some feminists feel that it is still impossible to work in the mainstream media and remain true to themselves. Out on the margins, many of them have bent their efforts instead to developing alternative, pro-women media and the results are everywhere to be seen: feminist newspapers, journals, literary magazines, book presses, and one radio station (Vancouver Co-op Radio). For many women, accommodating their identity and sensitivities to the main-stream environment exacts too great a toll. "There is no female equivalent for the word emasculate," said one woman,

"but that is what I feel is happening to me and I cannot stay."
Yet even the women who pass through and move on acknowledge the contribution and celebrate the success of the
women who remain.

How far, then, is a long way? Long enough to have
established an honourable women's tradition in the media;
long enough to have acquired, after determined effort, great
responsibility in important and occasionally visible places;
long enough to reap the rewards of Cora Hind's achievement.
And long enough to expect equality.

Index